This Book Belongs To
Michelle Campbell

Daily Marriage Builders for Couples

A DEVOTIONAL

Fred and Florence Littauer

WORD PUBLISHING
Nashville·London·Vancouver·Melbourne

DAILY MARRIAGE BUILDERS FOR COUPLES

Copyright © 1997 by Fred and Florence Littauer. All rights reserved. No portion of this book may be reproduced, stored in a retrieval system, or transmitted in any form or by any means—electronic, mechanical, photocopy, recording, or any other—except for brief quotations in printed reviews, without the prior permission of the publisher.

Unless otherwise indicated, Scripture quotations used in this book are from The New American Standard Bible (NASB) © 1960, 1962, 1963, 1968, 1971, 1972, 1973, 1977 by The Lockman Foundation. Used by permission. Other Scripture quotations are from:

The Amplified Bible (AMP): Old Testament, copyright © 1962, 1964 by Zondervan Publishing House. Used by permission. The Amplified New Testament, copyright © 1958 by the Lockman Foundation. Used by permission.

The Good News Bible, the Bible in Today's English Version (TEV) copyright © 1966, 1971, 1976 American Bible Society. Used by permission.

The Holy Bible, New International Version (NIV) copyright ©1973, 1978, 1984 International Bible Society. Used by permission of Zondervan Bible Publishers.

The Jerusalem Bible (JB) Copyright © 1968 by Darton, Longman, & Todd, Ltd., and Doubleday & Co., Inc. Used by permission.

The King James Version (KJV) of the Bible.

The Living Bible (TLB) copyright © 1971 by Tyndale House Publishers, Wheaton, Ill. Used by permission.

The Revised Standard Version of the Bible (RSV) copyright © 1946, 1952, © 1971, 1973 by the Division of Christian Education of the National Council of the Churches of Christ in the U.S.A. Used by permission.

ISBN 0-8499-1420-5

Printed in the United States of America

Contents

Part III. Wear the Dream: *How to continue to grow in all aspects of life, communicate on a positive and enjoyable level, and find meaning and pleasure in reading God's Word*

How to Get the Most from This Book

The 120 Daily Marriage Builders in this book are designed to add zest and meaning to your marriage by helping you improve your communication with your spouse and increase your understanding of his or her feelings, attitudes, and motivators. To help you achieve these goals, we suggest you keep a notebook handy to record your responses in the personalized sections. Next, as you share these thoughts with your spouse—and you may even want to share some of them with your children—jot down their reactions too.

These notes will be invaluable to you later on, not only in strengthening your marriage, but also in building cherished memories of your family's life together. We're so grateful, now that our children are grown, that I recorded stories and notes during their growing-up years and kept such mementos as report cards, achievement and athletic awards, and other memorabilia. Those notes and reminders about the times our family enjoyed together now trigger remembrances in us that help us enjoy those happy days all over again as we recall our shared memories.

Another reason to keep a notebook handy is that some of the verses and quotes in the Daily Marriage Builder chapters will be especially meaningful to you as you read them. We expect you will want to write them down where you can find them later—not on the back of the church bulletin or on the cover of the phone book. Have a Bible near at hand, too, because you will probably be curious about some verses cited and want to read what came before and after them. We have used selections from different versions of the Bible, both to add variety and also to bring your attention to the various ways of saying the same thing. Whatever version you use, the heart of the meaning will be the same. We have some Bibles that have two, four, or even six translations in a parallel arrangement, showing the different versions' translations. If you wish to study the Bible seriously, one of these would be an excellent investment. One of our favorite versions is the Amplified Bible. It does what its title says: It defines and explains complex words or phrases and enlarges and expands the meaning. (Fred says I talk like an Amplified Bible. If one word will do, I'll use ten.)

To get the maximum results from this book, it is important that you commit to reading the text and responding to the suggestions on a regular basis. Set your alarm ten minutes earlier and read together before getting out of bed. Or go to bed before you are exhausted and spend some time discussing the topics before going to sleep. Check off each day's chapter as you complete it.

We have divided the book into three sections. The first part, "Dare to Dream," answers the questions, Is there more to life than this? What can we do now to lift our vision beyond the ordinary? The second part, "Prepare the Dream," gives you specific ideas for how you can achieve a better married life and move toward a deeper spiritual relationship. And the third part, "Wear the Dream," describes how you can continue to grow in all aspects of your married life, communicate on a positive and enjoyable level, and find meaning and pleasure in reading God's Word together.

At this point you may be saying to yourselves, "All this sounds too much like work!" But remember, we're suggesting you start by spending just five or ten minutes a day in reading and discussing the ideas presented here. And we've started with very simple ideas and topics, so you can ease yourselves into the deeper discussions that come later. And after all, what is a good, better, or best marriage worth to you? Johnny Carson, when interviewed by the *Los Angeles Times*, explained, "If I had given as much to marriage as I gave to the *Tonight Show*, I'd probably have a great marriage. But the fact is I haven't given that, and there you have the simple reason for the failure of my marriages. I put the energy into the show."[1] Are you willing to put your energy into your marriage?

Fred and I have worked hard to make our marriage successful—but we didn't always do that. Over the years we've learned a lot about ourselves and about the art of making a marriage work. This book shares the methods and ideas we've found most helpful in our own relationship and in the things that have helped improve the marriages of thousands of couples who have come to us for help.

We shared the writing of this book, so you will find a variety of styles here as well as an assortment of topics. (So you'll know who's "speaking," the writer's name—Fred or Florence—appears at the top of each Marriage Builder.) Each chapter includes a verse or quotation, some information based on our forty-five years of marriage, our experience in working with other couples, and a daily challenge asking, "How about you?" meaning, "What are you going to do about this?" Finally, there's a closing prayer asking God for direction on that day's topic. Those of you who have an active prayer life won't need this written-out prayer, but we know from experience that many couples don't dare pray aloud together—or they end up preaching to each other and becoming angry instead of blessed.

We can guarantee if you spend ten minutes a day reading and thinking about these issues and suggestions, plus a little more time communicating about the ideas we share here, you will have a better marriage, a happier family, and a deeper relationship with the Lord. For those of you with children, there are frequent suggestions of topics to discuss with them, too, that will make them think creatively and help them rise above average.

Because we know the importance of practicing what we preach, we have worked through every lesson presented here ourselves. And we've had such a rewarding time researching on this project and writing this material that we can hardly wait for you to try it. Please let us know what happens in your life as a result of your diligence and dedication to improving your marriage.

Commit yourselves to building your marriage from wherever it is right now to where you both want it to be, and you will see results far beyond your expectations.

Florence and Fred Littauer

1611 South Rancho Santa Fe Road, Suite F2

San Marcos, California 92069

PART I

Dare
to
Dream

Is there more to life than this? Yes!

PART 1

Dare to Dream

Week 1, Day 1 ___

Building Your Marriage

> Except the LORD build the house, they labour in vain that build it.
>
> *Psalm 127:1 KJV*

Florence

Fred and I were on a writing vacation in a rustic cabin on Lake Sebago, Maine, when we received a call from a couple with marriage problems. They were visiting the area and after getting acquainted we learned they were Christian leaders in their community; she taught Bible studies, and he was on the board of elders in their church.

"What seems to be your basic problem?" I asked.

In unison they answered, "We don't communicate."

"You seem to talk quite freely," I mentioned.

"Well, anyone can talk," he said.

"That's right," Fred agreed. "Anyone can talk, but few can communicate."

There was a silence as I took the wife into one room and Fred sat with the husband in another. The minute they were apart they told us how difficult the other person was. Separately, each one was quite engaging, but when we came back together to discuss their future, they immediately began to argue over whose idea it had been to call us in the first place.

"Does it matter?" Fred asked.

With a grim look the husband answered, "Everything matters."

Actually, on the broad spectrum of life, there's much that doesn't matter at all, isn't there, such as who decides to make the call for help? Do we need to know everything?

This couple had no trouble talking, but they couldn't communicate.

Fred and I wrote this book for couples like this pair—couples who need to turn talking, or even arguing, into meaningful communication. Some of you do quite well at communicating and often enjoy your conversations. Some of you can communicate as long as you avoid certain touchy issues. And some of you just look at each other and either fight or refuse to talk at all.

In some marriages one spouse wants to discuss the problems of the moment, but the other won't respond. One man told me, "I haven't said anything but 'Yes, dear' in years." He thought he was noble not to argue—and she was furious that he wouldn't say a word. Do any of these problems sound familiar to you?

Even if your marriage is ideal, could it be even a little better? In the past, Fred and I talked, but we didn't communicate. In fact, we had more fun if we weren't together. At social functions we'd separate as soon as we entered. I'd find a little group who enjoyed my humor, and Fred would locate some serious person who could exchange deep thoughts with him. On the way home we'd report on our evening. We weren't really communicating; we were just reporting!

We learned to talk with each other on valid issues, but we both carefully monitored our words so we didn't upset each other. In retrospect we were acting much of the time. We'd learned our lines, and we knew better than to veer from the script.

How did we get from this stilted conversation to our current level of full and meaningful communication? How did we go from being happier apart to spending twenty-four hours a day together, seven days a week, traveling, speaking, and writing side by side—and loving it?

This book tells how we did it—and how you can too. It's arranged in brief, daily readings you can ingest quickly in ten minutes a day or discuss as suggested for whatever time is available. We start by suggesting some basic, fun, nostalgic topics for you to talk about together, subjects that aren't controversial and should help you get reacquainted with each other, even if you've been married for years.

Remember, Fred and I have done everything we suggest you do. For example, before we wrote the suggestion (in chapter 6) that you talk with each other about childhood differences that could affect your attitudes and behaviors as adults, we talked about our own childhoods. In fact, we carried the idea one step further and visited our childhood homes. We took a trip back to Larchmont, New York, and visited Fred's childhood home, his schools, and even his paper route. The next year my family had a reunion back in Haverhill, Massachusetts, and we went to the store where I grew up, to the high school I attended and later taught in, and even to the cemetery where my parents and other relatives are buried.

Our discussion of our premarriage jobs, houses, and schooling was the catalyst for these enjoyable and nostalgic trips that gave each of us a new understanding of our backgrounds and therefore, each other. This was one of the ways we've learned the benefits of meaningful communication!

In a June 6, 1997, *Newsweek* editorial entitled "Lost in the Big Blur," writer Jonathan Alter grieved that we, as a nation of individuals, no longer communicate with each other. We listen to talk shows, pick up moral values from immoral people, and consider what is showing on TV for guidance as to what we should wear and believe. Alter stated, "This is a world where communion is more important than what you communicate, where words are mistaken for deeds, and images are magically transformed into accomplishments."

How about You?

You'll learn how to communicate openly in a meaningful and not superficial way by using the Daily Marriage Builders, keeping meaningful notes, looking into God's Word, and discussing the subjects together. In short, you will learn the joy of open communication with each other. You will want to be honest and not mistake words for deeds. And as a result you will become known for your reality and your accountability more than for the image you exhibit in church and in the community.

Remember: Everyone can talk, but few can communicate!

Suggested Prayer for Today

Dear God and Heavenly Father, we are interested in what You may have planned for us as we go through this book, and at the same time, Lord, we are a little bit intimidated. Will You ask us to walk into areas of our lives we have never even talked about before with each other? We are working hard, because we want to be obedient to You. You are our God, our Almighty God, our Savior, and our Redeemer. You gave Your life, Lord, that we might have life. We are most thankful for Your gift to us. Is there any less that we can do for You?

We may waiver, we may falter, but we both commit to You today our desire to become all as a husband and wife that You desire and have planned for us. We need You, O gracious and patient Lord. We ask You to strengthen us when we weaken. Chastise us if we refuse. Lift us if we stumble. Thank You, Father, for hearing our prayer, which we ask in the Name of Jesus. Amen.

Change in the Home Starts with Me

> Why do you look at the speck that is in your [partner's] eye, but do not notice the log that is in your own eye? . . . First take the log out of your own eye.
>
> *Matthew 7:3, 5*

Fred

"Why do I look at the speck in your eye instead of the log in my own? Frankly dear, I think the 'speck' is in my eye, and the 'log' is in yours! Your faults are so easy to see, and mine seem so minor by comparison!"

"If only she would shape up and be the wife she is supposed to be, we could get along just fine."

"I know I'm not perfect, but I can't go on any longer with his constant nitpicking and criticizing."

Sound familiar? These are the kinds of things couples tell us all the time when they come asking for help.

Florence has often been heard to state, "If it were possible for one person to change another, Fred would be an expert and I would be perfect. He surely worked as diligently as could be expected of any husband to make me into the wife he thought I should be."

I can't disagree with her description, as painful as it is. I was diligent and persistent for many years! However, in the end, even I had to admit I had been a total failure! In my view, Florence wasn't any better; in fact, if anything she was worse! How could this be with two intelligent people who had had such optimistic aspirations at the beginning of their marriage and such good intentions and perseverance to make it work? We are not quitters. So why didn't our marriage work?

Answer: We didn't understand that God's Word is truth, and truth must be properly applied. There is no other way. After becoming Christians, we both studied the Bible. We both saw the verses at the top of this page about the speck and the log in people's eyes. We understood the verses. But instead of applying the truth to ourselves we applied the truth to each other! Each one of us thought these were great verses, but we each thought of them in terms of what our spouse should do about it!

If only he would do what it said!

If only she would start to clean up her own act instead of trying to tell me what's wrong with me!

At last, we learned this very simple truth: CHANGE IN THE HOME STARTS WITH ME!

How about You?

Do you want to see changes in your home? Start by examining yourself. Give up trying to change or remake your partner. Learn to accept and appreciate the good qualities and traits God gave to the partner He created for you. Philippians 4:8 advises us to "think on these things" in our spouses that are "true, honest, just, pure, lovely, of good report, virtuous, and worthy of praise" (KJV). Pray and ask God to help you see yourself as He sees you, as your mate sees you. Pray and ask God to help you acknowledge and confess your weaknesses. Pray and ask your Father in heaven to do what you can't do for yourself: Erase and eradicate those things that are not pleasing to Him and to your mate. Pray that you will set and maintain forever your goal to make your mate the happiest person on earth. Pray and pray; continue to pray! There is no substitute for personal, heartfelt prayer; there is no other way, no easier way.

Ask God to change you! Then keep on asking Him to change you, your habits, your heart, and your desires. Thank Him for your partner. Thank Him, and then thank Him again. Find something new each day about your partner to thank your Father in Heaven for. You will be amazed. Soon you will be seeing your mate in a whole new way. And because you are now working persistently to effect change in yourself, soon your partner will see you in a wholly new light. Start with the log that is affecting your own vision. Forget about the speck in your mate's eye. Soon it will be washed away.

Soon you will forget it was ever there! When the change has come, you will know it has occurred because you decided to "START WITH ME"!

Suggested Prayer for Today

Wouldn't this be a good day for each of you to pray aloud from your heart to the Father—in the presence of each other? Husbands first: Call out to the Father, and in doing so, let your wife hear your heart. Women love a strong man who can cry out to his Savior in front of them without being ashamed or reticent. Be the leader your wife desires. To be a leader means to lead the way! So husbands first: "Thank You, Lord Jesus!"

3

Making Time for Each Other

> Speaking to one another in psalms and hymns and spiritual songs, singing and making melody with your heart to the Lord.
>
> *Ephesians 5:19*

Fred

A frequently shown television ad of the moment asks us, "Is this a great time to be alive, or what?" Oh, it is a great time in many respects. Technology is racing ahead so rapidly, last year's new products are already outdated by this year's new improvements. The electronic age has burst upon us with commonly available creations that were not even dreamed about a generation ago. Forecasters and futurists are promising there will be even more awesome advances in the years to come.

Wonderful? Yes. Amazing? Yes. Beneficial? Yes, generally all these advances help us with our tasks in countless ways. But so many of them tend to drive a wedge in the building of our relationships. Unless we seek a balance and are thoughtful and careful, we will see the gradual disintegration of our own marriage union. What is the answer? Is there any hope that we can be the exception rather than becoming another divorce statistic?

If you and your spouse are to become and remain best friends, you must learn now to take time for cultivating and developing the bond between you. We all have heard of couples who sadly found out that when their children left home they had nothing to talk about. All of their interaction had revolved around their children. When the children were gone, the husband and wife had nothing left. They were no longer needed as parents. They didn't know each other as friends, and often they found they really didn't even like each other! Result: another broken marriage.

Learn to make time for each other. That means learn to take time to talk, to share, to communicate, to listen, and to care about what each other is thinking and feeling. Making time for each other means treating your spouse as the most important person in your life. It means learning to treasure every moment you spend together, even when your inner thoughts are saying, *What a waste of time. I've got so much to do.* It means developing a ready sense of humor. It means going places together to have fun and learning to enjoy each other's company.

Have you ever noticed that the couples who have learned to live and love together have also learned to laugh together?

As Florence and I have walked through the peaks and valleys of our life together, we have learned that, after the Lord Himself, there is no other person more important to each of us than each other. We do not ever like to be apart. We have simply learned to have fun together, to enjoy each other's company, to be interested in what is important to the other. Therefore we share with you what we have learned so that you can know and use our experience now, rather than learning it over a span of decades, as we did!

How about You?

Is life racing past you? Are you afraid of what will happen to your marriage when the children grow up and fly out of the nest you have so carefully constructed? Is one or both of you too busy to even see what is happening around you? Have you taken time lately to stop and simply enjoy the life you've created for your family?

Young couples always think there's lots of time because they live as if there will always be a tomorrow. At this early stage of marriage many husbands and wives haven't even come to grips with the reality that life is finite, that it is going to end one day, and we human beings are only here for a short "season." Whatever stage of marriage you're in, think about tomorrow and build investments in your relationship that will pay a healthy dividend later.

Thankfully, Florence and I have always been relatively healthy, even though in the past we thought very little about the condition of our bodies. We were not careless, but health just wasn't a focal point for us. In the last year or two, however, as we both approach the blessed seventy-year mark, we have realized there are no trade-ins! These are the only bodies we will have, so we had better take good care of them today! Believe me, we are! We consider our healthy lifestyle an investment in our future.

You can apply this same axiom to your relationship with each other. Just as you undoubtedly want to give careful thought, attention, and action to planning for your physical health in the future, as well as your retirement security and income, in the same way you can start now to invest in the future of your life together by finding ways—and making the time—to do things together.

Suggested Prayer for Today

Gracious Heavenly Father, help us to be thankful each day for each other. Help us, Lord, to learn to have fun together, to enjoy each other. Lord, we don't want to ever be another divorce statistic. We want to be living examples of how a husband and wife, joined together by You, become one in every sense of the word. We are committed to this marriage, Father. Open our eyes, Lord, that we may see every area where we need to become more selfless and more Christ centered. If our lives are pleasing to You, Lord, we believe by faith that our partner will be pleased as well by our efforts to be the helpmate that we both want to be. We thank You, Lord Jesus, for giving us Your clear guidelines. In Your Name we pray. Amen.

4

When the Going Gets Tough

Enter by the narrow gate; for the gate is wide, and the way is broad that leads to destruction, and many are those who enter by it. . . . The gate is small, and the way is narrow that leads to life, and few are those who find it.   *Matthew 7:13–14*

Fred

Terry-Jo Myers, a Ladies Professional Golf Association tournament contender, "vividly remembers the day in 1992 when she decided to commit suicide." For nine years she had been battling an incurable bladder disease that pushed her to the limit of human endurance. It forced her into the bathroom up to sixty times a day and sometimes as often as every two minutes.

One morning at 3:00 A.M. Terry-Jo "had just returned home to Ft. Myers, Fla., after playing a two-day charity event in Tampa. She hadn't slept since the middle of the previous night, . . . was going to the bathroom every couple of minutes. Wracked with pelvic pain, she picked up a kitchen knife that November morning, intending to cut her wrists. First she decided to take a look at her sleeping daughter, Taylor-Jo, . . . who was 3.

"'I looked at her, and I realized I couldn't kill myself,' she says. 'I couldn't leave Taylor-Jo without her mother.'"

Terry-Jo didn't quit. She hung in there when the going got tough. And as a result she lived long enough that a new drug, still in its experimental stage, finally brought the relief she desperately needed. Dr. C. Lowell Parsons of [the University of California] San Diego said, "The impressive thing with Terry-Jo is she was able to function at such a high level for so long."

"'I was never able to concentrate on a shot,' Terry-Jo said. 'My focus was on getting through the pain and two more holes so I could make a mad dash for the next port-a-john.'"

LPGA Tour champion Nancy Lopez said of Terry-Jo, "'Life is full of people who don't try to help themselves. Terry-Jo kept fighting back. I really admire her.'"

Finally Terry-Jo is free of her symptoms and pain and successfully back on the professional tour. In the first six months of 1997 she won two tournaments, the Sara Lee Classic and the Los Angeles Women's Tournament. In her final round, Terry-Jo came back to win from five shots behind with a six-under-par 66, walking the last 'two holes with tears streaming down her face, overcome with the emotion of the moment.'"

When the going got tough, Terry-Jo didn't quit! "'The struggle made everything much more worthwhile. I've learned a lot. It's been a blessing,'" she said.[1]

How about You?

Have you felt at times there was no hope for your marriage? Have you been ready to quit when things got tough? To quote Nancy Lopez, "Life is full of people who don't try to help themselves." Florence and I didn't give up on our marriage, although there were certainly times when we both wondered, *Is there any hope?*

There is always hope, because God is now and will always be in the miracle-working business.

In an era of no-fault, "quickie" divorces, several states are now enacting laws such as the "Covenant Marriage" law in Louisiana. Under the new statute, time, counseling, and efforts to reconcile and resolve the issues are required before terminating the marriage contract can even be considered.

Jesus said, "The gate is small, and the way is narrow . . . , and few are those who find it." Oswald Chambers adds, "Thank God He does give us difficult things to do! . . . Jesus is bringing many 'sons' unto glory, and God will not shield us from the requirements of a son. God's grace turns out men and women with a strong family likeness to Jesus Christ. . . . It takes a tremendous amount of discipline to live the noble life of a disciple of Jesus in actual things."[2] When the going gets tough, the tough get on their knees! What about you?

Suggested Prayer for Today

Dear God and Heavenly Father, we need to know there is hope for us. Lord, please show us how we can learn to treat each other as friends. Sometimes words come out of my mouth that I wouldn't even think of saying to anyone else! We "always seem to hurt the one [we] love, the one [we] shouldn't hurt at all." We pray to You, Lord, for You are our only hope. We are somewhat ashamed to admit that we have tried everything else first. Nothing has worked enough. Now, Lord, we come to You wholeheartedly. We are ready to do whatever You would have us do. Guide us and teach us, O Lord our God. If we need help, Lord, I ask that You send us someone who can help us. We thank You, Lord Jesus Christ, that You already know and understand all our needs and desires. In Your Name we pray. Amen.

5

Reaping Bountifully

> He who sows sparingly shall also reap sparingly; and he who sows bountifully shall also reap bountifully. . . . Do not be deceived, God is not mocked; for whatsoever a man sows, this he will also reap.
>
> *2 Corinthians 9:6, Galatians 6:7*

Fred

"Get an idea, carry it through. You'll be amazed at what You can do!"

These are words I have never forgotten. They were indelibly inscribed on my mind and on my heart forever during a pivotal time in my life.

I was ten years old that summer at Camp Agawam on Crescent Lake in Maine, where my three brothers and I had spent many active and memorable summers, first as campers and then as counselors. Two or three times during each summer, an outside speaker or entertainer would come into the camp to put on his program. Hans Helms came that summer. He spoke with a strong German accent. I remember that in addition to his program in the assembly hall he did a presentation at the waterfront with his collapsible kayak. That was interesting—no, it was amazing! I had never heard of, or even imagined, a boat you could condense into a package small enough to stow in your car!

Maybe he was trying to sell the kayaks to the camp; I never did know. What I do know is that I have never forgotten Hans Helms. I wonder how many of my fellow campers that summer still remember him as clearly as I do. Why do I remember him so well? He "sowed" a challenge in a young boy's mind, an inspiration to dream, to imagine, to go forth and fulfill his greatest hopes: "Get an idea, carry it through. You'll be amazed at what you can do."

Have I already exceeded all my hopes? No, I have not achieved all that I set out to accomplish originally. I never became the millionaire I listed as one of my goals at age sixteen. And yes, there have been a number of stumblings, misplays, and poorly thought-through decisions in the years that have followed. But the words Hans Helms shared have stayed with me and inspired me. I have persevered. I have never given up. Now God has changed my own self-focused material goals and converted them into Christ-centered spiritual aspirations: to be like Him, to serve Him, and to grow in Him more and more each day.

Today, as I pray and thank Him daily, I am truly amazed at what He has done with me, amazed at the gifts He has given to me, amazed at the ways He is using me—fulfilling purposes I could never have even dreamed about. I did not know that such fulfillment was possible. I have not sown sparingly in my relationship with the Lord. I have not hesitated to give liberally of myself wherever He has sent me and to whomever He has sent me. I count myself as most blessed among men. He has transformed my mind and my marriage to follow His will and purpose.

The wife I formerly thought lacked understanding and was uncaring and unloving has become my closest friend and consummate companion, someone from whom I never want to be apart. Joyfully, I can at last say with conviction and certainty, "Life is good!"

Unless you knew me for the first six decades of my life, you might not recognize the extraordinary changes God has worked in me. God has sown spiritual seeds into my life. I am thankful I knew enough to cultivate them, and now I am able to reap the bountiful harvest.

How about You?

There is nothing worth having in this life that is not worth working for. Is your marriage worth working for? God has said what He has joined together, "Let not man put asunder."[1] God says your marriage is worth working for!

Begin your "work" by refocusing on those characteristics in each other that drew you together in the first place. Today tell each other, "Honey, three things I have always appreciated about you are . . ." You'll be glad tomorrow that you said this today!

"Get an idea, carry it through. You'll be amazed at what you can do" . . . when it is the Lord who is directing your path!

Suggested Prayer for Today

Blessed Savior and Redeemer, I have dreams too. I have dreamed of achieving many things in this lifetime. As I look back on the years that have already passed, Lord, I see two things: First, I am not where I expected to be and second, I am not as close to You as I think I ought to be. I know it is up to me to do something to change the course of my life. I do not want to look back again ten years from now and find myself saying the same things all over again. Therefore I surrender my will to Your will, Lord, and give You permission to do with me what You will, whatever You desire to do. I ask You to help me become what You have planned and purposed me to be. Help me, O Lord, to sow skillfully now so that later I can reap bountifully a harvest that is not for my indulgence but for Your glory. I thank You for the knowledge that You care much more about me than I have ever cared about myself. I thank You, my Lord and my Redeemer. I pray in Your powerful Name, the Name that changes lives! Amen.

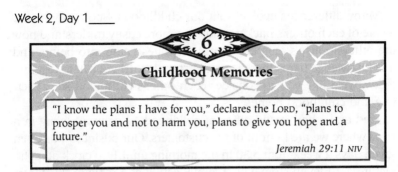

Childhood Memories

"I know the plans I have for you," declares the LORD, "plans to prosper you and not to harm you, plans to give you hope and a future."

Jeremiah 29:11 NIV

Florence

Very little would be accomplished in life if we didn't set goals, if we didn't sit down occasionally and say, "Where are we going?" We set goals for business, for careers, for finance, even for our physical fitness, yet few of us seem to have goals for our marriages. With all our present-day enlightenment, we still hold to the old-fashioned wishful thinking that we can simply get married and live happily ever after. We plan the wedding, we schedule the honeymoon, and some of us may even decide ahead of time how many children we want. But the mythical union of a successful marriage is supposed to materialize out of the mist with little planning on our part.

If you're willing to work on improving your marriage, you'll need to set some goals—some benchmarks that will let you know you're making progress. The first step in establishing your goals is to identify where you are. One of the easiest starting points to evaluate your relationship is to examine your differences and see how you're coping with them.

Take a few minutes right now to become aware of your differences. In evaluating and working on our own marriage, and during our years of helping countless other couples with theirs, Fred and I have realized that the more differences two people have the more difficult the relationship can be. Those differences are most painfully apparent when disappointments come and the spouses react differently, pulling back, adjusting independently, and silently deciding where they are or where their marriage should be going.

Many differences evolve from our childhoods. Spouses who are aware of each other's backgrounds can more easily understand how the other spouse's temperament and values came into being, and this knowledge helps increase understanding. In your time together today, we'd like you to consider each other's childhood social setting and childhood home.

Fred and I had vastly different childhoods. I grew up living in a store where we ate in front of the customers. Our business was open seven days a week from 6:30 in the morning until 11 o'clock at night. Picture a 7-Eleven store with a family eating at a table in the center of it, and you have our social setting. In contrast, Fred lived in what I saw as a mansion in a posh neighborhood; his family's meals were served by the maid in the dining room. They belonged to a country club by the seashore while our only sight of any sizable body of water was during the yearly Sunday school picnic at a distant lake.

We lived in a shoe-factory town that was losing its factories to the South. Unemployment was all around us, and for me, the glamorous life existed only in the movies. When I saw Fred's home for the first time and stood in the spacious foyer facing the circular staircase to the second floor, I said to myself, *Florence, this is for you!* I just knew I could be happy in a lavish home in prestigious Westchester County, New York.

My desire to live the "good life" surpassed my love for Fred. I thought more about the possibilities for my future than I did about how I could please Fred. The big house, lots of exquisite furnishings, and a lofty social status were the normal perks of life for Fred, and he could never see why my desire for a real house with a front door was so important to me and why the thought of belonging to a country club was a major goal in my life. He had what I wanted, and I knew I could "adjust up." I was Cinderella, and he was Prince Charming.

Luckily, these differences in our backgrounds were not serious for us, as I got more excited each time we "moved up" and Fred simply accepted me as I was, even though he didn't understand my need for possessions.

However, for many couples, background differences form underlying, unspoken problems. One adorable girl I talked with told me she was brought up in a pastor's household, and the whole family was steeped in scriptural knowledge. She knew every Christian cliché and how to overcome all problems through prayer. But then there was her husband, Bob. "His family didn't know the Lord at all," she explained. "His father was crude, and his mother pitiful. There's no hope Bob will ever become my spiritual leader." And she was right. When I talked with him, he told me she was a walking Bible and no matter what came up, she had a spiritual pill to cure it. "I could never compete with her, so I just don't try."

Whether our background differences are in material goods or in spiritual knowledge, the more extreme they are, the more problems they may cause in the future.

How about You?

What are your differences in background? Discuss with each other what you remember about your childhood surroundings. Share honestly how you felt about each other's family dwelling and his or her family's apparent status when you visited for the first time. What problems have these differences caused in your marriage? Can you lay these difficulties out before you as you talk, identify any resentment or grudges, and repair any misconceptions? Can you look at your backgrounds with objectivity—and even with a sense of humor?

Before you can move on to setting goals for the future, you need to examine your attitudes from the past.

Suggested Prayer for Today

Dear Lord Jesus, we never noticed before that we held some grudges about our family backgrounds. We had some misconceptions and judgments that we had never looked at. Thank You for bringing these things to our attention. Give us the ability to accept our differences in the future and the desire to restore to wholeness what we have broken.

We love You and praise You. In Jesus' Name. Amen.

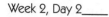

Money Problems

> Neither a borrower, nor a lender be; for loan oft loses both itself and friend, and borrowing dulls the edge of husbandry.
> *Polonius, in Shakespeare's* Hamlet, *act 1, scene 3*

Florence

Of all the conflicts we see in marriages, financial disagreements rank at the head of the line. Statistics show that 80 percent of Americans are pressured by overdue bills. As the fights or the bouts of depression boil on, one of the most helpful actions a couple can take is to sit down during a time of peace and examine where their attitudes on money came from and, with that understanding, work toward a compromise position. What did each of your families think about money? Where did you get your ideas on how to handle your finances? Knowing how you developed your attitudes about money will help you understand your actions and, where necessary, make changes in your actions.

Because I grew up poor and lived behind my father's store, I had a fear of poverty deep within me. Each night as I'd go to sleep I'd hear my parents counting the day's cash and my mother saying, "Will there be enough money to eat next week?" We didn't use the few good dishes we had; we saved them for some mythical day in the future when our fortunes would change and the queen would come to call. Despite all this, our family was very proud. We had no credit cards; we paid cash for everything, and we were considered honest and upright citizens of the community. My grandmother would walk two miles to the electric and gas company on the day the bill arrived in the mail. "We want them to know we pay our bills on time," she would state proudly. In her senior years when she was eligible for social security payments, she refused to accept them. "I've never taken handouts from the government before, and I won't do it now," she said.

"But you deserve it," we'd explain.

"No one's going to think I'm a charity case!" she would reply.

After Grandmother died we found forty years of milk bills from the house delivery in a kitchen cabinet. In the bottom right corner of each one she had neatly written the date she'd paid it and then added her initials.

Yes, we were both poor and proud at the same time.

I was ashamed because I had so few clothes compared with my friends. When I had my first job selling chocolates by the pound in Mitchell's Department Store, I had only two outfits to wear. One was a pink-and-white-striped seersucker two-piece suit, and the other—made from the same Simplicity pattern—was light blue. Why do I remember those two outfits so clearly after fifty years or so? Because to me these two sad little dresses were a badge of humility, perhaps even humiliation, during my teenage years.

Shoes were another problem because my parents could only afford one pair a year no matter how fast their children's feet grew. Because I had big feet, size 9 in eighth grade, there were few choices available, and I ended up with whatever the store had in my size.

My mother had only one pair of black tie-on oxfords with clunky heels, but I vowed that when I grew up I would have pretty shoes and never wear ugly shoes again. Recently I saw a teenager wearing my mother's shoes! I couldn't believe, given a free choice, that anyone would want black tie-on oxfords with clunky heels, but I heard the girl tell her friend that her new shoes were the latest fashion and "really cool"!

Do either of you relate to how I felt about money, clothes, and possessions?

Fred had a totally different outlook on money. His parents and grandparents were in the millinery business in New York City, where they worked long hours each day. Grandpa had started out as a street sweeper in New York and progressed to substantial wealth and a reputation as a shrewd businessman. As Fred grew up, money was never an issue. The children were not spoiled and they learned the value of hard work, but there was no tension about the paying of bills.

Can you see the difference in our attitudes toward money?

In the early years of our marriage we could never discuss money issues. It wasn't until we learned to communicate about emotional hurts and pains that we began to understand our differences. I had been trying to hold my strong feelings under wraps, and I felt Fred was taunting me. How many years of financial tension we went through before we were able to deal with the problem without accusing each other of treason.

When we got married, I wanted every bill paid immediately. I panicked if an overdue notice came, and I feared the FBI would come after us if Fred didn't keep all our records straight. He couldn't understand my fears, and he took risks in business that scared me. I felt he was ridiculing me. When he told me money was none of my business and when he lost money in the stock market, I thought he did it on purpose to upset me.

How about You?

Can you see how our different background views on money caused serious problems? What did you each learn about money from your families? Did your parents agree on finances or not? Tell each other about these attitudes and listen without making judgments. This is not the time to argue but to look at your differences objectively and say, "Oh, now I see why you do that."

Finding where your opinions about money come from is the first step toward financial responsibility. Be willing to listen to each other without interrupting. This is not the time to accuse each other of bad choices but to start a discussion about attitudes on money and possessions. Talk about your differing backgrounds and show each other that you can discuss money without getting angry.

The old and wise Polonius, in the quote at the beginning of today's chapter, gave Hamlet sound advice when he told him to keep his finances in order. Don't borrow or you won't keep your budget in a reasonable line. Don't lend because you may never see your money or your friend again. Money has always been a problem, but today there are financial counselors available to help you function within your income. Don't argue; take action.

Suggested Prayer for Today

Dear Father God, oh how we need You when we delve into talks about money. What a touchy subject that is! Eliminate our negative feelings toward each other. Give us understanding for each other's background and opinions. Let us accept each other's reasons even if we don't agree with them. How our parents handled money is history, right or wrong, but it is history that explains the present. Watch over us as we enter into this discussion. Give us a healthy attitude toward each other's opinions.

We thank You and praise You. In Jesus' Name. Amen.

8

Baked Beans on Saturday Night

We have so many excuses to eat. God not only wants to change what we eat, but He wants to change why we eat.
Carole Lewis, Choosing to Change

Florence

So many of us eat too much. We eat at celebrations when we're happy. We eat at funerals when we're sad. We eat when we arise; we eat before we go to sleep. We just love to eat. Carole Lewis, national director of First Place, a Christ-centered health program, says that when we get to Heaven we'll recognize the Baptists because they'll all be carrying a covered dish!

First Place teaches that before we can change our old eating habits, we must find out why we eat too much. In my childhood family, food was expensive, so we couldn't waste a thing. My mother could stretch one can of Spam to feed five of us and make hash from the leftovers. We were taught never to take more than we could eat and never to leave anything on our plates. The only time my mother ever laid a hand on me was one Sunday when I didn't finish my dinner and she reminded me about the starving children in China. I replied, "So send it to them!" Whack! I never gave that answer again!

On this subject Fred and I had the same upbringing, and we've had to train ourselves that we don't need to eat everything handed to us. With the number of luncheons and banquets we attend, we could gain weight every single day with no thought to those starving children in China.

The subject of food is not often mentioned in premarital counseling, but different backgrounds can cause very different expectations about what we eat, when we eat, and even what we call a meal. Although Fred and I were both taught to be stars in the Clean Plate Club, we had some subtle misunderstandings. In Massachusetts everyone had three meals a day called breakfast, lunch, and supper. Our one dinner a week was on Sunday, after church. When we got married Fred let me know right off that these labels were wrong. We would eat breakfast, lunch, and dinner every day. There are no suppers (except church potlucks), he said, and anything between meals is a snack.

I also had to cease "wiping the dishes" after washing them. I had to "dry" them. How could I have been so stupid as to "eat supper" and "wipe dishes"?

Another cultural difference was Saturday's supper, now dinner. In the Boston area the most common Saturday night meal was hot dogs, baked beans, and canned brown bread. I had never stopped to think that citizens of Paris, Rome, and Hong Kong, along with the Littauers of New York, didn't all know about Saturday's beans. The first time I presented Fred with my traditional Saturday meal, he asked, "What is this?" When I tried to explain the background for my choices, he did not say, "Oh, how nice to follow your Boston tradition." Instead he said, "No one eats hot dogs in a house. They belong in Yankee Stadium!" We ate silently that night, and whether it was dinner or supper hardly mattered.

Fred was in the restaurant business when we got married, and he carried his supervisory talents into our little apartment. When he walked in each evening after work he immediately checked to see if I had done everything properly. I had to preheat the dinner plates, chill salad plates and forks, be sure not to put two vegetables of the same color or same consistency on the same plate at the same time, and always have a perky garnish decorating the presentation.

These rules were not abusive, but as we look back on them, we both see that this training program was unnecessary and degrading to me. Gratefully, by the time Fred quit my do-it-yourself improvement program, I'd learned enough from him to be a gourmet cook.

How about You?

What were you taught about food? Do you feel that eating big meals keeps you healthy? Can you uncover why you have some distorted ideas about eating? Do you both share the same attitudes or do you not see eye to eye? Discuss where your feelings on food first came from. You may be surprised to find out why you eat. Was dessert a reward? When you are depressed do you eat to cheer yourself up?

Did either set of parents have unusual eating habits or odd choices of what they would or wouldn't eat? Did either father put unnecessary demands on the mother? Assess the answers to all these questions and see how many of these background oddities are still floating around in your present family. Who would ever think food could be such a problem? But it certainly can be!

Suggested Prayer for Today

Dear Lord Jesus, we know food was important to You and Your disciples. We remember the feeding of the thousands and the significance of the Last Supper (not the Last Dinner). We know we are to ask Your blessing on each meal. Help us to keep from disagreeing on the plates and the parsley and focus our minds on the purpose of the meal and the fellowship around the table. We thank You for Your provision for our health, and we pledge to take better care of how, when, and what we eat.

In the precious Name of Jesus we pray. Amen.

9

Call the Doctor

Is there no balm in Gilead? Is there no physician there? Why then is there no healing for the wound of my people?

Jeremiah 8:22 NIV

Florence

Different attitudes about health and the care of our bodies can bring conflict into our marriages. Some people grow up believing they should wait until they're close to death before going to a doctor, and they usually marry ones who run for help at the first sniffle. As a child I was rarely sick but when I was, my mother paid extra attention to me. She put a cool cloth on my fevered brow and let me have ice cream for supper.

As Fred grew up his family was involved in a cult that denied sickness of any kind. They took no medicine and sought no help. Not understanding Fred's background attitudes about health, the first time I got the flu after we were married, I expected Fred to baby me as my mother had done. Instead Fred suggested he could go to a movie since there was nothing much to do with me so sick. I couldn't believe he would abandon me! Later, as our children came along, our differences on health care became even more obvious.

We had never discussed these differences before we got married. I simply assumed Fred would show great concern and hover over me if I ever got sick, and he worked on the premise that we wouldn't get sick! Gratefully, we didn't. When I was pregnant with our first child, my mother-in-law let me know it was acceptable to go to an obstetrician. I would have gone anyway, but it was a lot easier with the Littauer family's blessing. As Fred and I discussed the health issue early in our marriage we saw our background differences and came to a mutual agreement. If I felt a doctor was needed, Fred accepted my judgment. I didn't have to plead, but I also didn't run off to the doctor without a good reason.

Once we got beyond our background extremes, Fred became the compassionate parent who would get up in the night with the children, and he has cared for me with concern and tenderness whenever I've been in need. Now that we can look at our former differences with humor, we hope Fred never has a long illness because I have what my children call a "lack of nurseness": "You're sick? Go to bed. No TV. When you feel better, come out."

It wasn't really this bad, but they had good attendance records at school. Staying home was no fun.

How about You?

Discuss the differences in your two families' attitudes about doctors, healthcare, medicine, vitamins. If this has been a problem with you, talk about why you believe as you do and don't argue about it. Often when you look at the foundation of your belief system, you find that it doesn't really make sense, and you become willing to modify your stance. On many issues, there is no right or wrong way until you mutually establish one.

If you have had no marriage conflicts over health issues, praise the Lord and move on. Few couples agree on everything, but the goal is to come to a middle-of-the-road compromise both spouses can live with. Once you accept this point of agreement, don't continue to bring it up or give sarcastic comments about who won.

Ogden Nash, my favorite comic poet wrote:

> I believe a little incompatibility is the spice of life, particularly if he has income and she is pattable.

Suggested Prayer for Today

Dear Lord Jesus, thank You for giving us good health and a compassionate concern for each other. So many families have conflict over medical issues and we ask You to help us deal with those issues compassionately. Thank You for Your continued blessing on our health and on our attitudes toward each other. Thank You for caring for us and protecting us. We pray in the precious Name of Jesus. Amen.

Love Makes the World Go Round

> Love embraces the totality of the other person. . . . We will never
> know who a person is until we understand where they have been.
> *T. D. Jakes*, Woman, Thou Art Loosed

Florence

The poets tell us that love is a many-splendored thing, that love makes the world go round, that love is like a lovely rose, and like a dizziness. Were you brought up on the romantic notion that human love transcends all other emotions and can keep you happy "ever after"? Or were you in a family full of realists who debunked flowery phrases and long-stemmed roses? What is love to you?

What examples of true love did you see in your home? So often in marriage we don't discuss what we expected love to be. Without letting our spouses know what our expectations are, we look for love and find disappointments instead, and we store them up in our mental banks. We don't dare talk about such issues. Some of us assume all the blame for our disappointment, and some of us put it all on our mates. Either way there is no healthy resolution.

In my humble childhood, love was spending time having fun, playing games, and making up stories. My father encouraged us to speak clearly and improve our vocabulary. Between helping customers in the store, Dad would sit down with us and challenge us to think creatively. My mother was a music teacher, and she tried to teach us to play the violin and enjoy singing hymns.

For us, love was being together and topping each other's funny stories. Love was music. Love was words. Love was poetry. Love had nothing to do with money.

When I first visited Fred's family, I found they were all too busy to have fun; to them, love was wrapped up in dollar bills. If you kissed Grandpa, you got money; if you didn't, you were left out when the silver dollars were passed around. Those who had the gold made the rules. When we would visit the family on a Sunday afternoon, our children would have to line up with their cousins to receive their money. One day Lauren refused to kiss Grandpa because he hadn't shaved and she could tell his face was prickly. When he called her over, she wouldn't go and he said, "Then you don't get your dollar today. Maybe that will teach you a lesson." It did teach her that love and money go hand in hand, that if you don't give the token of love, you don't get to touch the money.

Fred and I, from the fabric of our different backgrounds, had to weave together a new love to show our children. As we became believing Christians we saw what God intended love to be: selfless, giving, not keeping records of wrongs. Love didn't seem to depend on fun or on money. It wasn't until we'd been married fifteen years that we began to talk about love and not just look for it. We saw how differently we had been brought up and that neither situation was ideal—poor with fun or well off with no fun.

Is there value in looking behind us for the roots of our attitudes on any subject? Since Fred and I have been doing this for years we have grown closer to each other; we have developed new understanding because we've walked in each other's footsteps. We've gone back to our childhood areas, visited our churches together, our grammar schools, our old houses, our play areas. We've walked these paths together and deeply increased our understanding of where we have been.

In his book *Woman, Thou Are Loosed*, Bishop T. D. Jakes says we need to be included in each other's history, because that's what made us who we are. All the events of our childhoods, both good and bad, have shaped our lives to this point.

How about You?

Bishop Jakes says you don't really know who a person is until you understand where he or she has been. Do you know where your mate has been? Are you willing to talk about your differences in your expectations about married love? Is one of you continuing to disappoint the other because you don't understand each other's needs? Is it possible that you are married strangers?

In our book *Freeing Your Mind from Memories That Bind* there are fifty pages of questions spouses can ask each other about their feelings when they were children. Asking these questions to each other now would be a positive and eye-opening experience. Then you will really know each other because you'll know where you've been.

Set aside the time to talk about your childhood experiences as they relate to houses, status, money, food, health, and love. The average couple spends less than ten minutes a week in meaningful conversation, and then they wonder why their relationship is steadily deteriorating. You can't build a marriage when your only communication is crisis management. Spend time in the next few days discussing peaceably the differences in your background and your expectations. We seldom get what we only perceive we deserve. We have to share our expectations and perceptions!

Actress Katharine Hepburn in *An Affair to Remember* tells Spencer Tracy, "Love has nothing to do with what you are expecting to get—only with what you are expecting to give—which is everything."

It's time to get to know each other!

Suggested Prayer for Today

Dear Lord Jesus, we both realize we are selfish by nature, and we have been waiting for the other one to change and see things our way. We each want love, but we see it from two different points of view. Give us the desire to talk over some of our background differences and get to know each other by discussing where we have been. Give us the kind of love that empowers us to want to give all we have to each other, expecting nothing in return. Help us to see our love for each other as a gift we willingly choose to give.

Lord, we love You, and we want to love each other more than we ever have before.

In the Name of Jesus we pray. Amen.

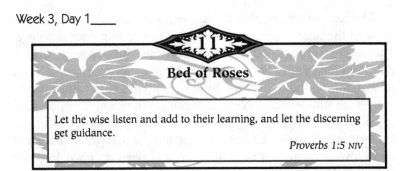

11

Bed of Roses

Let the wise listen and add to their learning, and let the discerning get guidance.

Proverbs 1:5 NIV

Florence

For forty-five years Fred and I have been building a marriage. You might wonder, *Does it take that long?* Yes, it takes forever. But that should not be a discouraging thought because getting there is half the fun. Wouldn't it be dull if we received a certificate at the wedding service that said we had five years to put our marriage together and once we achieved that limit we could never get any better? We would have to stay at that level, with no growth, no improvements, from that point on.

I look back at where we were about five years into our marriage. We were about thirty, and Fred was on the cover of a restaurant magazine as the "Boy Wonder of the Food Service Industry." He was offered a large sum of money for the business he had built, but he knew he could make it worth even more, so he didn't sell. By the time he was ready to sell, the business was worth little, and he ultimately gave it to a key employee. Not only was Fred deflated and depressed, but I was angry. How could he have done this to me? How could he have humiliated me and put me in this embarrassing situation? What if the Lord had sent a notice to let us know at that point our training time was over. "You've been married five years, and you've learned all you ever can learn. One of you is depressed; the other angry. It's too bad, but that's where you are going to stay for life."

Gratefully, the Lord let us keep on learning. Fred profited from his mistakes, and I learned my happiness didn't depend on money. These lessons took time, and they're continuing to this day; yes, we are still growing.

Why are we writing this book? Because we want to spare you some of the heartaches we went through in building our marriage. There were few books on marriage available when we were starting out. We didn't dare ask our mothers for help because they'd judge us as failures, and to ask our fathers to discuss such issues would have been unthinkable. We had to put up the good front, pretend to be happy, and let everyone think we were a model couple. We surely couldn't ask about sex, because our parents played innocent and naive and seemed to believe we had been dropped into our cribs by a large stork flying by with a bundle. They let us know we should be grateful that they accepted us instead of sending the stork off to search for another chimney. Once I asked my mother some minor marriage question, and she said, "You made your bed, now lie in it." This didn't help much, but I did learn not to ask her anything remotely intimate.

Isn't it great that we live in a time when nothing is too private to ask about? When solutions for every problem are sitting on a bookshelf waiting for us to reach out and read one? When God's Word gives us principles to live by and there are pastors, writers, and speakers to help us apply these truths to our lives?

How about You?

"Marriage is like life . . . ," Robert Louis Stevenson wrote. "It is a field of battle, and not a bed of roses." Let's look at our moments together as a friendly, challenging time of building a marriage from wherever it is to wherever you want it to be. Each day we will share from our lengthy experience God's plan for each one of us. Some days my words will be lighthearted and uplifting. Some days Fred's words will take you deeply into God's truth, and you will be newly inspired and invigorated. The potential for growth is within each one of us, and we'll hope to give you a fresh thought each day that you can learn, practice, and discuss. We want to help you move your marriage from a field of battle to a bed of roses.

Will it take forty-five years? Probably not for you as it did for us.

I'm sure you are fast learners and someday Fred and I will look up and see you passing us by. Well, won't you?

Suggested Prayer for Today

Dear God our Father, we know You have a plan for our lives, and we want to live that plan to our fullest. Open our hearts that we may desire to know truth and be willing to change ourselves and not each other. We await Your instructions with excitement. You have told us to build upon the solid rock and not the shifting sand. Sometimes we feel that our foundation is weak, and we want to begin to build our marriage on a firm foundation. We pledge to read and pray each day, and we know You will change us when we do our part, even if it takes forty-five years!

    In Jesus' Name we pray. Amen.

12

The Porch Swing of Life

Where there is no vision, the people perish.

Proverbs 29:18 KJV

Florence

Now that your eyes are open and your spirits are willing, what is your first step? Do you need to make lists and establish five-year plans? Or do you dare to dream beyond the ordinary?

The Rev. Robert Schuller, on his first trip to Russia, stated on the radio, "You and you alone can determine your dreams." We can all see why the Russians had not dared to dream. There was no hope. Their lives were so controlled that there was no opportunity to rise above the norm. But in our country there is endless opportunity. We can make goals, follow plans, and achieve more than our parents did.

Fred and I were in Berlin shortly after the wall was torn down, and we had the opportunity to walk from the West to the East. Each side had been equally devastated at the end of World War II, but the recovery was drastically different on the two sides of the city. The Allies—primarily the United States, England, and France—had given free aid to the West side. Residents of West Berlin were told to get up from their defeat and rebuild. They were given a vision, a possibility.

Conversely, the East was under Communist control and was allowed no vision. Nothing changed. When we walked from the West, with its wide boulevards brightened by flowered medians, glitzy boutiques, tall trees, and robust people, into the East side, it was like going from life into death. Bombed-out buildings still stood as they'd been since the bombs fell fifty years ago. There were no flowers, the trees were without leaves, no birds were singing, and the people looked sad and drab.

Without a vision, the people perish.

Other nations see Americans as compulsive workers, dying for the dollar. Yet with all this ambition and desire for success, why don't we enjoy the climb more? Why don't we dare to dream?

For some of us the first reason may be that we weren't encouraged as children to think we could be successful. Some of us may have had parents who thought we wouldn't amount to "a row of pins." Some of us may have little education or a feeling that we're not smart enough to become anything worthwhile.

A few of us may have achieved great goals or made a lot of money but still feel insecure inside. Perhaps we've asked ourselves, "Who am I?" and not heard a clear answer.

No matter where we are in our self-evaluation today, we can move on. We can dare to dream.

After all, as poet Robert Browning asserted, "A man's reach should exceed his grasp, or what's a Heaven for?"

It's always easier to relax than to reach, to give up than to grasp, but we want to stretch rather than to just settle into the status quo. If we rested until the perfect path to success opened before us, we would all be sitting on the porch swing of life waiting for directions.

How about You?

Let's pretend that's where we are today, lined up on that glider on the veranda looking out to blue skies and sunshine forever. We can smell the sweet flowers of success, but if we're going to pick them we'll have to get up out of the glider, step off the porch, and take action. We can see ideas flitting around like hummingbirds, but to use one of those ideas we'll have to get a net and capture it. Some of us would prefer to rock where we are, to watch life glide by from our safe spot on the porch swing, than to get up and move on. Some prefer to accept what's good rather than to aim for the best. Some would rather sit on the sofa than to dare to dream.

The Bible tells us, "Where there is no vision the people perish," and yet many of us are without a vision. We're taking the fatalistic approach that "if God wanted me to have a better job He'd send a personnel manager to my front porch."

Don't be a porch-swing person any longer. Don't stuff your laurels into a pillow and rest upon them. Don't rock in indecision and inertia.

Fred and I are calling you off the porch so we can all dare to dream together.

Suggested Prayer for Today

Dear Lord Jesus, as our inspirational leader, You are always there to move us on. You don't get discouraged or give up. You've lived Your life on earth, suffered abuse for doing right, kept Your eyes on Your Father God, and walked the path He laid out before You. You went willingly to the cross so that we today could be free. We thank You for Your sacrifice of Your life. You never became the human leader You could have been, and yet we complain if we don't get promoted or our teens don't get accepted at Harvard. Lord, lift our eyes above the temporal. Give us a vision so that we will not perish. Help us to dare to dream. In the precious Name of Jesus we pray. Amen.

.

13

Establish Peace

If possible, so far as it depends on you, be at peace with all men.
Romans 12:18

Florence

If you've been using the porch swing as an excuse for inaction, we hope you now recognize the problems your inertia is causing and you're committed to moving on together. Don't wait for a three-point plan from Heaven to drop in your laps, but pray for the exciting creativity that is uniquely yours.

If God didn't want us to have positive, productive marriages, He would not have created the family as an institution. He could have left us all single and wandering around doing our own thing, but instead He decreed man shall not live alone. To live together means we can't do our own thing; we must learn to share not just our bed but our ideas. We must communicate openly with each other without fear of retribution. If you have kept your thoughts to yourself because you're afraid your mate won't agree with you or will think your ideas are stupid, let's change that today. Let's agree that we'll share our dreams with each other, and we'll listen without condemnation. My friend Evelyn Davison told me her husband looked at her one day and said, "You'd communicate a lot better if you didn't talk so much." Does that sound like some of us? Are we all talk and no listen?

How about You?

Why do husbands and wives hesitate to be open with each other? There are two usual reasons. One is we were put down as a child with such comments as, "That's the dumbest thing I've ever heard!"

"When you have something worthwhile to say, let us know. Until then, keep quiet." "Children are to be seen and not heard." Did either of you hear things like this as children? Share any such comments with each other.

The second reason you or your spouse may hesitate to communicate is because one or both of you has shut the other one down so hurtfully that you don't want to try again. You've learned the hard way it's better to keep quiet and stay out of trouble. Can you right now tell your mate just one thing he or she has said that made you feel stupid? Will you listen to each other? Don't get defensive, but think about your comment. Did you intend to be funny? Were you trying to teach the other one something? Did this comment come from your own pain? Could you both have lived more happily if it had not been said? Was there a better way to get your point across? Did you each push the other one back to childhood hurts? Did you "sound just like my mother"?

If you will take the time right now to tackle these questions openly, you will be ready to move on. If one of you reacts in fear, stop and explain why you're reacting this way. This is not a time to straighten out each other but to listen, apologize, forgive, and then move on. You don't need to establish blame. It's over; whoever "started it" doesn't matter. Just learn and don't do it again.

Remember when you first met? What was it that made you enjoy each other's company? Could you talk with each other by the hour in a way you had never dared try with anyone else before? Tell each other how you felt. When did this free exchange cease to be? Did one of you attack and the other withdraw? What can you do to change this pattern? The first step in any healing is to admit there is a problem. Is there one? If one of you says yes and the other no, there is a problem!

A couple came to Fred one day for help. The man stated loudly, "My wife here is depressed. Do something with her."

Fred asked the man, "And what is wrong with you?"

"Oh, there's nothing wrong with me. She's the one who's depressed. I don't have a problem."

Fred said, "If you have a depressed wife, you do have a problem."

Do you have a problem? What is it? What can you each do to improve your current situation and communication? This lesson today is to help you be open with each other so that you will be able to get the maximum out of your time together each day.

Our verse today states: "So far as it depends on you, be at peace with all [people]." Start now with your partner. Establish peace. Peace, not contention, leads on to love.

Suggested Prayer for Today

Our Father in Heaven, we need Your guidance. When we start to talk, we get defensive. We each want to prove our point. We know You don't care about our point. Who's right or wrong doesn't matter to You. We know it's all right for each of us to have opinions— even different opinions. But we ask You to give us an extra portion of love today that will lift us above our differences, that will give us peace. We really want this peace; we don't want to be pinning blame on the other person. Why do we do this? Is it because we are protecting ourselves? Oh, Father embrace us and forgive us so we can move on in love.

In the Name of the Father, the Son, and Holy Spirit, Amen.

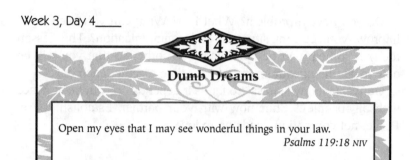

14

Dumb Dreams

Open my eyes that I may see wonderful things in your law.
Psalms 119:18 NIV

Florence

Now that you've found you can talk together without getting angry, let's look at the dreams each of you has had that you haven't dared to share. Is there someplace you've always wanted to go? A career you've always dreamed of having? A ministry you'd like to pursue? Listen, and don't laugh at each other's thoughts. Ideas are very personal; they belong to us alone, and we don't want someone else to scoff at them. You may have some dreams you've never told anyone. Maybe your parents didn't ask or seem to care, and you didn't dare to tell others for fear of ridicule. Isn't it a shame that some of our most brilliant thoughts have died a solitary death with no one even coming to the funeral?

A teacher told me she had tried an experiment to see how well parents know their children's desires and dreams. The day before a PTA meeting, she gave out blank sheets of paper to her students and asked them to write down their dreams. "What do you really want in life?" she asked them. "What would you like to be?" The room became quiet as each child was allowed to dream—not only allowed but encouraged to dream. The teacher collected the papers, and then had the pupils share orally from their hearts. The rule was that no one could scoff at others. Each one had permission to go beyond the norm. Some were so impressed they had new respect for each other.

When the parents assembled in the classroom, the teacher again passed out pieces of paper and asked them to write down their children's dreams. A look of mystery fell upon them as they pondered, *What does my child dream?* When the papers were collected, most of them were blank. Some said, "My child has no dreams," and one said, "All his dreams are dumb dreams."

The teacher then read some of the children's answers without identifying who wrote them. The parents were stunned to find that their children actually had some desires beyond the norm. Their children had actually been thinking.

How about You?

Share your dreams with each other. And then consider your children's dreams. Are you aware of their dreams? Have they dared to tell you? Are they afraid you'll make fun of them? Why not make this idea into a family project? Ask around the dinner table: "If money or education were no obstacle, what would you really want to do in life?" Let each one share, and don't allow anyone to sneer at another's thoughts, at those inner ideas that we own as a part of ourselves.

> "For my thoughts are not your thoughts,
> neither are your ways my ways," declares the LORD.
>
> *Isaiah 55:8* NIV

What if you don't have any dreams? Where can you look to receive inspiration? Start with the Scriptures and look at the life of Abraham, who had enough faith to follow God's direction even when he didn't know where he was going; of Isaac, who found his beautiful wife, Rebecca, standing alone at a well; of Jacob, who worked so hard to win the lovely Rachel and was given sad wall-eyed Leah instead; of Joseph, who kept his faith in prison and became the highest-ranking official in Egypt. Study these Bible heroes and discover how they held on to their dreams even in the face of tremendous obstacles. Teach your children these stories as biographies of real people. Use these lives for discussion and inspiration in your family. What does your family know about the life of Jesus? Have you seen how He forgave others, how He ministered to the poor and sick, how He loved the unlovely? What strength we can draw from the lives of the real people in the Bible! Start today to study God's Word in a practical sense.

Back when I was first teaching Bible studies and growing in my knowledge of the Lord Jesus, I assigned myself to do a series on the Old Testament. I had never really read it completely through, but I knew I would force myself to study if I had to teach it to others. What a wealth of inspiration I tapped into. I became so enthralled with the plots and the people that I wanted to teach everything I learned.

If you haven't opened God's Word and prayed, "Show me your wondrous truths, Lord," you have a treat in store for you as a couple and as a family. These characters are not religious goody-goodies. They are people who often made poor choices, but who learned from their mistakes. A recent survey showed that the only Bible character a majority of schoolchildren could identify was David as he killed Goliath. Make sure your children can do better than that. Study, share, and apply the truths to your life and then to theirs, and you will all dare to dream with a new excitement.

Suggested Prayer for Today

Dear Lord Jesus, Your life alone should be an example for our family of the one perfect man. We should be learning of Your love and Your forgiving spirit, and yet we confess we have worshiped You without seeing You as a real person who faced real problems and dealt with real temptations. Lord, help us to see You as an inspiration for our lives and not just as an icon to revere. We pray in anticipation of our new life. In the Name of the Lord Jesus we ask it. Amen.

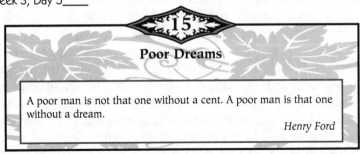

15

Poor Dreams

A poor man is not that one without a cent. A poor man is that one without a dream.

Henry Ford

Florence

So often we hear people say, "If I'd only had more money, I would have amounted to something." Is that true? Or is Henry Ford's statement true when he says it's not lack of money that keeps us down but lack of a dream? As a nation we have often tied potential success to money, and yet in my own personal case that wasn't true. As my two brothers and I grew up in the three rooms behind our father's store, we had none of the trappings of success. Our living room was the store; we had no car, no phone, no hot water tap, no washing machine, no refrigerator. We ate only what we sold in the store. If it didn't come out of a can, we didn't eat it.

I remember one lady who came into the store and said to my mother, "It's a shame there's no hope for those children, for they appear so bright." We were bright, and we didn't let that lady take away our dreams. We studied hard, took music and elocution lessons, held fast to our dreams, and without money, we all made it in life. With scholarships and personal dedication to our dreams, we all became successful communicators: I as a teacher and then as a speaker/writer, Jim as a career chaplain in the Air Force, and Ron as the top radio personality in Dallas for more than twenty-five years. How did this happen? How did three children with no money and "no hope" achieve success?

In looking back on our lives, I can see that the ingredient we had that most children lack was the ever-presence of our parents. They didn't go to work; we lived in their work. There was never a moment when our parents weren't available. Our customers were our extended family. They looked at our report cards and came to our amateur performances at the church talent shows. Our parents and our customers were our enthusiastic encouragers.

Our father, born and brought up in England, taught us Bible verses, poems, and vocabulary. Our mother, a violin and cello teacher, gave us a love and understanding of classical music, and Aunt Sadie, the church organist, taught us piano lessons at no charge. The values of words and of music were instilled in our minds, and we have used everything we were taught at some point in our lives.

In her book *What Money Can't Buy,* author Susan Mayer concludes that income has a smaller impact on how poor children fare than we might think. In following families over decades, she has decided that if by some miracle our government could double the income of the lowest 20 percent, it would make almost no measurable difference in the major social problems of pregnant teens, single mothers, behavioral development, or mental health, and it might even increase idleness of young men by reducing incentives to work. In its review of the book, *U.S. News & World Report* said, "Reluctantly, Mayer reaches a very unliberal conclusion: Parents' character—their skills, diligence, honesty, good health—probably matter more to children's prospects than money."[1] I am grateful as I look back that even without a choice, I had a very nurturing childhood. My brothers and I were low on money but rich in parental attention.

In our experience, we find many families with both parents working, overwhelming debt, emotional stress, and no energy left to spend creative and study time with the children. Whether a family has the biggest house or the newest car makes little difference if the children feel neglected. Being blessed with material goods and a comfortable lifestyle doesn't mean you are neglectful parents, but no matter what your economic situation is, make sure your children don't feel that everything else comes before them.

How about You?

Ask your children if they need any more of your time, and if so when. Do they need help with homework, or do they need you to sit next to them when they practice the piano? Do they want to shop for clothes when you're in a hurry? Carpooling children around doesn't count as quality time. Remember, the dream isn't the money and the possessions but what you pour into your children one at a time: your character, honesty, moral values, manners, and your love of God and His Word. These are things that make the big difference in the long run and that few children have enough of in our busy society.

I once heard author Nora Ephron say, "Most children would rather have their mother in the next room having a nervous breakdown than have her in good health lying on a beach in Hawaii."

I didn't work or travel for speaking engagements when I was raising my children, and I thought I was the model for Super Mom. Yet one of my children once said, "You never came to anything I did." I was stopped in my tracks by that remark, wondering how my child could have forgotten all the school events, sports activities, and countless other performances I'd attended. When we reviewed the truth, it turned out there was only one major event I had missed, but that was the one that had stayed in the negative memory bank.

We spend time with our children to give them all the benefits we can, not just so they will rise up and call us blessed. But a little applause would be rewarding now and then.

Suggested Prayer for Today

Dear Lord, today we thank You for the time our parents spent with us and for what they taught us. Bring to our minds something special they did just for us. Show us what we need to do better as parents. Help us to pay eye-to-eye attention to our children. Slow us down, Lord, so we don't seem to them to be in a hurried frenzy all the time. Give us a better attention span for what our mate has to say, too, and help us keep our focus first on You and then on our family. We know we won't have a second chance to raise these children. Help us to continue to think on these things. We ask this in Jesus' Name. Amen.

16

Lifters or Leaners

A happy heart makes the face cheerful, but heartache crushes the spirit.

Proverbs 15:13 NIV

Florence

By now we hope you realize how important it is to have a dream to lift yourselves beyond the ordinary walk through life. We've talked about how couples need to accept each other's thoughts even if they don't agree. We've seen that looking into God's Word will give us inspiration. Now what new steps do you need to take to pursue your dream?

At the turn of the last century poetess Ella Wheeler Wilcox wrote:

> The two kinds of people on earth that I mean
> Are the people who lift and the people who lean.

Read that couplet and recognize the truth in that simple statement. How many of us could divide our friends, or even ourselves, into those who lift and those who lean? The ones who encourage us and the ones who push us down? Some people grow up in families of leaners, people who don't lift them up, people who burst childhood bubbles.

Picture for a moment a bathtub. It's empty, cold, and hard. Now turn on the faucet and adjust it to the perfect temperature for you. Something cold is warming up. Now pour in some bubble bath, and suddenly the ordinary becomes exciting. The aroma is pleasant, but the best part is watching the bubbles grow. Out of one tablespoon of liquid comes a mountain of bubbles. So little becomes so much. The stronger the force of the water, the bigger the bubbles become. Is there anyone of us who can resist the temptation of sliding into such pleasure? (Some of you may want to go right now and start running the water, throw in some magic bath beads, hop in, and continue to read!)

But what happens if you get called to the phone before you get in the tub? You shut off the faucet and leave the warm bubbles that may have mounded even higher than the tub itself, intending to come right back. However, the cares of the world detain you, and when you return, the fluff and the fun have gone out of the bubbles. They've died down a bit; if you were gone too long they have disappeared altogether. But all is not lost. You turn on the water again full force, and with the new "encouragement" fresh bubbles reappear. The water gets warm again. You've revived what seemed to be dying.

Now consider our childhood minds. We've each been given at least a "capful" of creativity. Left in the bottle, it doesn't produce any new ideas, but poured out into a warm environment it begins to bubble. The stronger the encouragement, the fuller the force, the more bubbles appear. So many of us are just bubbling over with enthusiasm and excitement, our minds overflowing with creative thoughts. But what happens if we get left alone with no one stirring up the waters, no one keeping the bubbles alive? After a while the enthusiasm cools down. The bubbles burst, and we're left with just a tub of cold water and perhaps the remnant of a few tiny bubbles here and there.

But don't despair. We can turn on the tap again. We can bring some of the bubbles back to life. They may not be as big or as lively, but they can be stirred up one more time.

How about You?

Think about your creativity and about how you respond to your spouse's creativity. Is your creativity heated up and encouraged? When you pour yourself out, are you allowed to bubble to the surface? Or are you left alone with no one fluffing up your bubbles until one by one they pop and disappear? Has someone beaten down your bubbles, taken a paddle to them and pushed them under until there are none left alive? When one pops up here or there does someone say, "Don't try that. What a dumb idea. It'll never work"? There go your bubbles down the drain.

I want to help you put the bubbles back into your life, to encourage you to dare to dream.

Start by asking each other right now to describe the lifters and the leaners in your childhood. Think of those who really encouraged you, those who blew bubbles with you. Discuss the leaners, those who pushed you down and burst your bubbles. Were these people your parents, your teachers, your pastor, your friends? Which were lifters and which leaned heavily upon you?

How are you doing with your children? With each other? Which one of you lifts? Is one of you leaning on someone else—your spouse or a child—for your emotional support? Have you made that person your personal happiness pill?

How do your children view you two? Do they see Mother lifting up, making excuses for Dad's anger, covering up his failures? Do they see Dad lifting Mom up, explaining why she's always tired, excusing her forgetfulness, putting a blanket over her depression? Or do they see you both as heavy leaners? Children start out with an innate intuition. They know which end is up. They see the difference between the lifter and the leaner.

Share Ella Wheeler Wilcox's little verse with your children and ask them who among their friends lifts them up and who pushes them down. How do they think their friends view them? Are any changes needed in their attitudes and behaviors?

If you are really brave and can stay calm no matter what, ask them how they see the two of you. If they blanch and look frightened, you will know they are afraid of at least one of you. Let them know you won't get angry (and don't), and ask them to tell you what they really think of your differences. Is one of you a lifter and one a leaner? Ask them for examples and really listen to what they say. Don't defend yourself or make excuses. Thank them and don't throw their remarks back at them in the future. If you can handle all this, you may open communication on a more honest level than you've ever had before.

Suggested Prayer for Today

Dear God, our Father, how we want to be lifters to each other and to our children! Give us the ability to look into our own lives and see if we're lifters or leaners. Give us the courage to ask our children their opinions and not get angry when they give them. Give us discernment to know if they're honest or just saying what they think we want to hear. Don't let us be parents who burst our family members' bubbles but ones who encourage each other and our children as we go out daily to a difficult world.

O Lord, lift us up! Don't let us lean! We pray in Jesus' precious Name. Amen.

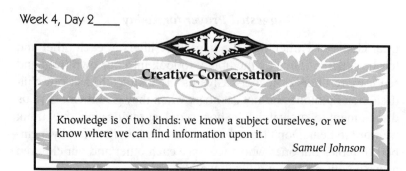

Creative Conversation

> Knowledge is of two kinds: we know a subject ourselves, or we know where we can find information upon it.
>
> *Samuel Johnson*

Florence

When a group of Rhodes Scholars was tested to discover any common threads among them, one consistency was the fact that these students came from homes where the families ate dinner together. At first the researchers probably thought this was hardly a great intellectual conclusion but rather a cultural happenstance. Or was it? As they interviewed these outstanding students, they soon learned it wasn't the food but the quality of the conversation that made the difference. Sitting around the table encouraged young people to share their thoughts and feelings and kept the whole family in touch with and in support of each other's activities.

As I grew up in my father's store, we had no dining room. We ate in the store! As I look back on this odd arrangement, I realize that where we sat didn't shape our lives but what we said did. My father gave us challenges each morning, and we were to report our conclusions at the supper table. Before we left for school, Dad had read several of the newspapers we sold, and he would give us a brief but clear summary of the major news of the day. In the evening, even with customers milling about, Dad would call for our creative answers to his challenge and ask how we had used his news summary at school. Usually we had worked it into our conversation, and often we were the only students who were aware of the news item when the teacher asked about it.

None of us became Rhodes Scholars, but we have all made our living with words and with our ability to make an interesting story out of the skimpiest of facts.

A friend of mine spent a summer working at the Kennedy family's Hyannis Port, Massachusetts, compound back during World War II. She was so impressed with the fact that Joseph and Rose Kennedy asked questions of their children about current events, listened to their answers, and complimented them on their grasp of national politics and global affairs.

In a *Newsweek* cover story some fifty years later, the writer reviewed how one segment of the Kennedys had turned out. "At dinner at Bobby Kennedy's, each child had to come to the table ready to discuss one current event; at the age of 12, the requirement was raised to three current events."[1] This large family followed the same pattern as Bobby Kennedy's parents had done before them, the same as I repeated what my father had done to challenge my family.

No matter what any of us might think of Kennedy morals, we could agree that as a family they have stood center stage in the political arena. Did talking around the dinner table have anything to do with their grasp of national and world affairs? Did my father's example make an impact on our lives? Our children tend to follow what was taught to them even if they didn't like it at the time.

As Fred and I raised our children amid a variety of dinner guests, we did the same thing my father had done. I kept the conversation lively, topical, and up to date, and Fred kept track of what percentage of the sharing each person was allowed so that one would not monopolize the whole time. Fred would divide the number of people by 100 to come up with each person's percentage of "talk time" during each one of our meals. If there were 10 people, each person was supposed to get 10 percent of the mealtime to express his or her views, then someone would inevitably pipe up, "Your 10 percent is up now." We all liked quiet guests who would say, "You can have my 10 percent."

How about You?

Did you grow up in a family that conversed at the table and learned to be respectful of others' opinions? Did one of you come from a family where no one talked to each other? Discuss these differences as soon as possible and see how you are doing with yourselves and with your children.

Marita once had a boyfriend who got nervous at our house because we talked. When she went to his house, she found out why. They all had dinner sitting in a row facing the TV and eating from TV tables. No one talked. They could only say, "Pass the salt" during commercials. In an era where conversation is a lost art, give your children an edge by encouraging intelligent, creative discussions around your dinner table. You might even produce a Rhodes Scholar or two!

Suggested Prayer for Today

Dear Lord, show us how to converse with each other and with our children, how to make our time together really count. Help us to be willing to make the effort to know what's going on in the world and to show our children by example the value of keeping up with current events. We see now the importance in helping our children rise above the monotony of TV and learn how to converse intelligently with adults.

Thank You for Your care and Your patience. In Jesus' Name. Amen.

18

Evaluating Ourselves

> Oh wad some power the giftie gie us
> To see oursels as others see us!
>
> *Robert Burns*

Florence

From the time I was a child, I heard this verse from the mouth of my Scottish mother, Katie MacDougall.

All three of us children were strong-minded young people, and our mother would caution us that not everyone would think we were as great as we thought we were. She would do us a favor by pointing out some fault that we had seen as a virtue and letting us know we should pray to see ourselves as others see us. Mother was always concerned about outside opinion, often wondering, What will THEY think? Even though we never met these "they" people (they must have lived in another town), our lives were influenced by them as we had to ask ourselves before every venture, "What will THEY think?"

In today's society of "anything goes," we seem to have put aside the concern of what other people will think of our actions; we seem not to care about anyone's opinion but our own. "Do your own thing" has become an accepted slogan for free-thinkers.

Is there a middle road between constantly worrying over other people's opinions and blatantly disregarding acceptable behavior? Which way were you both brought up? Was it with similar regard for other people's opinions, or were your families different? Fred and I tried to create a balance in our home, but as we became known in the Christian arena, our children were subjects of scrutiny, and many THEYs arose to watch over them. We had to tread a fine line between letting others' opinions control our children's lives and allowing them to "let it all hang out."

In the process of striving for this balance, Fred and I began a family evaluation plan. We devised a way to expose all of us Littauers to an in-house analysis of the best of our traits and the areas in which we needed to improve. In order to make this idea work, Fred and I had to be willing to be examined also. We chose New Year's Day as a good time to test each other and to make new goals for the future. Fred made out a big chart with all our names across the top and two categories to be answered: What I like about each person and where he or she needs improvement. We all got promptly to work and were able to be completely honest because no one would know who wrote each comment except Father Fred, who tallied up our responses.

Naturally, Fred had a master chart, and when he had inserted all of the entries, he read them off to us. We tried to guess who had said what about us as we each listened to comments about ourselves. This was such an eye-opening experience that I saved the first chart and still have it before me as I write.

The things the children liked about me were: cooking ability; teaches lovingness to the kids; makes fondue suppers; is happy and loving; has true concern; has various talents; is able to have fun; has a loving, sweet spirit; is a good, helpful teacher; is an understanding friend; and makes home a fun place. My negatives were: shouldn't talk so much on the phone, shouldn't lecture so much, shouldn't tell us we're in a bad mood, shouldn't get upset so easily, should be better prepared earlier, should be more humble and patient.

Father Fred dressed well; was neat and organized; had a consistent life; applied what he taught others to himself; was kind, sweet, thoughtful, considerate, and loving; and was understanding, fair; and friendly. He needed to improve in being more pleasant to Marita's friends, in getting over bad moods, not being so serious all the time, not getting upset or moody over little things, being more joyful and fun to be with, and not being grumpy.

When Fred read all the comments, he listed them for each person, emphasizing each person's strengths and encouraging him or her in any perceived weaknesses. We kept the discussion on a positive level, so that we each ended the day feeling good about ourselves and were determined to improve even more in the new year.

Because we emphasized the best and not the worst, our children responded well and were willing to work on their weaknesses. Lauren had to stop being so bossy, bubbly Marita had to tone down and not talk so much, and young Fred needed to cheer up and not be so gloomy. This insightful activity was such a growth experience that we repeated it each New Year's Day for several years.

How about You?

Why don't you try this in-house evaluation? Make a little chart, as shown here, for each person to use. Each one writes his or her own best quality and how he or she has tried to improve. Then each person notes the same things about everyone else. One of you tallies the comments and reads them off in a positive manner. You may want to do this each New Year's Day also. If you do not have children, talk over these points together and use the chart. Who knows what you could learn from each one!

Name _____

My best quality is _____

In the last year I have tried to improve in_____

_____

As for others:	Best Quality:	Needs Improvement in:
_____	_____	_____
_____	_____	_____
_____	_____	_____
_____	_____	_____
_____	_____	_____
_____	_____	_____

Master Chart

Date_____

	Husband	Wife	Child 1	Child 2
Best Qualities 1.				
2.				
3.				
4.				
Needs Improvement 1.				
2.				
3.				
4.				

Suggested Prayer for Today

Dear Lord Jesus, thank You that You encourage us to examine ourselves. We know You don't want us to be anxious over others' opinions, nor do You want us to be rude and not care. Help us to use these ideas we've shared today to start our family on the road to improvement. We are willing to be open to what our children have to say about us and show them our desire to please them. Keep our eyes focused on what is best for us as we become closer to You. Help our children to aim to be the best they can be and to encourage each other. We thank You and praise You in Jesus' Name. Amen.

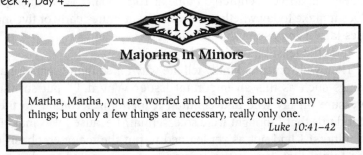

Majoring in Minors

Martha, Martha, you are worried and bothered about so many things; but only a few things are necessary, really only one.

Luke 10:41–42

Fred

Think of your family conversation at the dinner table. What is it like? Or do you all watch television at that hour? If you do, that probably means there is no conversation at all. The program becomes the family's focus.

As with most couples, Florence and I came from very different backgrounds with numerous disparities in the way our childhood homes functioned. Television was never an issue; it was too new. In Florence's family, mealtimes were filled with lively conversation emphasizing sharing, learning, and humor. At my home, it seemed that the focus was more on form, sitting up straight, keeping your elbows off the table, not talking with food in your mouth. Whose turn it was to do the dishes and family chores were major concerns.

As Florence and I began our own family, we both tried to bring elements of what had been made important in our childhood families to our new family table. Florence tried to encourage meaningful conversation, and I was determined that our children would grow up with good table manners!

I carried this concern for "appearance" into every aspect of our marriage. I felt that punctuality was next to godliness. As someone with many melancholy traits, I stressed the importance of being on time for everyone, especially my sanguine wife. She never seemed to know what time it was and would frequently get distracted when I thought she should have been getting ready.

Now, I'm going to ask you what today seems likely a perfectly absurd question: "How important was it on Sunday, July 11, 1971, that we all arrive at church on time at 10:55 A.M.?" What difference does it make today whether we were five minutes early or five minutes late? What is the truthful answer?

"Not the least bit!"

Then will someone kindly tell me why for so many years I made things such as this an important issue? Why did I put so much pressure on my wife and children to perform according to these standards that I thought were so essential? Because I was majoring in minors! I had not as yet learned to put the major emphasis on the things that were actually important as opposed to what only seemed important at the time. Table manners are important, this is true, but they are not life itself! And do you know that with or without the benefit of my training, my wife has excellent table manners! There must be a lesson here.

In recent years, my major focus has been to make sure my wife is safe, secure, and happy. I strive to make sure I never interrupt her, correct her, or expect anything of her, especially being on time! I'm not perfect at it yet, and I may never be, but she appreciates the fact that I am always sincerely trying. When I do stumble she is much less threatened and can more readily overlook my oversight.

I am now majoring in the things that are important to my wife. My goal is to please her in everything I do. What is the result? I'm a far better husband, and Florence is a far happier and contented wife. This translates into, "I love you."

How about You?

Since we know that opposites attract, chances are that one of you tends to be more of a perfectionist and the other is more casual. Typically the proper and perfect spouse tends to instill his or her standards on the carefree and more haphazard spouse. Understanding our personality differences helps all of us to recognize our God-given individualities and to accept each other as we are without the need to effect change. Florence always wanted to be loved just the way she was and for who she was, not when she might become perfect.

Where are the two of you today in accepting each other just the way you are? Take some time today to discuss those areas in your relationship where either or both of you might be majoring in minors. Share with each other honestly and from your heart what your desires are, how you wish to be viewed and treated by your mate. Speak of the things that are sometimes said that are hurtful and tend to cause you to become cool and aloof.

The time you invest in this kind of disclosure and introspection will reap huge dividends in the future. Every day that you delay helps to further seal the cap on the emotional freedom you could be enjoying together.

Suggested Prayer for Today

Heavenly Father, this kind of openness and introspection is apt to be threatening to me. It is sometimes much easier to bottle up my feelings and say nothing. Yet down deep in my heart, Lord, I know that unless we deal together with some of these things that bother us we will never grow closer together. Instead we'll build walls that are even higher and thicker. Father God, I want to be obedient to You. I want us to have the kind of relationship with each other that You have always intended for us. Therefore I ask You to remove the fear from my heart and give me the strength to be willing to delve into the unknown. I thank You, my Lord and my God, that You already know both of our hearts and all of our needs. In Your patient Name I pray. Amen.

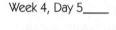

Silver Boxes

> Let no corrupt communication proceed out of your mouth, but that which is good to the use of edifying, that it might minister grace unto the hearers.
>
> *Ephesians 4:29 KJV*

Florence

In the last several days' readings we have suggested that you ask yourselves, Am I a lifter or a leaner? Do I encourage creative conversation? Am I willing to evaluate myself and my family? Am I majoring in minors? All of these introspective questions together will change your outlook on life if you put them into practice. If you dare to dream that you will move on to a more exciting marriage than what you have right now, today's verse and its application can make all the difference.

It was years ago when I was called upon to give a spontaneous children's sermon. Praying quickly for an idea, I thought of the verse Ephesians 4:29, a verse we had taught our children to remind them to say kind words to each other at the dinner table. We had reduced the message down to three little words: "Is it edifying?" If a child insulted one of the others, we would ask, "Was that edifying?" The child would then have to take it back and apologize. The children were allowed to ask the same question of Fred and me if we spoke too harshly. I explained this system to the church children that day when I was called forward with no warning. I reviewed the verse with them. No bad words should come out of my mouth, only good words that will lift up and not knock down, words that will do a favor, be like a gift to the hearer.

As we completed the lesson, a little girl stepped into the aisle and said, "What she means is our words should be like a little silver box with a bow on top." The audience responded so well to her comment that I kept the thought and began to build a message from it.

First I asked myself how I had done in giving out silver boxes. Did my children look upon my words as gifts? Did they say to their friends, "Wait till you hear my mother. Every word she says is like a gift. At my house, it's Christmas every day"?

As I reviewed this idea in my mind, I remembered my son looking at me one day and stating as only teenagers can do, "It amazes me that people pay money to hear you talk. That must be because they don't have to listen to you for nothing." Hardly a silver box! I tried to rationalize that he hadn't really meant that, but then I thought of some things I'd said to him . . .

One day he came home from a friend's house and reported, "Mrs. Johnson says I have a charming personality."

Obviously I should have said, "Mrs. Johnson's right." But considering he hardly talked at home, I snapped, "I'd sure like to see some of that charm around here."

As I look back on this incident, I realize Mrs. Johnson gave young Fred a Silver Box for his charm. He brought the gift home to his mother, and I tossed it away. He could go to Mrs. Johnson's every day next week, and she could continue to give him Silver Boxes, but it wouldn't really help if he knew that when he handed it to me I'd throw the gift away.

Before I could teach a lesson on Silver Boxes, I had to make sure I was giving them. The Lord kept disciplining me and saying, "Florence, is that edifying?" As I prayerfully worked on changing my attitude, my son responded, and our relationship developed to the positive one we have today.

I look back on my childhood and realize my father was my most dependable encourager. He was always optimistic and told me daily that I could make it. In spite of our lack of money, he gave me hope that if I studied hard enough I could get a scholarship to college—and I did! During Christmas vacation my senior year my father showed me a box he had hidden behind our piano. The box was full of newspaper clippings written by my father and published in Boston papers. I had no idea he could write, and when I asked why he hadn't told me about those articles, he replied, "Your mother told me because I didn't have much education I shouldn't try to write. It might not be good, she said, and we'd all be humiliated."

My father explained how he'd written secretly, sent the articles in, watched until they were published, and then cut them out and saved them in the box. "Today," he said, "I just felt like showing you this box. I won't be leaving you any money, but this box is for you."

The next day my parents went to Boston, and while he was there my father dropped dead of a sudden heart attack. It's true he left no money, but I have his box of clippings, his box of broken dreams, the evidence of what could have been if only someone had given him some encouraging words.

How about You?

Do you lift up your mate and give him or her Silver Boxes every day? Or are you negative, critical, and demeaning? So many marriages fail because spouses cut each other down instead of building each other up.

And while you're handing out Silver Boxes to each other—and we hope to your children as well—consider how you are doing with your own parents. No matter what their age, they long for praise and appreciation just like everyone else. They often feel useless and wonder if their grown children remember anything they did for them as they were growing up. Try saying, "I'll never forget how you sacrificed to help me get an education—or piano lessons—or my first car."

Talk openly today about how you are doing with each other, with your children, and with your parents. Be willing to accept what your mate says without becoming defensive or angry. If you react negatively, it shows you are not yet mature enough to take a deep look at yourself. Start today to give out Silver Boxes, gifts of encouraging words.

Suggested Prayer for Today

Dear Lord Jesus, You are a gift to us, and You provide us with enough love to give out over and over. We want to be encouragers.

We want people to look forward to seeing us enter a room because they know we will lift them up and never knock them down. Dear Lord, help us to speak kindly to all and make each sentence one that edifies others. Help us to be role models for our children so they will see You, Jesus, in us. May our words be gifts from here on. In the precious Name of Jesus we pray. Amen.

Improving Communication:
Venturing Beyond Your Comfort Zone

Let not your heart be troubled, nor let it be fearful.

John 14:27

Fred

Most husbands and wives communicate quite well on objective subjects: world events, sports, neighborhood news, etc. They feel free to share their opinions and understanding on a wide variety of rather general subjects with no hesitation. They chat amicably and cheerfully at the dinner table, when they're out with friends, and in front of the children. If couples are talking so easily, why are there so many books and articles in magazines about communications in marriage? Why do so many couples tell us, "We don't communicate"?

The problem comes when the subject becomes personal and involves feelings. Most of us are only willing to talk about those things or subjects in which we feel comfortable. We all have a "comfort zone" beyond which we will not venture, and we all have an area of "private property" we will allow no one to enter. When discussion comes close to those boundaries, most of us tend to clam up and erect "no trespassing" signs.

What happens when that person we're keeping out of our comfort zone is our spouse, the one to whom we should be the closest? Wouldn't you prefer to be able to share openly all those deeper feelings and needs with the mate God has given you instead of a counselor?

In the next few chapters we will share with you how to identify your areas of private property and offer some steps to help you open the gate or even break down the wall that may be separating you. If you are already aware that you have built such a wall of protection, you may be frightened at the thought of allowing that wall to be removed. From God's Word, and from our experience, we can share with you that there will never be the oneness and the unity that God intended for your marriage until those walls are dismantled. Only then can you experience the true peace and joy our Lord Jesus has already granted to us according to John 14:27.

Breaking down these walls may be hard to think of at the moment. They have represented safety to you for so long, but they are providing a false sense of security. They are also keeping out the best that God wants you to have. Remember that the Scripture says (in five different places!), that a man shall leave his father and mother and cleave unto his wife, and the two shall become one flesh. All of the relationship between husband and wife is dependent on the two becoming one. How can you and your spouse possibly become one when walls stand between you, keeping you emotionally apart?

How about You?

Will you agree together today to be willing to explore those areas of your marriage, those areas of your oneness, where there might be a wall that is keeping you apart? That's the first step: to be willing! Scripture tells us that God is always at work in us to make us willing and able to obey His good purpose. Now each of you decide: Are you willing to settle for anything less than your rightful inheritance from your Father in Heaven?

If you, as do most couples, have some barriers between you, we would like to suggest to you that you probably have only three choices: One, STATUS QUO—remain the same, stay right where you are in your relationship. Two, GIVE UP—chuck the whole situation because there is no hope. Or, three, CHANGE— work to bring the best into your married life, knowing that with God's help you can. Are there any other choices? Do you have any other options? Which one of these three choices will you make?

Surely it is best if each of you decides to do the work necessary to bring about change and improvement. However, if at the moment one of you is unwilling, the other can still do his or her part as God desires. There is never any loss from being in the will of God! Your marriage will still benefit, for the partner who may be unwilling at the moment will more than likely begin to see the changes that are taking place and then become a willing partner also!

Starting tomorrow, with the next chapter, you will have the opportunity to spotlight some of those areas of "private property" within yourself that may be blocking you from receiving God's best.

Suggested Prayer for Today

Dear God and Heavenly Father, yes, we do desire the best for our marriage. We desire the relationship You intended for us to have. We ask You today to open our spiritual eyes and open our emotional hearts that we may both be willing to see those areas that we have set aside for no one to see. We know, Lord, that You see everything. We are not fooling You, and truly, Lord, we don't want to fool each other. Nor do we want to fool ourselves into thinking there is no such area if there really is. So, Lord, we ask You today to shine Your Light of truth into our innermost beings. We ask You to reveal that which has been hidden in the darkness and bring it into the light. We thank You, Almighty God, for we know You are always patient with us, Your children, You are always gentle, and You are always compassionate. You understand each one of us and what goes on inside of us. We thank You, Lord, that we can trust some of these delicate issues to You. We thank You, Lord, and we praise You, our God Almighty, and Father of our Lord Jesus. Amen.

22

Improving Communication:
Spotlighting Trouble Spots #1

The Sovereign LORD has given me an instructed tongue, to know the word that sustains the weary. He wakens me morning by morning, wakens my ear to listen like one being taught.

Isaiah 50:4 NIV

Fred

Beside each of the following questions, there is a line for each of you to individually score yourself. Give yourself a rating according to how the statement applies to this scale:

> 0 – Almost never
> 1 – Seldom
> 2 – Sometimes
> 3 – Much of the time
> 4 – Almost always

This insightful but simple tool will be of no value to you unless you are totally honest with yourself and respond with what you feel is your true answer without regard to what your spouse marks.

	Wife	Husband
1. My mate is generally available to listen when I want to talk.	____	____
2. My mate is sympathetic and understanding when I want to share some deeper feelings with him/her.	____	____
3. My mate does not generally have to weigh his or her words carefully to keep me from getting angry or upset.	____	____

4. My mate and I usually have interesting
things to talk about with each other.   _____   _____

5. My mate is my best friend. I feel free
to share my hurts and frustrations
with him or her.   _____   _____

When you have scored yourselves from 0 to 4 on each question, compare your numbers in the two columns. The first thing to look for is similarity of answers. If they are the same or similar for a particular question, at least you are in agreement with the statement as it applies to the two of you. If they are not similar, then clearly there is an absence of harmony on that point. It is something you will need to discuss. If there is a significant discrepancy, we suggest you merely agree that this is something you both need to talk about . . . later. In a subsequent chapter we will give you some important guidelines to agree upon before opening up these topics for in-depth discussion.

Further, if one of you has marked 0 or 1 to one of the statements while the other has marked 3 or 4, you may be looking at one of the areas of your communication with each other that is a trouble spot. It may even be one of those areas of "private property" into which you will not permit the other to venture. These are danger spots! They do not need to be dealt with today, but they must not be forgotten or ignored if you intend to fulfill your dreams and attain what God has designed for you both.

To help you so that this item is not forgotten or ignored, you might want to put a big circle with a colored marker around the differing scores, or mark the whole line with a yellow highlighter. Later, when skimming through the pages, this highlighted or circled item will stand out and call for attention.

Tomorrow you will have a whole new set of five statements to score. Once again a caution: Since some of these statements may open up deep wounds from the past, wait for the guidelines that follow before you commence heavy discussion about these topics.

Suggested Prayer for Today

Blessed Lord Jesus, You are our hope. We can see now that our marriage—any marriage—doesn't stand a chance of fulfillment without You. We see now that knowing You is not enough. We need to grow deeper in our relationship with You, so that we can grow deeper in our relationship with each other. How else can we gain the victory or the cleansing, Lord, from our natural tendencies to be self-centered and to think first about our own needs.

Lord Jesus, I ask You to give me a selfless nature just like Yours. I want to be a fragrant aroma, a delight to You. I commit to You anew today, Lord Jesus, that I will do my part. I know You will do Your part, which is only to help me, to encourage me, and to lift me up when I stumble. Thank You, blessed Savior and Redeemer, for hearing my prayer. I love You, Lord Jesus. Amen.

23

Improving Communication:
Spotlighting Trouble Spots #2

In the Lord, neither is woman independent of man, nor is man independent of woman.

1 Corinthians 11:11

Fred

Once again for each of the five following statements, rate yourself according to the scale. Be sure to read the statements carefully. Missing one word could completely change the meaning and the intent of the sentence.

0 – Almost never
1 – Seldom
2 – Sometimes
3 – Much of the time
4 – Almost always

	Wife	Husband
6. I feel free to share my feelings with my mate even when my feelings don't agree with his or hers.	____	____
7. I generally do not interrupt my mate when he or she is speaking.	____	____
8. My mate rarely belittles me or puts me down in front of other people.	____	____
9. We are generally able to discuss our feelings about sex quite openly.	____	____

10. My husband/wife is generally satisfied with
my efforts to please him or her sexually.   _____   _____

Once again, compare your scores. Are you pretty much in agreement on each of these statements? It is interesting for Florence and me to think back now on our own past inability to understand each other. To put it bluntly, for the most part we didn't! Because I was more or less oblivious to my own shortcomings and to the stresses I was putting on Florence, I would have scored most of the statements for myself with a confident 3 or 4! If I were to score the statements for her, I would have given her anywhere from 0 to 2 on virtually all of them! In other words, I thought I was doing a pretty good job, but didn't think she was doing well at all.

Florence, on the other hand, would have put down very low scores as to her feelings about me. For one example, on question number 3 above, in the husband's column I would have put down a 4, since Florence almost never, even in the worst of times, belittled me or put me down in front of others. For her part, Florence would have scored me with a 0 or 1 since I was constantly doing that to her. I wasn't even aware of what I was doing, and because I thought I was "the righteous one," Florence didn't even think she could discuss her feelings with me.

We had some steep mountains to climb, and even though the going was tough at times, we never gave up. We forged our way to the top. That's where we are now. Let me tell you, the work was worth it! We are enjoying our life together so much now, we are still doing whatever it takes to keep our communications lines open and alive. Neither of us wants to ever slide back down that mountain even one tiny bit. We invite you to come up and join us. The view from the top is everything we hoped it would be!

Suggested Prayer for Today

I thank You, Heavenly Father for the hope that You have given to us. You have given us life *eternal,* and we are now able to see that

Your promise of life *abundant* applies to us as well. We see now, Lord, that You expect us to do our part. We see that we must come to You. We see that we must be yoked together with You, first as individuals and then as a couple. When we are yoked together with You, we cannot stray. Your yoke over our shoulders keeps us walking that straight and narrow road with You. It is only when we slip out of the yoke that we stray.

O Lord, I ask You to put blinders on me as I walk with You so that I am not able to even look for greener pastures. Lord, I will climb every mountain that I must cross. Though I may grow weak I will come to You for a fresh outpouring of Your strength and Spirit upon my soul. I am so thankful to You, my Master and my Lord. In Your precious Name I pray. Amen.

24

Improving Communication:
Spotlighting Trouble Spots #3

Soft speech breaks down the most bonelike resistance.

Proverbs 25:15 AMP

Fred

In the self-evaluations in the past two readings, did you find some issues you don't agree on? Were there some surprises? Most couples find as they go through these questions that the paper, or the book, is impartial and has no favorites. When questions are answered honestly and are written down in black and white, one cannot say to the other, "That's not true. You *couldn't* feel that way." Because it is there in plain sight, all one can say then is, "Why, honey? Tell me why you feel that way."

In face-to-face conversation, or in confrontation, the stronger personality of the two has often been heard to say, "That's not true. I don't do that," or something such as "You have no right to say that!"

What is the result? The other mate feels shut down, as if he or she has no right to those feelings and certainly should not express them, and that no one will listen anyway, so why bother? These pages are designed to help you get beyond that barrier to the point where you can have a meaningful dialogue without one or both of you erupting in anger or denial.

Let's look now at the final seven statements to see if they spotlight any flash points. Remember the scale:

0 – Almost never
1 – Seldom
2 – Sometimes
3 – Much of the time
4 – Almost always

	Wife	Husband
11. My husband/wife generally does not criticize me.	____	____
12. I help my mate feel good about himself/ herself and let him or her know he or she is important to me.	____	____
13. We generally discuss family problems and questions together and then reach decisions on which we both can agree.	____	____
14. My mate understands and respects my desire for occasional privacy and times to be alone.	____	____
15. My mate is generally quick to apologize when I have been hurt or offended.	____	____
16. We are generally able to discuss our spiritual walk with the Lord with each other.	____	____
17. I feel I understand fairly well what my mate desires from me emotionally.	____	____

Are there any trouble spots in these seven statements? Did you find some areas where one of you has a completely different perception of what the answer is than the other spouse did? If so, do not be discouraged or think it is unusual or even that your marriage is hopeless. It is not. It would be a rare couple indeed who could go through those seventeen statements without finding one where they were not in agreement.

Now look up! Look to Him. When the Lord Jesus is in our lives and we are willing to come to Him, there is always hope, for *He* is our hope. We do not have to rely on ourselves. We do not have to be able to break down those old habit patterns on our own. We have to do our part, but when we go to Him He will help us do what we cannot do on our own.

Tomorrow we will look at the three essential rules of good communication in marriage. When we follow these simple principles it's amazing how we can talk about deep and sensitive feelings without ending up in a disaster. Florence and I have learned these steps. We know that you can too.

Suggested Prayer for Today

Lord God Almighty, I bring to You today my thankful heart. I believe, Father, that there is a way to bring harmony into our home. The Lord Jesus said He is the way. I want to walk in that way. I will trust You, Lord, to give me the ability to look into some of these trouble spots that I have seen in myself these past few days. Lord, I have kept them hidden and out of sight for so long, it will be difficult to be vulnerable and to let anyone else into those areas that I have protected so zealously. I ask for the strength to open those doors. As my partner and friend opens his or her doors in the same way, help me to be gentle and compassionate in the same way that You are compassionate. I don't want to trample on his or her efforts to share deep feelings and needs with me. Father God, I ask You to open my heart to listen without interrupting, to hear without denying, to learn without defending. I thank You, my Lord and my God, and in Your Name I pray. Amen.

25

Improving Communication: The Three Essentials

> It is better to keep one's mouth shut and be thought a fool, than to open it and remove all doubt.
>
> *Mark Twain*

Fred

Communicating in the marriage relationship is different from any other form of communication in all the world! Most communicating—the conveying of ideas, information, and feelings—outside the home is *objective*. Emotions are not involved. Inside the home, however, communication is frequently mired in deep and often repressed feelings and is therefore *subjective*. It is very easy for one or the other spouse to get upset at what seems to the partner to be the most trivial request or statement. All the hurts, pains, and discouragements of life are apt to color how we respond to each other. So let us not forget the importance of *feelings* in marriage communications.

There are no rights or wrongs to feelings, and therefore we *must allow our partners to express their feelings without interrupting, without correcting, without criticizing, and without disagreeing!* Anything less will stifle meaningful communication between a husband and wife.

I wish I had learned these essentials much sooner than I did. Maybe I would not have totally stifled my wife's ability and right to share her feelings with me. Because of what I did to her, it took many years before she felt safe enough to express her true feelings. She had learned over too many years to effectively water them down to what she knew would suit me! All too many spouses—wives especially—have told us the same tale. It's better to say nothing or what the husband wants to hear rather than deal with the consequences of his anger. This is not communicating! This is playing a charade! Hence:

Rule #1. No Interrupting! You must allow your partner to express feelings without interrupting, correcting, criticizing, or disagreeing. Before you even begin to discuss the possible trouble spots you may have spotlighted in the seventeen statements in the previous self-evaluation, you must agree that you will both abide by this first essential rule. Do not be surprised when you break the agreement yourself. One of the most difficult things to do is to not interrupt. When one of you does stumble, the other, by your prior mutual agreement, must have the right to say, "Wait a minute, honey. I was still talking, and I was interrupted." (Please note that this is carefully worded so as not to say, "You interrupted me!" because this is a *you statement,* something to be avoided, as we discuss next.)

Rule #2. No YOU Statements. Such words as "You said . . ." or "You got angry . . ." or "You made me feel stupid . . ." or "You caused . . ." serve only one purpose: They immediately put the other person on the defensive. He or she is literally being forced into a protective or defensive mode. Not only is the other person then not hearing what you are saying, he or she is very likely to forget rule #1 and interrupt and attack you. Let's agree then: no *you* statements. Instead, say "I feel . . . ," or "I felt hurt by . . . ," or "I feel I'm not worth anything to You," or "It would be better for me if, . . ." These statements are much less threatening to the listener, and may even evoke compassion within the other person for how he or she may have unintentionally made you feel! Everyone has a right to express his or her feelings. Make rule #2 a platform in your agreement.

Rule #3. No ALWAYS or NEVER Statements. Agree to absolutely avoid using these two instant-blockade words. The moment you say to your partner, "Yes, but you always . . ." you force him or her to put up an immediate wall. The other person begins to plan how to refute your untrue and unfair statement. Now instead of learning and listening to you, he or she is planning the counterattack. Once again, communication for the moment has ended. There is no longer the sense of freedom that feelings, thoughts, and ideas will be openly received by the other person.

How about You?

Make an agreement now with each other that when one of you unintentionally breaks one of these three rules, the other person can stop and immediately say, for example, "Wait a minute. I wasn't finished. Please let me finish, and then I'll listen to you." It is neither spiritual nor wise to hide or suppress your real feelings. However, it is also neither spiritual or wise to dump them on another person in an explosion of anger or rage. Emotions must be appropriately expressed without bringing pain or hurt to someone else. Work at it. It's worth the effort!

Suggested Prayer for Today

Lord I have learned today that it is neither fair nor right for me to interrupt my mate. I confess to You, Lord, and at the same time to you, my (husband/wife), that I have done this all too often in the past. Lord Jesus, I ask You to make me sensitive so that I can hear when I do interrupt.

To you, my mate and my beloved partner, I give permission to let me know when I do it to you. Together we can grow out of this, and with the Lord helping us we will both overcome this nasty habit of mine.

We thank You, Lord, for we know that your desire for us both is to experience your best. We love You, Lord. You are so patient and gentle with us. You give us so much slack in the rope before You say that's enough. Lord, I ask You to help us both to be as patient and gentle with each other as You are with us. We thank You, Lord Jesus, and we praise Your Holy and Glorious Name. Amen.

26

Strengthening Our Foundation: Personality Weaknesses

Everyone should examine himself first.

1 Corinthians 11:28 TEV

Fred

One of the enlightening facets of Florence's and my studies of the four basic personalities, or understanding our differences according to the Sanguine, Choleric, Melancholy, and Phlegmatic temperaments, is that it enables us to see that we were each created with strengths as well as weaknesses. By seeing in an objective manner that God gave to each one of us at birth a set of traits, the evaluation becomes fun and informative instead of accusing and threatening. No one is pointing a finger at anyone and saying, "This is your problem!" Instead, you can see yourself plainly in black and white. Areas that need to be strengthened are quickly obvious to all.

Being willing to admit that we have weaknesses and then telling our mates that we want to work and improve in this area is one of the most profound ways we can say "I love you" to each other. By doing so we are letting our mates know that we desire to please them in every way we can. We want to erase some of those sore spots and strengthen our foundation.

The challenge for today's "assignment" may not be quite as easy as previous ones have been, but believe us when we tell you the time you spend on this task will be well worth your effort! Each of you should write out your own answers. Do not be influenced by what your spouse writes.

First read the statement and then, on a separate piece of paper, write out the two things you would like to tell your mate. When you have both written your two responses—and only two!—then you can each write them on this page in the book.

For Wives: The two personality weaknesses in my husband that I would like to see strengthened are:

1. _____

2. _____

For Husbands: The two personality weaknesses in my wife that I would like to see strengthened are:

1. _____

2. _____

When couples seek help with their marriages they must both be willing to listen, to change, and to resist placing the blame on the other person. We have met with couples who wanted to prove to us that the fault was the other person's. Sometimes couples try to out-shout each other in a desperate attempt to win. When each one is trying to win, both people lose!

How about You?

We all have weaknesses. In the Personality Profile evaluation found at the back of this book, you will note that twenty strengths and twenty weaknesses are listed for each of the four temperament types. The evaluation helps you see which weaknesses are inherently part of your personality. In this assignment you have been asked by your partner to look at only two of your weaknesses, the two that, when changed, would make your mate most happy. Is that too much to ask?

Remember, we cannot effectively change ourselves. The habit patterns we have developed over the years, these traits that we were born with, are firmly entrenched. However, they can be uprooted—*IF!* . . . If you will ask God to help you to recognize them, and if you are willing to ask your mate on an ongoing basis how well you are doing in your efforts to rid yourself of the two things he or she listed for you above.

One of the best things you can do for yourself and for each other is to sit on your bed tonight, before you go to sleep, and allow one another to share why these two items are important and then for each of you to pray today's suggested prayer out loud. As with each day's suggested prayer, feel free to modify, add to, or replace it in any way that seems good to you. Always remember that in these prayers you are praying only for yourself and for your needs, not that the Lord would change or make your mate better!

Suggested Prayer for Today

Dear Lord Jesus, You are really getting into the heart of my soul. But that is good. I want to be made aware of everything that is keeping me from being all that I can be for You—and for my beloved partner as well. I thank You, Lord, for bringing us together. I thank You, Lord, for making us one. Now I ask You to help me understand these two weaknesses that are most important to my mate. Even if they don't seem so important to me, they apparently are to him or her. Because of my desire to be a pleasing and loving partner, I want to do whatever will help him or her the most. But I need Your help, Lord. I know I can't change on my own. I have already tried and have seen that it doesn't work. But I am trusting You, Lord. I am trusting that You can do for me what I can't do on my own. I commit today that I will do more than try. I will work diligently to come to You as You instruct us to do. I thank You for Your promises and Your truth. In Your Name I pray. Amen.

Week 6, Day 2____

27

Strengthening Our Foundation: Emotional Needs

Grant her honor as a fellow heir of the grace of life.

1 Peter 3:7

Fred

All of us according to our gender, our personality type, our background, and whatever "baggage" we brought into marriage have different emotional needs. We don't always stop and analyze what they are or put a label on them, but we do know that we are apt to be unhappy when these needs are not met—or even depressed if they are never met. The most interesting phenomenon of the marriage relationship is that we tend to give to our partners what we want to receive from them—when this may be the direct opposite of what they need and want from us. Instead of giving to our mates what they need, we give them what we want back, hoping they will catch on and give us the same!

I came into marriage with a deep, even desperate, need to be loved. Therefore, being young and with no knowledge or understanding, I gave love to Florence in every conceivable form I could think of, assuming in my youthful naiveté, that she would be so appreciative that she would simply pour it back on me and we would live happily ever after! Did it work? Of course not!

Florence quite readily saw through what I was doing to her and began to resent it. Once she began to resent what she perceived was my manipulation of her, she pulled back and gave less and less of herself. We both functioned in the same natural roles of self-centeredness. Was this spiritual? Of course not! But we weren't even Christians at the time. When we did finally submit our lives to the Lord some fifteen years later, these patterns and traits were well established and not easily broken.

86

Florence came into our marriage from a family where she felt loved, appreciated, and encouraged, but hers was a background of never-ending financial stress and need. Was *love* an emotional need for her? Not really, because she had always felt loved throughout her childhood. Therefore she was not seeking it from the marriage relationship. What *was* she seeking?

One of her most significant emotional needs was not love but *security,* confidence that her financial needs would always be taken care of. Did I have an emotional need for security? Not at all. I was confident in my abilities to provide it. When later we went through our very rough times financially, Florence had the feeling that I was doing it *to her.* I wasn't meeting her needs at all, and she wasn't meeting mine. Was it a miracle we stayed together? Ah, yes! But then Jesus is in the miracle business!

How about You?

Now it is time to think about your emotional needs. Once again write them down on a separate piece of paper and when you have both done so, enter them on this page.

For Wives: The three major emotional needs I would like my husband to meet for me are:

1. _____

2. _____

3. _____

For Husbands: The three major emotional needs I would like my wife to meet for me are:

1. _____

2. _____

3. _____

Once again you have plenty of food for thought for a friendly, positive, and meaningful discussion. If tonight is a good time, that's great. But we know there are days when the family schedule makes such a meeting time difficult or impossible. If this is one of those days, it might be better to hold up on tomorrow's lesson until you can first complete today's suggestions and then proceed with the next day's chapter. You decide. Ask the Lord Jesus. He'll help you make the right decision.

Suggested Prayer for Today

(Today, one of you pray from your heart in the presence of the other. We have given you suggestions every day; today, let's be different. You have many models and suggestions from previous days' suggested prayers. We know that for some, oral personal prayer is difficult. That is a barrier you should strive to break. The Lord already knows your needs, your desires, and your heart even before you ask. Nevertheless, He does like to hear you ask. So now, one or even both of you pray in the presence of the other. Remember your prayer is to the Father and is not for the benefit of your mate, although he or she can certainly be blessed by your heartfelt prayer.)

28

Strengthening Our Foundation: Dismantling Walls

For he himself is our peace, who has made the two one and has destroyed the barrier, the dividing wall of hostility.

Ephesians 2:14 NIV

Fred

If you have been married for a number of years, you probably know there are some areas of your life together that you very much try to hide or avoid talking about. We all have them to some extent. These are generally highly sensitive areas we just can't allow into the open. We've tried to be open in the past, and what happened? Later, in a moment of anger or hostility, our mate threw those sensitive hurts right back at us.

When that happens we wish we had never allowed anyone to get inside of us. That day we vow, "Never again!" And we add a few more bricks to the top of the wall; we make sure we are tightly enclosed and that no one can get inside. It is just too painful. *I've tried and it didn't work,* we think to ourselves. So we shut down and begin to live more and more in emotional isolation.

But why did we get married, to live alone? No one does that, but all too many of us are doing that now! Be advised, things do not automatically get better with age or with the passing of years. If we don't invest some effort and time in our marriages, they get worse and more hardened. If life's a journey, what a shame not to enjoy the trip.

Florence and I are now fully enjoying our trip. Are you enjoying yours? Our whole and sole focus in this book is to help you to look forward to each new day of your journey together while focusing your mind and your heart securely on the Lord Jesus, the author and finisher of your faith.

How about You?

Are there some walls in your marriage that ought to be dismantled? Often we do not think so. We are relatively comfortable, dealing only with surface issues. But just ask your partner, "Are there some walls?" You might be in for a surprise. Let's find out.

For Wives: Three things in our marriage that I do not feel my husband and I can discuss are:

1. _____

2. _____

3. _____

For Husbands: Three things in our marriage that I do not feel my wife and I can discuss are:

1. _____

2. _____

3. _____

As in the past two days, so that one's listings do not influence the other, write down your responses on another piece of paper. When you both have written your own responses independently, you can enter them here on these pages.

When you compare your answers you will inevitably find that there are some walls separating you from being the close "ONE" that God the Father planned and purposed for the two of you; satan* loves these walls. He loves to keep God's people in bondage. But you don't have to be subject to his snares. You can begin now by discussing with each other why these walls ever went up in the first place. You can agree to be understanding, patient, and com-

---

*In my writing I intentionally avoid using capital letters regarding satan, for I specifically wish to do nothing that might be construed to ascribe dignity to him.

passionate with each other. You might then dare risk dismantling these emotional walls that you have built and steadfastly maintained. God's purpose for your home, your marriage, and your relationship is oneness, unity, and harmony in the Lord Jesus Christ. He is our peace. He has made us to be one. If we let Him, He will destroy that barrier between us, the wall of hostility and emotional privacy.

Suggested Prayer for Today

Dear God and Heavenly Father, it sounds so good that we might someday act like one, think like one, and *be* one. I confess to You, Lord, that I have erected some barriers. I felt I had to do it to protect myself from the pain that would too often result. When I look at your life here on earth, Lord Jesus, I never see that You did any such thing to protect yourself. You suffered far more than I will ever suffer. Not only did You suffer at the hands of your enemies, your friends weren't always that much better. I know You understand how I feel sometimes. I am thankful that You know every desire of my heart. You already know, Lord, that I do desire better—better than I *have* right now and better than I *am* right now. I ask You, O Lord, to help us as a couple to grow closer to You, to develop and strengthen our faith, and to grow closer together as husband and wife. We thank You, Lord Jesus, for we know that when we ask, You hear, and when You hear You grant our petitions when they are Your will for us. We thank You, Lord Jesus Christ. We pray together as one in Your precious and Holy Name. Amen.

Strengthening Our Foundation:
Progress through Prayer

After Jesus had gone indoors, his disciples asked him privately, "Why couldn't we drive it out?" He replied, "This kind can come out only by prayer."

Mark 9:28–29 NIV

Fred

In the past three days you have looked at some things that may have been emotionally challenging for you. If, as suggested, you sat together in the evening to talk about your responses and your feelings, you have very likely touched on some areas that you have never really opened up before. This can be very painful, but it is also very healthy to do.

Now one of the most important things you can do for yourself and for each other is to agree to have a meeting like this at least once a week. Review together what you have talked about. Ask each other for an appraisal of the past week: Are we making progress? Are we growing closer together? What else do we need to do? How can we help each other without becoming domineering or controlling? How can we talk about these issues without becoming angry or ending up in a fight?

You did not fall to your present level of communicating with each other overnight. It is the result of years of some good and some disappointing experiences, both before and after marriage. You will not see changes in your relationship overnight either. It will take time. It will also take commitment from both of you. Change will require persistence. Last and most importantly, change will require prayer—consistent personal prayer.

In the verse above, the disciples asked the Lord Jesus privately why they could not cast the demon out of an epileptic boy when his father had asked them to. Jesus' answer was most significant then and still is for us as well today: "This kind can come out by nothing but prayer." Jesus was telling the disciples that there are certain things that can only be changed through prayer. Willpower is not sufficient. Determination is not sufficient. Knowledge and wisdom are not sufficient. Education is not sufficient. Commitment is not sufficient.

In this book we are not talking about demons but of long-entrenched habit patterns and hurts that sometimes we do not want to give up at all. If you will look at the rest of this passage in Mark, you will see that the demon was well entrenched and had no intention of giving up at all. We know from Scripture that the Lord Jesus, even though He was God incarnate here on earth, still found it necessary to be in regular and consistent prayer communion with His Father in Heaven. If Jesus found it necessary, how essential it must be for each one of us!

These changes in your marriage that you are discussing with each other this week can come about by nothing but prayer! Without prayer you are working in the natural, not in the spiritual. Without prayer you are striving to cast out hurts and habits from your relationship without power, without God's power! You are relying on your own human power.

How about You?

Before you get into your nightly or weekly meeting to discuss your personality weaknesses, the emotional needs that are not being met or the walls that you may have built, we urge you to begin with prayer. Pray aloud from your heart to the Father. Pray that you might have the very nature of the Lord Jesus Himself as described in Philippians 2:3–7 as you talk and communicate with each other. Finally, remember there is one who doesn't want you to meet, to talk, or to grow together. He must be dealt with. Since the husband is the protector of the family, we strongly suggest that he pray the prayer rebuking satan as found on page 286. Pray it aloud with the authority that You already possess in the Name of the Lord Jesus Christ. A further suggestion: Pray it every single night before you go to sleep. Pray against the enemy whether or not you think he is attacking you. Remember: A strong offense is the best defense! When exercising your authority over him, always command him out loud, never silently. That's what Jesus did. He never commanded the demons or satan silently or under His breath. Jesus always let him know who was in charge! We are in charge over ALL the powers of darkness because he has already given to us His power and authority (see Luke 10:19).

With consistent personal prayer as your foundation, you will rejoice as you see God moving in your hearts and then in your marriage. With prayer you will make real progress. You will not be relying on human power or willpower but on God's power to change lives!

Suggested Prayer for Today

Thank You, Lord Jesus that we have your power to depend on. You never turn off the power; You never dim the lights! The switch at Your end is always turned on. I confess, Lord, that there have been times when I turned off the switch at my end. Now I want to keep that switch in the "on" position forever. Lord Jesus, I ask You to give us both a quiet and understanding heart as we try to talk with each other about these issues that have kept us apart, about the walls we have built to protect ourselves. Lord, help me to become more like You. Instill in me Your own nature and character. I want to be like You. I want my family to see in me Your Spirit, Your love, and Your gentleness. I thank You, O blessed Savior and Lord. I call You Lord because You *are* my Lord, and I want You to be my Lord in every sense that the word implies. Thank You, Lord Jesus. Amen.

30

Strengthening Our Foundation: Who Goes First?

> Wives . . .
>
> *Ephesians 5:22 and Colossians 3:18*
>
> Likewise, ye wives . . .
>
> *1 Peter 3:1 KJV*

Fred

The Scriptures that inspire today's reading are the three specific places in the Bible where God gives direct instructions to the husband and the wife for their marital relationship. Look at these three citations. There is something unique about them. What is the first word in each of the three verses? Who gets the commandment first? Each time, God speaks first to the woman.

Three verses later, Ephesians 5:25 then addresses "Husbands. . . ." Similarly, the next verse in Colossians, 3:19, starts out "Husbands. . . ." and 1 Peter 3:7 starts out by saying, "Likewise, ye husbands. . . ." This is an interesting structure. In each of these three epistles of Paul, the instruction is first given to the wife and then to the husband. Why is this? Let us bear in mind that "all Scripture is given by inspiration of God"; it is given exactly as God determined it should be. All Scripture was penned by men who worked under the direct inspiration of the Holy Spirit. Therefore nothing can be attributed to the original author's personal preference or individual quirks. Why do you think God chose to give these instructions first to wives?

Take a few moments now and discuss with each other why you think God chose to do this. There are no right or wrong answers, because the answer is never spelled out in the Bible. So any answer you come up with may be perfectly valid. When your discussion has brought up some plausible and feasible explanations, write them down in the spaces provided.

1. _____

2. _____

3. _____

We have asked this question many times of groups and received a variety of responses. Some say that women's hearts are more tender to the Lord, and knowing this He spoke first to them. Some have said that men tend more to have a pride barrier and are therefore less responsive. Another reason given is that men, being what men are, have more difficulty in submitting their will and life to the Lord's will. Still another reason sometimes given is that in general women spend more time studying Scripture and are therefore more likely to see and obey God's will for them. Do your reasons coincide with these reasons?

The fact is, we do not know God's reason. One thing is clear, though: In each case He has given the directive first to wives and then to husbands. How can you apply this directive to your home and marriage?

Usually there is one person in the couple who has more enthusiasm about doing something to improve the present state of the relationship. If you were to ask most counselors, pastors, or family therapists which spouse usually comes first to ask for help, you would get one consistent answer. Eighty percent of the time it is the wife. And if you were to ask, "When couples come in for help, which one tends to quit first?" 80 percent of the time you would hear, "It is the husband."

How about You?

Men, why do we do this? Let's start now by taking the initiative and being the spiritual leaders in our homes that God intended and designed us to be. Let's say to our wives, "Honey, we can work this out. Let's work together to become what God wants us to be. Let's work together to achieve that level of harmony and happiness that we know is out there. Let's not wait until we're a statistic. Let's be an example of what God can do in two people's lives." Then tell her, "I'm going to do my part in working to please you, to become the husband that gives you the life you dreamed about when you said yes to my marriage proposal. I hope you will join me on this journey. Even if you are not ready to say you will, I am going to forge ahead anyway. You will see me improving, because with God all things are possible."

Suggested Prayer for Today

For Husbands: Lord, if I mean those words I just read to my wife, I have made a bold and daring, even frightening, commitment to her. I do mean them today, Lord, but what about tomorrow when she says something that upsets me? What will happen to my resolve? I don't want to be a part of that 80 percent who quit. I don't want to be known as one who gives up easily. You've told us that with You all things are possible. Well, now Lord, I'm asking you to show me that I can do it. I am asking You to help me, to give me the strength and perseverance I need. I thank You, dear Lord Jesus. Amen.

For Wives: Dear Lord, I would love for my husband to take the lead as my spiritual head, my protector, and my provider. I pray now for him, Lord, that he will be able to withstand the pressures to quit. I have longed for him to say to me that we will walk through this life together as one. I want to be his wife. I want to respect him and to love him as You love me. Show me, Lord, how to love him selflessly as You love both of us. I thank You, Lord Jesus, for caring so much about us that You will never give up on us, even if we want to give up on ourselves. In Your Name I pray. Amen.

The Best of Times

> The eye is the lamp of the body. If your eyes are good, your whole body will be full of light. But if your eyes are bad, your whole body will be full of darkness.
>
> *Matthew 6:22–23 NIV*

Florence

Where do we look for a dream? Let's pretend right now that one of you is bored, defeated, or discouraged. You have a job, but somehow it's routine and uninspiring. Other people seem to have it better. In the next few days we're going to look for dream-starters, ideas that might brighten your horizon. We'll examine our desires and seek ideas first from our own family backgrounds, from our own talent and experiences, then from the hope to help others by filling needs and finding areas of leadership potential. We'll also see that leaving our future to luck or chance is not a good choice.

Let's start with our family backgrounds. Charles Dickens, in the opening lines of his classic novel about the French Revolution, *A Tale of Two Cities*, wrote, "It was the best of times, it was the worst of times, it was the age of wisdom, it was the age of foolishness. . . . it was the season of Light, it was the season of Darkness, it was the spring of hope, it was the winter of despair, we had everything before us, we had nothing before us."

As I look back on those times of the Depression, I realize the move into our store was the end of the dream for my mother and father. They had lost their hope to raise their children in a normal house. For them and many others of that poverty era, it was the worst of times. But, as in Dickens's description, for us children it was often the best of times, living in a store full of ice cream and candy. For a while it was a season of light for us but a period of darkness for my mother. I would work hard and get a scholarship to college, for me that time was a spring of hope, but for our mother that store represented many winters of despair.

How do you make a house out of a store? How do you repair a lost dream? Where other people had a front porch, we had a public sidewalk adjoining the three cement steps that led up to the door. Where others had a lawn, we had weeds and a gas pump with customers honking for attention. Where other people had regular windows with curtains, we had store windows with Coca-Cola signs. Where others had white houses with black shutters, we had old brown clapboards with peeling paint and dingy yellow trim.

Where others had a living room, we had a store. Where they had furniture, we had a rack of newspapers, a table with cakes, jelly rolls, and whoopie pies, a long glass case full of penny candy and sticks of gum, two big ice tanks with bottles of milk and Canada Dry ginger ale bumping anxiously against each other as the ice melted and the water level rose. Behind the table where we ate and played Monopoly was an ice cream freezer stocked with Fudgesicles, Popsicles, and Creamsicles. (You can see why for us kids this environment wasn't so bad after all. In fact, my friends thought coming to my store was fun.) We had nothing, and yet we had everything.

Little did I realize at that time that the store would be the start of my dream. While it was the worst of times for my mother, it was an opportunity for me in many ways. The extended family created by our customers gave me a continuous audience for my memorized elocution pieces. The encouragement of my father told me I could make it. The constancy of the people taught me to speak kindly to everyone whether I happened to like them or not. We couldn't afford to lose a customer! The church across the street was our only social outlet, and our teachers there showed us how to love God.

I look back on those best and worst of times and realize that poverty is a great motivator that tells those in its grip, "You'll never make it out of my control unless you have a passion for success, unless you dare to dream."

How about You?

When you look back, do you remember some time in your child-hood when you saw the dream? Was it during the best of times or the worst? What was the dream? Did you have "nothing" that was really "everything" you needed for motivation? Have you followed your dream? Have you looked at the bright side of your childhood or at the darkness?

When you look back at your family you may see a spark you missed at the time, an event that looked like a negative when it happened but that God offered as the start of a dream. Are you liv-ing now in the best of times or the worst?

In our verse for today the Lord Jesus Himself speaks to us about spiritual vision. Our eyes take in the world around us; they rove like a video camera picking up pictures to record in our memories. If we have good eyesight and look at good scenes, we will be full of light. But if our eyes focus on the bad, we will live in darkness. Are you living in the light or in the dark? As a couple, share the best and the worst things that have happened to you in your lives. What do you think about each other's evaluation of these incidents?

Suggested Prayer for Today

Lord Jesus, we want our eyes to see the vision You have for us. Open our eyes that we may see a hope ahead of us that we may not have noticed before. We don't want to settle for living in three rooms behind a store for the rest of our lives. We promise to look on the bright side and not continue to live in darkness. We want the future to be the best of times. We know You are our hope, our eyes, our light. We praise You. In the Name of Jesus. Amen.

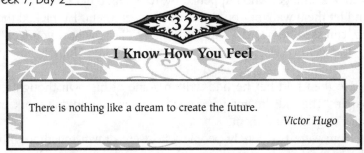

32

I Know How You Feel

> There is nothing like a dream to create the future.
>
> *Victor Hugo*

Florence

The future can't just be left to chance; we have to create it. We first dream of possibilities, picture the future, and then get on with creating it. Even though it doesn't always turn out the way we thought in childhood that it would, we need that extra excitement in order to dare to dream.

In the best-selling novel *The Bridges of Madison County* the leading lady is an English teacher who became a farmer's wife. She lives with her family in a rural community, and while life is predictable and pleasant, it's also a little dull. When photographer Richard Kincaid arrives in the area to take pictures of the quaint old bridges there, he brightens up Francesca's day. She finds herself communicating with him in a way she never would have talked with her husband. They discuss the poetry he writes in his spare time, along with a little fiction now and then. Her husband never wrote anything, and her love of literature, starved for so long, bonds with his love for poetry. They look each other straight in the eye when they talk. They listen to each other's thoughts and feelings. He doesn't tell her she's wrong to feel that way. She shares with the stranger that it's a nice town, people help each other, you can leave your car unlocked. "There are a lot of good things about the people here, and I respect them for these qualities," she tells him. Kincaid can tell she's trying to convince herself as she goes on about the virtues of small-town living. Then she adds, "But it's not what I dreamed about as a girl."

She'd never said those words before; she'd never dared to state such a disappointment, but those thoughts had been in her mind.

It took a stranger who happened by, to open up her hidden dreams and let them walk out on the table between them. He picked them up, caressed her words, and said simply, "I know how you feel."

The words a wife dreams her husband will say: "I know how you feel."

He then told her he had written some of his own thoughts on paper. "The old dreams were good dreams; they didn't work out, but I'm glad I had them."

Here were two lonely people who were drawn together with a sharing of their dreams, dreams that somehow didn't work out, but the dreamers were glad they had had them.

Do you two have some dreams? Have you ever shared them openly with each other? Have you sat quietly with no one else around, looked each other in the eye, and listened, intently enraptured with each other's words?

Isn't it amazing how little time we find to listen to each other, to really sit down and draw out words that aren't practical, that won't solve a crisis? And yet how easy it is for a stranger to hang on your partner's every word. In today's loose society, a lonely friend can be found on any corner, in any business, at any church who would stop everything and listen. Shouldn't you be listening to each other and prevent your mate from needing a confessor?

How about You?

Set aside some time today—it could be right now—to communicate with each other. Sometimes Fred and I pretend we've just met. We have a date and tell each other of our dreams. Even though many people at our age have no dreams and don't even count on a future, we still talk as if we had another fifty years ahead of us. We still get excited over each other's ideas. Francesca wanted to talk about art and dreams, "not about realities that kept the music silent, the dreams in a box."

Based on your individual talents, desires, and interests, tell your mate what you have dreamed about and how that dream might come to reality. What would you both have to do to fulfill your dream? Do you need to go back to school? Get more training? Start a business? Have some help in the home? What would you need to fulfill your true desires?

Now have your partner share his or her dreams. Listen to each other. Look at each other. Hang on every word. Don't leave those words drifting out there for someone else to pick up.

Suggested Prayer for Today

Dear Lord, I realize that we have both held dreams in our minds that we haven't shared. Like Francesca, they aren't what we dreamed as a child. They're a little closer to possibility, toned down by age and experience and disappointments. Lord, give us the ability to listen to each other. It costs nothing but a little time. Help us to really care about each other and not to leave our dreams in a box. We thank You and praise You for helping us dare to dream. In Jesus' Name. Amen.

❖33❖

Filling Needs

Turn my eyes away from worthless things; revive my life according to Your Word.

Psalm 119:37

Florence

A few years ago in the midst of talks of a national recession, I tuned into a television show where a perky lady was telling how she had gone into business for herself. With her was an exuberant man who interjected, "When the economy is down, it is time for you to look around, find a need, and fill it."

The host asked the woman how she had gone from being a corporate manager to her current business, and she explained that when she found herself out of a job she asked herself what she had needed most when she was working. She realized she never had time to go shopping or do errands, so she decided she'd do that for busy people. She started her own business doing other people's marketing, walking their dog, taking their shirts to the laundry, or sitting and waiting for the television repairman to come to their house. Her hours are flexible, and her profit is clear. She has always loved to shop, so now she has time to shop all day and earn a living while doing it.

Do your dreams sound outlandish? Are you afraid of what others will say or that they will laugh? Perhaps your dream is something many of us have thought about and said, "I wish someone would come up with . . ."

In our country today with so many major companies "downsizing," people who wish to get ahead have had to take their lives into their own hands and become creative. No one today can be sure, as their parents were when they launched their careers, that if they start working at General Motors or IBM right out of college they will progress each year and retire with a pension. When the culture's old security disappears, we have an even greater need to dare to dream.

It's helpful at this point to look back to our ancestors and see if there is a theme among them. Did they all seem to have a certain talent? Perhaps you have the same touch and have not put it into action. It's never too late to start. How about your own ability and your personal experiences? We always do better working at something we enjoy.

Do you like your current profession or employment? If not, what have your experiences prepared you for that could become an occupation? As you are thinking of these possibilities, stretch beyond the norm and ask one major question: What need do people have today that is not being filled? What could you do about it?

When she found herself without a job, the perky lady on TV asked herself what she had needed most when she was working. Her own answer was someone to do her errands, so she started a business to help. I know I could use her. I love shopping but in the limited time I have at home, I can't possibly get to the cleaners, the shoe-repair shop, or the drugstore before I have to leave again.

In my book *Dare to Dream* I tell the story of Ralph Lagergren, who spent over ten years trying to get his Bi-Rotor invention produced and marketed. This harvesting combine is engineered to reap grain with 70 percent fewer moving parts than existing combines and will enable farmers to harvest faster while losing less grain and yielding fewer damaged kernels than anything on the market. Ralph and his cousin Mark Underwood fluctuated between frustration and exhilaration for years until they finally received some money from the state of Kansas to help finance the lab tests. Then Ralph quit his sales job to go into the promotion of his invention.

When Ralph heard my tape on *Silver Boxes*, where I state that many of us die with the music still in us, he wrote to tell me of his dream and said, "I'm banging my cymbals and playing every other instrument I can. The music is *not* going to die in me."

Since the time I wrote Ralph's story, many articles have been written about how he has dared to dream that he could produce and sell a combine that filled a farmer's need. I've become acquainted with Ralph—we keep in touch—and I am thrilled that his dream not only succeeded but that he sold the invention and the whole business for what sounded to me like a fortune. His last note to me included a picture of his Bi-Rotor combine, several new articles about him, and a note that said, "We are on the brink of making it very big. Daring to dream is what life is about."

How about You?

What needs are there in your community that your skills could fill? Start asking around and buy special magazines that tell about new possibilities. Make a discussion at dinner tonight. Who can think of anything that hasn't been tried yet? Who can think of a service people need someone to do for them? In New York City there are professional dogwalkers for people who are too busy to give their pet exercise. One man in Japan started a business as a "stand-in." Whatever you couldn't get to, he'd go and stand in for you. He could produce wedding guests so you'd look more popular or fill up a TV audience at the last minute so the filming would show a full house. There's no end to the possibilities when you find a need and fill it. Keep daring to dream. As a couple, don't enter into some new business if one of you feels uncomfortable about it. Even though no one likes a negative opinion, *listen.* God uses us to check each other. Unity is better than failure.

Suggested Prayer for Today

(Pray this prayer individually.)

Dear Lord Jesus, I've never been a really creative person, but I'm in need of a different career or an improvement in my current one. Give me ideas of what people need done for them that I can do.

Help me to think clearly about each possibility and to listen to my spouse, who may have fresh ideas. Lord, I want so much to be of unusual use to this world, and I need Your inspiration. I await Your answer. In the Name of Jesus . . . in anticipation. Amen.

Moral Leadership

> If it is serving, let him serve; . . . if it is encouraging, let him encourage; if it is contributing to the needs of others, let him give generously; if it is leadership, let him govern diligently, if it is showing mercy, let him do it cheerfully."   *Romans 12:7–8 NIV*

Florence

In Romans the great apostle Paul writes to tell his people that no matter what they are called to do they must do it cheerfully and to the best of their ability, not looking for financial reward alone. He mentions serving: finding someone's need and filling it; teaching: sharing your knowledge and wisdom with those who need it; encouraging: lifting up those who are downcast and discouraged. Paul also talks to those who have made money and tells them to give generously to those who need it and to show mercy to the hurting. Do it all cheerfully, not as a burden, but realizing the Lord has gifted you, and it is your obligation to bless all those who need help. Paul knew way back then that many people couldn't minister to their own needs; they required help.

The Lord Himself explained to His disciples, "The poor you will always have with you."[1] From the beginning of time there have been those who are successful and there have been multitudes who need help. Where are you on this scale? Jesus doesn't say if we get enough poverty programs under way we can eliminate the indigent. He says simply, there will always be people who need help.

As Paul pointed out the different ways we all can serve, he mentioned leadership. There will always be people who by hook or by crook will ultimately succeed and who will encourage others to follow. Paul commended those with leadership abilities to govern diligently, honestly.

Many of you reading these words today have leadership ability you haven't tapped yet. How can you put it into practice? When we think of being leaders, we often consider becoming politicians to join those who govern and make rules (although few of us will actually run for office), but Paul was speaking of our providing spiritual and civic leadership.

Czechoslovakia, invaded and conquered by Hitler, had all but perished when the embers of its dream began to ignite. After forty years of hearing lies, the people were ready to hear the truth. In Vaclav Havel's 1990 New Year's Day address to his country, he presented the reality: "Our country is not prospering. The great creative and spiritual potential of our nation is not being used to its fullest. Our outdated economy is squandering energy, a country once proud of the standard of education ranks seventy-second in the world, [and] we have [ecologically] the worst environment in all of Europe, but the worst thing is we are living in a decayed moral environment."

Although these statements were intended to stir up a deprived country with a decayed moral environment, the principle could apply to our nation today. We have always been on the winning side, and yet with each election we have lowered our standards of leadership. Immoral behavior that sank presidential candidate Gary Hart in 1987 is considered acceptable today. Adultery is overlooked in the presidency but strangely immoral in the military. Fraudulent financial dealings are wrong only if you're caught. Even in our church governing bodies, strict moral standards aren't always essential.

Paul is telling us to govern diligently, to pay attention to the needs of the people, to keep our standards high, and to do it all cheerfully.

How about You?

Do you feel a call to leadership? Many are called but few are chosen.[2] Putting oneself in a potential leadership position takes a daring spirit. The Lord has put a call on me to train Christian leaders, speakers, and writers to move to the front, to step out in faith. Many who didn't think they could be leaders have come to our training sessions, Christian Leaders and Speakers Seminars (CLASS) and opened up to the Lord's leading in their lives. Some have become political leaders, and many are now speakers and writers who are influencing thousands.

Could your dream be in leadership? Could the experiences in your life, uniquely yours, be used to help others in similar situations? Could you be open to teaching a youth group? Christian young people desperately need a warm, moral, adult friend who can set an example for them to follow.

Could you both be willing to host some couples in your home and help them with their marriages? That's how Fred and I got started in Christian ministry. We began to teach the principles of the personality types to ten couples in our living room. Then we moved to adult Sunday school classes in the church, then to retreats, seminars, conventions, and on to writing books. We didn't plan to do these things; we were just open to the leading of the Lord.

Perhaps the Lord is calling you both into leadership along with serving, encouraging, giving, and showing mercy. Are you willing to say, "Here am I, send me"?[3] Discuss what leadership skills you perceive in each other. How could you minister together?

Suggested Prayer for Today

Dear Lord, we weren't looking to be leaders, and yet we see the need. We see teenagers going astray, church couples getting divorced, local government with no ethical standards. Lord, are You calling us? Are You waiting for an answer? Lord Jesus, we never thought of dreams leading us to give ourselves to others, to show mercy and compassion to those less fortunate. We thought dreams led to wealth and castles, but You've shown us today that not all dreams are for our financial benefit. Lord, make us willing to dream to make a difference in the lives of others. In Jesus' Name we pray. Amen.

Bad Luck Happens

For in a multitude of dreams there is futility and worthlessness, and ruin in a flood of words.   *Ecclesiastes 5:7* AMP

Bad luck happens to everyone.   *Ecclesiastes 9:11* TEV

Florence

In these verses we see a different approach to dreams: Don't just sit there with a continuous line of wishful thoughts wafting through your mind. This is futile living. These daydreams are worthless, a waste of time. Don't be talking about the great deals you are making, flooding your friends with words about your future success. Not every deal works out; bad luck happens to everyone.

We've all had a friend who looked smart, spoke well, and always had one more get-rich-quick deal to offer you. And yet he never quite got rich himself. Scripture warns us not to be like that ourselves. It's fine to dream of success, but we need to focus on our future, not fantasize ourselves into futility. How many wives come to us with this kind of cry for help: "He's always looking for the big deal, but he never really gets to work. We've been hanging on the brink of disaster all the time"? Bad luck happens to everyone.

My brother Ron, for many years a top radio personality in Dallas, once asked his listeners to send him twenty dollars if they loved him. He made this request on April Fool's Day just for fun. Within three days he had received a quarter of a million dollars, no strings attached! The media picked up this miracle, and he was on major talk shows and written up in *People* magazine. He was branded as an overnight success. What luck!

Was he an overnight success? Was this a visit from Lady Luck? When asked these questions, he replied, "It's a lot easier to be an overnight success when you've worked hard for thirty years getting ready for it." He gave the money away to the Salvation Army and other local charities, and he's still working. He's up every morning before the crack of dawn, and on the air by 6:00 sharing topical humor and encouraging words until 9:00.

A few of us may win the big prize, but we'll have better odds if we work hard getting ready for it.

As we travel and speak, Fred and I meet many successful people who had dreams, focused their energy, worked hard, and accomplished their goals. On one occasion we were met at the airport by Billy, the personal valet and chauffeur of Brig Hart, the energetic and enthusiastic host of our weekend seminar. Brig was the center of attention and a bundle of energy. Everywhere he went, people seemed to follow him. He and his adorable wife, Lita, seemed to be born to a life of riches and excitement.

But Billy told me about a different Brig, long before he ever dared to dream.

Brig had once been in the marines, but he found life at the beaches to be more his style. Billy and Brig spent their days surfing, and in his spare time Brig operated a floundering surf shop. Surfing and partying were his main interests, and Billy told me he doubted back then that Brig would ever amount to anything. Brig was just another beach bum who rented a room from Billy's mother.

Brig's surfing shop was failing miserably, and he knew he needed help. So when someone suggested he attend a meeting for local businessmen, he jumped at the chance. With his long, blond hair and deeply tanned skin, Brig looked out of place among the other businessmen there.

The speaker that night had driven several hundred miles to share the plan of network marketing. Only a handful of people were in attendance, a couple of well-dressed businessmen and that long-haired beach bum. The speaker quickly discounted Brig as a network marketing potential and focused his attention on the other men present.

It wasn't long until the smartly dressed businessmen concluded that the concept of network marketing wasn't for them, and they left in the middle of the presentation. Only Brig remained in the audience. Disheartened, the speaker stopped and prepared to pack up his materials when Brig said, "Hey, man, I'm here. Get on with the program." Although he figured he was just wasting his time with this long-haired beach bum, the speaker continued his presentation. At the conclusion, Brig decided to join the business.

The minute Brig saw the possibility for his future, he began to prepare the dream. He attended a weekend event for the business, and while he was there two things happened that changed his life. He saw his dream actually being lived out by others. They became his friends and his mentors. He also saw another dimension to their lives, and he committed his life to the Lord. Following the guidance of these men, he began to mature both professionally and spiritually.

In just a matter of years, Brig has been transformed from an aimless surfer struggling to survive to the head of a large networking group. The room he rented from Billy's mother now has been replaced with a ten-room waterfront home of his own, a motor coach, a boat, and other "toys." Brig dared to dream, and as a result, his whole life has changed. He no longer worries about how he can pay the rent. His main problem these days is finding a convention center large enough to hold everyone who wants to come hear him share his dream. Brig Hart has become the motivation to thousands of others, teaching them how they too can dare to dream.

How about You?

There are still many possibilities to achieve the great American dream but they don't come from courting Lady Luck. There are many second-income opportunities, but make sure they are legitimate and well established and that you know someone who has done well in the business. Don't jump into something that sounds too good to be true, lots of money with no work. If it seems too good to be true, it usually is.

Remember, it's a lot easier to become an overnight success if you've worked hard for thirty years getting ready for it.

Suggested Prayer for Today

Dear Father God, we need Your wisdom. So often we want the pleasures of life so much that we look for ways to get rich quick. We know You don't honor that kind of wishful thinking; instead You want us to focus on our future and take the steps that lead to hard work and success. As different opportunities come up, give us the discernment to know right from wrong, to not be led astray by something that sounds too good to be true. Lord, we dare to dream that our marriage and our finances can be much better in the future when You open the right doors for us to go through. We pray for Your all-knowing wisdom. In Jesus' Name. Amen.

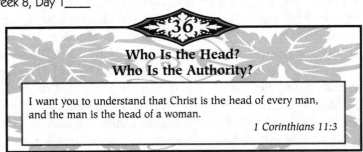

36

Who Is the Head?
Who Is the Authority?

I want you to understand that Christ is the head of every man, and the man is the head of a woman.

1 Corinthians 11:3

Fred

Many Christian men have made honest mistakes by trying to be something God never intended us to be. We thought we had all the answers, that we must make all the decisions, that we were the authority in the home, that only men received the word directly from the Lord, and that therefore our wives must obey us. As a result our wives have been hurt and brushed aside while we have taken on the lonely responsibility for our families without the benefit of our wives' insight, wisdom, and guidance.

Now we must wake up and know the mind of the Lord. Hearing someone else's understanding of the Lord's Word is not sufficient. We must diligently search the Scriptures ourselves to know the truth. We must ask in prayer for the peace that passes understanding so we may know we are in fact hearing the mind of the Lord as He intended.

Doesn't the husband have authority in his own home? Isn't that what Scripture teaches? A careful search of God's word will clearly show us that the husband is the *head* of the wife, but . . . not the *authority over* the wife![1] Why? Because the Lord Jesus Christ is to be the only authority in the home! He Himself has said, "All authority has been given to Me in Heaven and on earth."[2]

While this understanding of God's will seems obvious to many Christians, it is not easy for some to accept this interpretation. I believe the Scripture clearly teaches that only the Lord can be the authority in the home. The husband and wife, being one in the scriptural and spiritual sense, must be submitted *to one another.*

Both must be submitted and surrendered to the Lord. God created a man and his wife to be one flesh. He created them as spiritual equals.

Then how can the husband be the head of the wife? The answer lies very simply in the fact that as the head the husband has a separate and distinct *function of responsibility* from the wife rather than a *position of authority*. Therefore the husband's functions in the home are very different from his wife's functions. When we understand this differentiation, our homes can operate in the harmony and unity that is the intent, purpose, and will of God. Whenever we are out of the will of God in any respect we can only expect discord—perhaps even chaos—and frustration leading to emotional separation. This is where Florence and I were in our relationship after many years of not understanding God's order for the home. Today it is exactly the opposite: rewarding, fulfilling, and satisfying to both of us in every way.

How about You?

Where would you place your marriage on your personal satisfaction scale? Talk it over together. Use all the tools and resources that are available to you to strengthen any areas that are short of where you would like to be. Do not settle for second best. The Lord has given you eternal life as Christians. He also wants you to have abundant life. It's His promise to you. Abundant life leads to life that is rewarding and satisfying.

Each of you should take over and fulfill your God-given roles in the marriage. Let the husband fulfill his functions as the head, as the spiritual leader. Let him be the provider, the presenter, and the partner. When the husband is in his right position, the wife can more effectively fulfill her functions as God intended.

Suggested Prayer for Today

Dear God and Heavenly Father, we thank You for your Word, which always is truth we can rely upon. We never have to wonder, *Are we in your will?* Your Word is clear and sharp. Help us, O Lord, to gain understanding and to see your perfect plans and purposes. Open our eyes, O Lord, that we may behold wondrous things out of thy law. Help us, O Lord, to establish our home on an ever-strengthened foundation. We thank You for Your divine standard of holiness and Your example of selflessness. Father God, we worship You, and we praise You. We give thanks to You forever and ever. We sing Hallelujah unto Your Glorious and Precious Name. We Bless You and offer up to You our sacrifice of thanksgiving in the Name of the Lord Jesus Christ. Amen.

The Husband, the Protector

> Husbands . . . , live with your wives in an understanding way, as with a weaker vessel, since she is a woman; and grant her honor as a fellow heir of the grace of life.
>
> *1 Peter 3:7*

Fred

The Lord Jesus Christ provided all the spiritual weapons we need to protect ourselves, the church, and our families against the spiritual attacks of the enemy (see Ephesians 6:10–18). We are to be the spiritual leader, the head. We men should also be the first in scriptural knowledge, understanding, and wisdom. One of the tragedies of modern life is that in many homes the wife is spiritually far ahead of the husband. On average, women spend far more time in Bible study and prayer than men do.

Men, we are also to protect our wives emotionally as well as physically. What man would not willingly and without hesitation lay down his own life to save the lives of his wife and children? Most of us would do it instinctively, without a thought, in a moment of danger. But what about protecting them emotionally?

Generally we men are created to be stronger emotionally. We don't tend to fall apart as easily or have a low point each month as many women are apt to experience. God created us to see things, particularly stressful things, from a different perspective. We are to be the calming influence in the home, the shield that fends off the stress and the strain. Does that give you something to think about? Are you the shield that protects your wife and family from emotional interference?

We know from Scripture that we have the authority to stand against the enemy and command his obedience in the Name of the Lord Jesus Christ. We know that men are created stronger physically and are by nature not unwilling to use that greater strength to protect our loved ones. Virtually any man is ready and willing to stand up against any and all attacks from outside the family that cause his wife or children emotional grief or strain.

The question then is: Who will protect them from the emotional attacks that originate from our mouths, from within our souls? Who will protect your wife when the frustration, the anger, the rage are spewing from the depths within you?

I have never in forty-four years of marriage hit Florence. I was never physically abusive. I do acknowledge that in the past I had a critical and judgmental spirit. I often corrected her in front of other people. Perhaps I was not emotionally abusive, but I was surely emotionally overbearing and demanding. If someone had tried to tell me that I was hurting Florence, that I was damaging her, if I heard it at all I could rationally prove that I was not. I could quickly summon up a list of the things and areas in which she fell short as a wife and helpmate. This would clearly exonerate me and show, I thought, where the real issues were: with Florence, naturally. Where else?

My own attitudes and logic, my own inner pain and struggles, were so typical of male thinking. It took a long time for me to see that I was filtering my views through cloudy lenses that prohibited me from discerning reality. Now at last I see clearly!

I was the one who needed to change. I needed to cease justifying my emotions, my moodiness, and coldness to my wife when I was hurt or displeased. In short, I needed to start working on myself with no regard to what Florence was doing to improve herself or to become more spiritual! There was only one person I could effectively work on. It was me!

How about You?

Men, God has assigned to us the role of *protector*. Let us gladly march into battle ready to stand up against anyone or anything, any force that tries to steal or interfere with the peace and harmony that we desire for our homes. Let us also be man enough to recognize when the source of that intrusion is within us ourselves.

Suggested Prayer for Today

(For husbands)

Dear Lord Jesus, I ask You to open my eyes so I can see where I may be contributing to any dissension that takes place in our home. I want to demonstrate to my wife and family Your nature and Your character. I know I fall short. I pray today that You will give me a desire to look at myself and see what is in me that is stealing my ability to be the emotional protector You have assigned me to be.

Father God, I ask You to give me the strength to be willing to go to my wife and ask her in what areas I am not measuring up to be the husband who loves, nourishes, cherishes, and protects his wife. Give me, O Lord, the patience to listen without interrupting and help me with the other areas in which I need to improve. I thank You, my Lord and my God. In the precious Name of Jesus I pray. Amen.

The Husband, the Provider

> Husbands ought also to love their own wives as their own bodies.
> . . . For no one ever hated his own flesh, but nourishes and cher-
> ishes it, just as Christ also does the church.
>
> *Ephesians 5:28–29*

Fred

Jesus, always our example, teaches us in these verses that He nourishes and cherishes His Church, and that we husbands are to regard
our wives in the same way. We are to provide for their material
needs, their natural needs, and their emotional needs. We are to be
the bulwarks they can lean on.

Looking back to an earlier chapter in Ephesians, we see that
"We are to grow up in all aspects into Him, who is the head, even
Christ, from whom the whole body, being fitted and held together
by that which every joint supplies, according to the proper working of each individual part" (Ephesians 4:15–16). As we "grow up
in all aspects into Him" we become an integral part of the supply
system, and all the parts work together in harmony. This is an awesome responsibility the Father places on each of us husbands.
Look at yourself. Are you fulfilling this role He has established for
you? Ask your wife. Are you willing to ask her how well she thinks
you are doing?

A long time ago I decided that one of the most important things
I could do to build our marriage was to provide for every one of
Florence's needs that I possibly could. There have been many
times I have had to make a conscious choice: Is this what I want
or is this best for her? I have never regretted making the choice to
provide for Florence's needs and desires. The result is that now,
even after many years of living with a controlling and manipulative
husband, she is able to completely trust me emotionally. She
knows deep down in her heart that I am always putting her needs

ahead of my own. I always try to provide for every desire of her heart.

I always want to be the *provider* for her. I want to supply her with everything I can that will give her peace of mind. One of the most frequent comments we now get from others, especially as we travel is, "You two seem to be so happy together; you seem so relaxed with each other." I'm glad a little bit of the love of the Lord Jesus is shining through both of us, that we may be a witness to others by just the way we treat each other, talk to each other, and respond to each other.

What are some of the simple things I do to provide for her needs and desires? Florence likes to have a cup of coffee when she first wakes up in the morning. I make the coffee and bring it to her. Then we sit down together in our bedroom and have our coffee together. There is no television, no newspaper; we just talk and visit. She likes that. She likes my undivided attention. I'm glad to give it to her because it makes her happy. Next, when we're at home I make breakfast for her every morning and call her just two minutes before it is ready to be served. She likes that! To her this is another way of saying I love you.

These two activities are just the beginning of the many things I do each morning to try to make her day as light and easy as possible. I also try to do all the tasks she does not enjoy doing. Does this make me less of a man? On the contrary, I am a man who is fulfilled, satisfied, and thankful for his marriage.

How about You?

Think now of what additional things you could do for your wife that would make her happy, that would remove stress from her life, that would be an example of your love to her, that would let her know you put her needs and desires ahead of your own. What better ways can you as a husband supply her human needs? How can you be a better *provider*? Not sure? Ask her!

You make a living by getting, you make a life by giving.

Suggested Prayer for Today

(For husbands)

Dear God, I want to be able to provide for my wife in the same way You provide for us. Lord, I confess that sometimes I feel so neglected myself. I don't feel my wife is sensitive to my needs. It is so easy to see my own needs and focus on whether or not they are being met, I confess that I forget to be selfless and fail to look to see what else I can do for my wife, to provide for her needs.

You have shown us in Scripture that in Your earthly walk among us You never took regard for Yourself over the needs of those You came to minister to. You always had time for the sick, the lame, the needy. You never said, "Don't bother Me. I'm busy." Lord, I ask You to help me to be like You. I even want my wife to know that I diligently desire to be the husband she wants me to be and that You want me to be. Thank You, Lord Jesus. Amen.

The Husband, the Presenter

> Husbands, love . . . , just as Christ also loved the church and gave Himself up for her . . . that He might present to Himself the church . . . , having no spot or wrinkle or any such thing.
>
> *Ephesians 5:25, 27*

Fred

Jesus desired to "present to Himself the church in all her glory, having no spot or wrinkle or any such thing." This scripture gives us additional insight as to how we are to regard and love our wives. Husbands are to become so Christlike that through the process and the journey of the marital union with us our wives will become spotless and "wrinkle-free." We are to create such an atmosphere in our marriages that our wives will be seen by the Lord as holy and blameless. Think on this for a moment. Is this not an awesome assignment?

Let me repeat that. According to this scripture, we husbands are to become so Christlike that our wives will become spotless and wrinkle-free as a result of living with us and from the positive influence we have had on their spiritual lives.

This does not imply that the wife has no responsibility of her own to reach for these objectives. She surely does. The verse is only speaking of the Lord's expectations of the husband. Similarly you might recall that the wife's instruction to be subject to her husband speaks only of what is expected of her and the attitude that she is to have. It neither speaks of nor implies any authority of the husband.

As mere mortals how can we accomplish such a seemingly impossible task as to present our wives spotless to the Lord? On our own, we cannot. With the power of the risen Christ freely flowing through our lives, our minds, and our bodies, however, we can make surprising strides in that direction.

His expectation of us places upon us another awesome challenge to become so "at one" with Him that we become like Him.

This means continuing to pursue our spiritual growth and maturity. Where are you today spiritually compared to five years ago? Have you made the progress that you should have? Where will you be five years from now? Determine today what your own spiritual future will be.

How about You?

Would it not be a good idea today for the two of you to sit down together and take some time for each of you to honestly express to the other where you are in your journey of spiritual growth. Not to challenge each other or point fingers at any shortfalls or failures but simply to discuss with each other where you are and where you'd like to be five years from now.

It is always a beneficial experience to take your mate into the inner recesses of your emotions and feelings and allow the other a glimpse—or, even better, when you are able, to give a full panoramic view—of what is going on inside you. You will be entering into the highest arenas of trust that a husband and wife can approach together. Not everyone is ready to do this. If you do not feel ready there should be no stigma attached to the need for this kind of personal privacy, nor should there be any pressure of one upon the other to open up in this area until you fully desire to do so.

These sensitive issues you may feel you need to hold back from your partner should still be shared privately with the Lord. He is never judgmental when you are open and honest with Him. He is always patient, compassionate, and kind. He can always be trusted. You never have to fear that He will throw your feelings back into your face. Talking them over with Him will be positive preparation for being able to share them with your partner later.

Once again, in our verse for today, the Lord has given us a seemingly monumental challenge as well as an objective He expects us to meet. Does it work? Can it actually happen? You should have seen the changes in my wife when I began to take seriously this injunction from my Master to be the husband He wants me to be. Now she is spotless and virtually wrinkle-free! She could be presented at any time!

Suggested Prayer for Today

(For husbands to pray aloud in the presence of their wives)

Dear God and Heavenly Father, I need help! At the rate I am going I will never be able to fulfill Your expectations of me. And Lord, truly, I do not want to disappoint You. You gave so much to me. You gave Your very life for me on the cross that I might have life. No one else has ever made such a sacrifice for me. I can't even conceive how You could find me worthy enough for such a great gift. I do not take lightly the gift of eternal life that I received as a result of Your willingness to so totally give of Yourself for me. Now, Lord Jesus, in my relationship with my wife I pray for the same selflessness that You had for me. Help me to be so "at one" with You that all the stress and strain that I have caused her in the past will be over, done and gone. Then she can begin to become what You have instructed me to present to you, a wife that is spotless and without wrinkle. I thank You, my Lord and my God. Amen.

40

The Husband, the Partner

Grant her honor as a fellow heir of the grace of life, so that your prayers may not be hindered.

1 Peter 3:7

Fred

What does it mean to be a fellow heir? The Scripture says my wife is the "fellow heir," or the "joint heir" (RSV), or the "heir together" (KJV), or "equally an heir" (JB) of the grace—the unmerited favor—of life. Surely that means we share equally spiritually in all that God wants to bestow upon us.

The Greek word used here is *sugkleronomos,* which describes "one who participates in the same lot . . . [referring] to a *personal equality* based on an equality of possession."[1] Scripture clearly shows us that man and woman, male and female, husband and wife are equal in the sight of God. My wife possesses as much of the grace of life as I possess. Therefore we are equal partners, sharing in all that we do, plan, or decide on as a family and as a couple. We are one in the Lord.

As the two of you actually become one in flesh, in mind, in spirit, in objectives, in decisions—as you become one in the Lord—you are truly equal partners. However, since the husband is the *head* we men have the additional awesome responsibility to *see that this equal partnership becomes a reality*. It is only by our leadership, which means by our example, that this can happen. Only then will we be fulfilled as men and our wives be fulfilled as women, for then we are functioning as God intended.

It has taken many years and many mistakes, but at last Florence and I are functioning as equal partners. We each have very definite and assigned roles and functions. I know I am to protect her in every way I can. I know I am to provide for her needs and desires

127

as much as I can. I know I am to grow up in Christ so I may provide a stress-free environment where she can grow as well, holy, and blameless. I know I am to make her feel that she is a fellow heir with me, my equal partner. And one more thing I have learned: These are my responsibilities as her husband. Therefore I am never to look over her shoulder and see how well she is doing on her part. This is what we call "playing the Junior Holy Spirit"! That is one responsibility God has never given to me.

Protect her, yes! Provide for her, yes! Prepare her to be presented, yes! Partner with her, yes! But check up to see how she is doing spiritually? No! And if I am not to check up on her spiritually, it probably holds true that she would prefer it if I didn't check up on her in any way. I know that I surely have never appreciated her checking up on me. I have said to her on more than one occasion, "Honey, what I want is a wife, not a mother." As clearly as we men understand this, isn't it strange how often words and directions come out of our mouths to our wives that are not those of a partner but of an overseer or a father?

How about You?

Are you sometimes an overseer or a supervisor to your wife? What does she think about your assuming this role? Take the time to ask her. She will appreciate your being interested enough to ask. It is a way of telling her that you care, that she is important to you.

It may have been some time ago that she last felt you had any deep concern for what was important to her or for how she felt. We men need to always remember that, generally, deep feelings are much more important to our wives than they are to us. They like to talk about the feelings they have. Too often wives feel that their husbands are too busy, too preoccupied, or just don't care. A partner cares about what is happening in the partnership.

Make the time now. Tell your partner that you'd like to set aside some time for her to share with you what she appreciates and what she would like to see more of in your marriage relationship.

Suggested Prayer for Today

(For husbands.)

Almighty God, I am so thankful today. I am the recipient of Your richest blessings. They are all available to me, and they are all available to my beloved wife as well in the same measure and portion. Lord, some of the greatest gifts You have to bestow upon us are Your peace and Your joy. I want these gifts, Lord. I want them every day in my life, in our home. I want my wife to be able to enjoy them as much as I desire them. Lord, if I am a stumbling block to my partner's ability to enjoy the reality and presence of these gifts, I ask You to open my mind so that I will be able to see without being defensive where the walls are that are keeping Your gifts from my wife. I want her to have them, Lord. The last thing I want to do is to interfere. Rather, I want to be a facilitator, a channel for her to receive every good gift and every perfect gift that You desire to give to each of us. I thank You, dear Lord Jesus. Amen.

Part II

Prepare
the
Dream

*What you can do to get moving
toward a better married life
and toward a deeper
spiritual relationship*

41

Commit to the Lord

Commit to the LORD whatever you do, and your plans will succeed.

Proverbs 16:3 NIV

Florence

So often when we make plans, we do it from our own human desires. We set goals about our future—where we want to be in five years or what size house we expect or what car we want to drive. We buy organizers to help us see the goals in writing and jog our minds and bodies into action—assuming we can find the planner when we need it. Some of us make New Year's resolutions that we'll go on diets, save money systematically, and have a new loving attitude toward our in-laws.

In general, these ideas for our future have little to do with spiritual matters, and often they fail, discouraging us from planning again. We gain weight, don't save a dime, and can't stand that leeching brother-in-law who hasn't paid back the two hundred dollars we were stupid enough to lend him! Why bother with goals when so often they just don't work out?

The Bible is not a text on household organization, but it does tell us to count the cost before building and to do all things decently and in order. But most importantly, the Word from God is to bring your ideas to Him first before you get involved in questionable ventures.

Frequently we talk with fine Christian people who have gotten into some kind of business trouble. An idea for a new venture seems attractive, and the partner who is more impulsive than the other decides to "go for it" without seeking any advice. In fact, the more risky the opportunity is, the less likely such people ask for counsel. They know sensible friends will say no, so they don't ask.

One couple we talked with were at a point of financial ruin and emotional divorce. They hadn't actually parted, but they weren't speaking except for emergencies. For both of them, much of life had become an emergency. It all started when a friend was "in on the ground floor" of a new multilevel business and convinced Sanguine Sam that he could make a fortune if he got in quickly. The company was going to make vitamin products and an amazing pill that would cause people to lose weight without dieting. Each of the lucky participants had a chance to sign up quickly, buy product at discount, and get their friends involved.

Sam had so many friends that he knew he could move this business off the ground in a hurry. His Melancholy wife, Marilyn, tried to discourage him, but he told her she was always a wet blanket. Sam set up meetings in their home, and Marilyn found herself a reluctant hostess. In the process Sam neglected his real estate business, and soon no money was coming in. The friends who said they'd sign up didn't share Sam's enthusiasm, and few put their hearts into the business as Sam had hoped. More than that, no one lost weight on the pill, and one had an allergic reaction and told others not to try it. By the time I met this pair at a convention for another company, Sam was angry and broke, and Marilyn was deeply depressed. They were both upset, and they blamed each other.

The Lord does not always bless Christians' businesses just because they jump into them. We are to bring our prospects to the Lord and seek His will. Any time someone wants you to get involved in some opportunity where you must leap in immediately, be immediately suspicious and check it out. If it's a good deal today, it will be a good idea tomorrow. Also, unless both of you agree and are willing to move on in harmony, you shouldn't be involved. The Lord doesn't bless us when we enter into something that our mate doesn't feel comfortable with.

Fred and I look back at some of our business mistakes and see that I had female intuition that this was wrong, and he did it anyway, over my objections. As Rudyard Kipling said, "A woman's guess is much more accurate than a man's certainty." How much we have learned the hard way, and how much we want to save you from failure! "Commit to the LORD whatever you do [take time, pray about it, seek advice, and agree on it],) and then [when you've done it decently and in order] you will have a better hope that it will succeed."

How about You?

Do you pray about the matter first, seek godly counsel, and then make a decision? Or do you plan things out and then ask the Lord to bless the matter you've placed before Him? He tells us that when we commit our plans to Him, we will succeed. Does one of you tend to jump into "opportunities" that your mate opposes? A house divided against itself will not stand!

What decision do you have before you right now? Are you thinking of a career change? Seeking a new house? Have you brought the matter to the Lord in serious prayer? Does your partner share your enthusiasm? When you do agree, He will open doors that you could never open yourself. His plan for you will succeed.

Suggested Prayer for Today

Dear Lord Jesus, we don't want to be angry at each other or make foolish decisions. Right now we are trying to decide about _____. Show us the right path to take. We don't want to make human decisions. We've made mistakes before. We won't be impulsive. We await your peace in our hearts. We love You and trust You. In Jesus' Name. Amen.

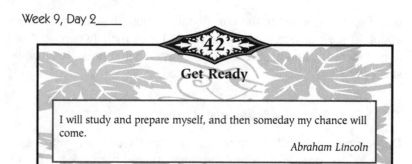

42

Get Ready

I will study and prepare myself, and then someday my chance will come.

Abraham Lincoln

Florence

Have you ever wondered how Abraham Lincoln made it to the top? I've looked at his pictures and wondered if he could be elected in today's world of political-image consultants. Can't you imagine the one assigned to Lincoln, complaining, "You gave me what? You must be kidding! The first thing we'll have to do is get rid of the scraggly beard—and then the clothes. How did he get this far in that worn-out black suit and the string tie?"

Gratefully, there was no television in those days, and Lincoln quietly got ready, made the right moves, and worked harder than the others.

No one had much hope for Abraham Lincoln. Even in his own party he was a loner. There were candidates who were better looking and had far more charisma, but while others gossiped and wondered, Lincoln studied and prepared, and when the call came, he was able to respond.

Few of us expect to be president, but what do we want to be? Have we thought beyond the moment to some realistic possibilities for the future? I talked with my favorite skycap, Eddie, one morning as Fred and I headed out for another trip. "Have you lost weight?" I asked.

"Thirty pounds," he answered proudly.

"How did you do it?" I hoped it was a miracle plan I could adopt for myself.

Eddie then explained that the skycaps had been taken over by a new company that cut their hours in half. Even though he had "good hours" and made excellent tips Eddie could see his future was going nowhere. So he took a night job at a discount warehouse store as a stocker. He could see that if he worked hard he could move up. "Most people there do as little as possible to get their money, so they noticed me right from the start," Eddie said. He was moved up to the cashier level, where he produced faster than the others while maintaining a cheerful attitude. He watched how the managers dressed and decided to exercise and lose weight. As he told me of his hopes for the future he added, "I've let them know I'm preparing to move ahead so when an opening comes they'll know Eddie's ready!"

How about You?

Skycap Eddie and President Lincoln wouldn't seem to have much in common, but they both knew the value of getting ready. Often women ask me how they can become a public speaker, and I say "get ready." Read everything you can on your subject, put together outlines for future messages, practice before any group who'll listen.

What do you need to do to get ready? Where do you want to be in five years? Start studying and preparing for the future, and someday your chance will come.

One Sunday morning I heard Dr. Charles Stanley speak on God's plan for our lives. He said some Christians assume if God has a plan they should sit and wait for it to happen, but he pointed out that God has the plan and our part is to find it! We have to be getting ready and seeking His will for our life. We need to be in prayer, not be lazy, look beyond the moment, and be accountable to God and our families.

What should you be doing to get ready? "I know the plans I have for you!" It's now our job to find the plans and follow the dream. Remember, Eddie's ready. Are you?

Suggested Prayer for Today

Dear Lord, we want to be obedient to Your will, but sometimes we don't ask what it is. We either change by ourselves, or we don't move at all. Our own desires get in the way, and sometimes we're lazy. We don't want to do the work to get ready. We watch TV instead of studying, praying, thinking, and preparing. Give us a fresh desire to move above average so we'll be ready when the opportunity appears. We thank You. In Jesus' Name we pray. Amen.

43

Pay Attention

> Next to entertaining or impressive talk, a thoroughgoing silence manages to intrigue most people.
>
> *Mrs. J. Borden Harriman,*
> *From* Pinafores to Politics

Florence

Silence has never been a goal of mine as I've always had so much to say. A number of years ago, Fred asked me, "Do you realize that when you are talking you are not learning anything?" As I let that thought flicker through my brain, he added, "You already know what *you're* saying. You only learn when you listen."

This was surely a fresh thought to me, and I did not respond with great enthusiasm, but I began to think about it. *You only learn while you listen.* I love to learn, but up until then I had not considered *listening* as a step toward knowledge. I had never thought of silence as something that would intrigue people and improve the listener.

Fred's challenge changed my life even though it was difficult at first to discipline myself to ask a person's name and then to listen to what he or she had to say. I'd be talking away to a person at a party when I would see Fred coming toward me. I knew he would ask me to introduce my new friend, so I'd whisper in desperation, "Your name! Tell me your name quickly—and where are you from?" Then when Fred asked I could use my emergency knowledge to introduce him to the person. After a few close calls, I was convinced I was not a born listener—but I knew I could learn.

As I asked questions of everyone I met and listened closely to their words, I began to gather examples and information that I have been able to use in my writing and speaking. I've found the pulse of the people on pressing issues and expanded my knowledge in a personal way. Listening is more than not talking. All of us know of times when we're sitting quietly but totally tuned out to what people are saying. How embarrassing when we hear, "Do you think so?" and we have no idea what we should have been thinking about.

Listening should be an active participation, not a rest period. We should be nodding, adding, "Yes, that's right," or "How amazing!" We should have questions to ask the other person: "When did you first get interested in this career?" "How did you happen to move here?" "What do you like best about your church or community?" Don't ask questions that invite one-word answers, such as "How many children do you have?" "How many miles do you drive to work?" or questions that get a yes or no answer. In our ministry we book authors on radio talk shows, and we have learned that even some of the hosts on the programs don't know how to ask creative questions—so we send them some samples. There's nothing worse on radio than having dead air while the two sit wondering what to say next!

Learning to listen and ask questions is well worth the discipline and will create a new interest in others. People will enjoy your company far more when they realize you really care about them.

Shakespeare wrote that it was "the disease of not listening" that troubled him. I don't ever want to have that disease again!

How about You?

We don't need to be brilliant conversationalists to be accepted by others; we just need to ask a few questions and then listen to the answers. Look the person in the eye, nod with affirmation, thank him or her for sharing words of wisdom. People will be delighted to realize that someone really cares what they think. Your silence will intrigue most people.

Today make a special effort to listen without interruption. Start with your spouse. Sometimes we are rude to our mates, tuning out or shutting them up.

As you go about your day, ask questions and show interest in people you might normally ignore. See how they brighten up when you ask about them. Report back to each other tonight and compare results.

Suggested Prayer for Today

Dear Lord, give us a new interest in others. We think we really care for others but we have cut people off; we've not listened actively. We want to be disciplined, and we want to slow down enough to ask questions as we rush through life. Give us a new love for each other and an interest in others we haven't had before. We pray this in the Name of Jesus. Amen.

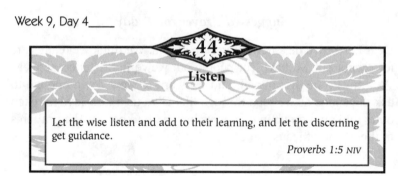

44

Listen

Let the wise listen and add to their learning, and let the discerning get guidance.

Proverbs 1:5 NIV

Florence

Scripture tells us that while fools babble away without thinking, the wise listen and learn, and the discerning look for experienced guidance. No matter what our personality pattern may be, we can learn to listen. In our marriage I was the talker and Fred the listener until that day when he challenged me to become a listener.

How do you change from being a talker to a listener? The first step is to ask the Lord to give you a love for people that you don't naturally have. I have learned that to be a listener you have to care more about the other person than you care about yourself. You want to learn more than you want to teach. For me this change of heart took specific prayer and conscious effort, but the results have become a blessing to me and to Fred. One of my favorite compliments is, "You are really a good listener."

One day Fred and I got on the plane in Palm Springs along with Henry Kissinger, former secretary of state under Presidents Nixon and Ford. By seat assignment I was directly in front of Kissinger and next to his special assistant in charge of security, James Taronto. I was fascinated by this handsome young man with a crew cut and preppy clothes; he looked like the All-American college boy of the fifties. He didn't look at all like a bodyguard. I asked him how he got into this unusual occupation, and he explained his time in the marines, his marksmanship awards, and his appointment to a high-level security position. After he got out of the marines, he interviewed for the Kissinger job and got it.

"Does the government pay your salary?" I asked.

"No, there's no security coverage for former cabinet members," he replied. "He pays for us himself. There are four of us, and we rotate so one of us is with him at all times, even while he sleeps."

During our two-and-a-half-hour trip, as I asked questions, James told me about his exciting trip to China, about his twin daughters, his beloved grandparents, and his plans "AK" (after Kissinger). "You can only take this intensity for about two years before you wear out," he said.

As we landed, he turned to me and thanked me for listening to him. "You are the most fascinating lady I've ever met," he said. "You seemed to care about me. Most people only talk to me to get to him. Sometimes I feel like a piece of furniture with no identity. Thank you for liking me for myself."

We exchanged business cards, and as the exit light blinked on, James jumped to his feet and snapped into his protective position. I watched as he opened a path for Henry Kissinger to walk through, and then they both disappeared into the crowd.

How about You?

How did you do yesterday in your listening practice? Did you question some people you might not have listened to before? Not everyone gets a chance to sit with Kissinger's bodyguard, but I've heard such interesting stories when I've questioned waitresses, skycaps, manicurists, and bellmen. Make a point today to ask someone about himself or herself, and then listen. One of our friends who doesn't get out much anymore does his communicating on the phone. When salespeople call to sell him things, he says he'll give them five minutes if they'll listen to him for five. He listens, and then he shares his faith in Jesus. Over the years he has led many strangers to the Lord over the phone by listening first.

For those of you who do any public speaking or leading of groups, the people you talk with provide you with excellent examples for your sharing. You've all seen those "man-on-the-street" interviews on TV. Why not become an interviewer yourself? Instead of having "another dull day" to report to each other, you will both have some new experiences to share. No longer will your dinner conversation go like this:

She: How's your day been?
He: Fair.
She: Just fair?
He: How about you?
She: Same as usual.
(*Silence from then on . . .*)

Wise people listen, learn, and bless others. Be aware, and then share!

Suggested Prayer for Today

Dear Lord, again today we ask for a special interest in other people. We ask that You give us the desire to listen and to really care. We're so busy and so preoccupied with our own activities that we don't pause to ask and listen to other people. You are all powerful. You care for us. We thank You and love You. In Jesus' Name. Amen.

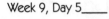

45

Practice

> Be ready for the sudden surprise visits of God. A ready person never needs to get ready. Think of the time we waste trying to get ready when God has called.
>
> Oswald Chambers, My Utmost for His Highest, *April 18*

Florence

If anyone of us had a natural ability to play tennis, would we wait until the day of a big tournament to begin learning the rules? If we could play chopsticks on the piano, would we sign up for the recital before taking lessons? If we were applying for a job that took typing skills, would we wait until the day of the interview to memorize the keyboard?

Foolish questions! We all know we have to practice, study, and prepare for any worthwhile pursuit in life, and yet in spiritual matters we postpone our preparation. There will be another day, a day when we'll have more time. Bible study and prayer become hobbies, leisure-time activities we will pursue someday . . . if we ever get done with the necessary things of life.

How do we get ready for God? This whole book was designed with preparation in mind. If you continue to read and discuss what is suggested each day, you will build a discipline of daily time with your partner and with your Lord. Don't spend this time as a chore you must do to check off your chart and win points with God. Instead, look at it as your morning phone call to your Father who loves you. According to your time, at least read the lesson section for the day. If possible, think about the verse or quote and decide how you can apply that to your personal life. Beyond that, try to take the time for discussion and practice in communication. Remember, we all can talk, but few of us can communicate. Reading is good, thinking is better, but communicating is best!

One couple we talked with as we began this book explained how they have used similar material. He travels much of the time while she is at home, and this pattern of life tends to cause couples to drift apart. What they do is talk on the phone each evening. When he is settled in his hotel room at night, he calls her, and they read the day's lesson together. They each have their own copy of the book, and they alternate reading out loud. Then they discuss the suggested material. He told me it always seems to be tied in somehow with what happened in their lives that day. Instead of just reporting the day's activities, they have something new to talk about. When they are done they read the prayer together, and he adds an extra prayer for her protection and restful night.

If you are apart at times, use this book as a bridge to connect you both in a meaningful way. Whether you are home or on the road, it is important to keep preparing for God's visits and for inviting Him into your lives each day.

Oswald Chambers points out to us that if we wish God to use us, we must be ready. We must do our homework before we are called. We must study in excited preparation, knowing that we are ready for whatever our Lord has in mind for us, whether our call is large or small. When he plans a recital He doesn't call on those who didn't have time to practice.

How about You?

How much time do you spend in Bible study or in personal prayer each day? Can you take at least a verse a day and ask the Lord to show you what He wants you to see in it? Get ready! Wouldn't it be a shame if God chose you for an exciting role in His drama and you had to say, "I'm sorry, I'm not ready"?

Start with these steps each day:

Be consistent in your marriage-building readings.

Memorize scripture as you go along.

Study further by reading God's Word before and after the verse of the day.

Spend meaningful time in conversation with your partner.

Do whatever programs may be suggested, such as taking the Personality Profile and doing the family evaluation.

Determine to make progress in your marriage and not assume it's your mate's responsibility.

Develop your prayer life beyond the brief suggested prayers. As you improve your communication with your partner, you'll improve it with the Lord. When you are ready, God's visits won't be a surprise.

Suggested Prayer for Today

Dear Lord, we have both been too busy to get ready fully. We've done our best, but we haven't been consistent. We praise You and love You, and we want to be closer than we've been before. We are looking at Your Word and Your instruction in a new way. Continue to shine Your light on us as we get ready for Your surprise visits. In the Name of Jesus we pray. Amen.

46

Keeping Alert in Prayer

Devote yourselves to prayer, keeping alert in it with an attitude of thanksgiving.

Colossians 4:2

Fred

Sometimes we see a verse in Scripture that we've seen many, many times before. We know it well, we know what it means, and then one day . . . suddenly it is flashing before us set in big, bold caps and bright neon lights! We see something new in it that we have never seen before. Colossians 4:2 was one such verse for me, especially the New American Standard translation shown above. (Different wordings often have a more significant impact on my mind.)

Devote myself to prayer? Did I really devote myself to communing with my Father in Heaven? Frankly, without any question, the answer was clearly NO! Prayer was the weakest part of my Christian life. Since that time when this verse made such an impact on me I have found that I am not alone. Most Christians will give the same answer. Either we're too busy to set aside time to spend with the Father or we doze off or our minds seem to wander from prayer to thinking about other things. Because I found my prayer time to be such a struggle, it was also ineffective, and there was a time, for several years, that I simply stopped having times of personal prayer. Perhaps such prayer was for others, I reasoned, but maybe it was not for me. Just what the enemy wanted me to think!

I prayed in church with everyone else. I prayed at mealtimes with no difficulty. I prayed sometimes on the way to work in the car. Was that "devoting myself to prayer"? My personal commitment to prayer didn't seem to measure up to what is expected of me in Colossians 4:2.

Keeping alert in it? No, I wasn't alert at all. Since I often dozed off or my mind switched from focusing on the Lord to something else, I had to give myself a fat "zero" on alertness. What was the solution? The scripture is clear; there is no mistaking what it says. It was for me. I simply was not doing what I needed to do. I had not learned how to have a disciplined and committed prayer life. I had little personal communion with my Lord and Heavenly Father.

With an attitude of thanksgiving. On this part I did not totally strike out. I was thankful for so much, and I was able to express that to my Savior.

Now everything about my old prayer life has changed. I have a disciplined, committed, daily prayer communion with Him. I am able to stay alert and focused. In this week's chapters I will share with you how I did it—and how you can too.

How about You?

Have you each been examining your own prayer life today? Take heed lest you fall into the trap of examining your partner's commitment instead of your own! Ask yourself, Am I devoted to prayer as the Scripture directs and the Lord desires? Do I set aside a specific time to be with Him and to stay alert? Am I willing to do that now, to make such a commitment to my mate and to the Lord?

Suggested Prayer for Today

Dear Lord Jesus, I come to You today to confess that I have not committed myself to daily prayer communion with You. I ask that You strengthen my desire to do what You have already directed me to do. Help me, Lord, to devote myself to spending specific time each day with You. There is so much I desire from You and so much I want to do for You. I know I will have not if I ask not. I know that I can never become like You unless I spend time with You, getting to know You, and trusting You in a rich and deeper way. Help me, Lord, to grow. Help me, Lord Jesus, to become like You. It is in Your precious and powerful Name that I pray, in thanksgiving. Amen.

Diligence in Prayer

Call upon me, and . . . pray unto me, and I will hearken unto you. And ye shall seek me, and find me, when ye shall search for me with all your heart.

Jeremiah 29:12–13 KJV

Fred

Read these verses to each other. Together look carefully at the words. What can you learn about prayer from this significant passage? What two thoughts are most penetrating to your spirit and to your mind?

Perhaps the first thing we see is God's promise that He will "hearken." He will hear. He will listen if we ask, if we pray! How can we expect Him to hearken if we do not pray?

The more I pray, the more I learn about prayer and the more I realize how little I know about prayer. The thing I ask of God most often is, "Lord, teach me more about prayer." True to His promise, He is teaching me, both from the Word and from the practical experience of seeing wondrous miracles and answers to prayer that I could never have known if I wasn't spending daily and regular time of prayer with Him.

In the human sense, prayer makes no sense at all. How can some unseen, unfelt, often unknown power hear our cries and respond to them in such a way that changes actually take place in our lives? Yet this is exactly what happens. He says that He wants us to come to Him as a child comes to his father, and He promises He will hear.

When you were little, did you go for a walk outside on the sidewalk with your daddy? Did you ever fall and scrape your knee? What did you immediately do but run back to your daddy and ask him to take away the pain and the bruise? You did it because you knew your daddy. You trusted him, and you knew he could help you. Do you know your Heavenly Father? Do you know Him well enough to go to Him with whatever is troubling you?

Years ago when Florence was teaching a ladies' Bible study at the women's club, a lady in her nineties, known to be a devoted Christian, was her most consistent student. This intrigued Florence so much she asked her why, despite her frailty she attended the class faithfully. The dear lady replied, "I'm cramming for my finals!"

How about You?

"Ye shall . . . find me, when ye search for me with all your heart." Does that phrase "with all your heart" describe your prayer life and your commitment to spending time with your Father? Would you like to see improvements in your marriage relationship? Begin by coming to Him daily and confessing to Him everything that you did or said today that caused discomfort, pain, or tears for your partner. At first you may want to do it privately. After all, it's just a matter between you and your Father in Heaven. You will find that when you are able to readily confess to Him you will soon be able to confess to your mate with equal ease. This is perhaps the first and most important step to enable real healing to take place.

Suggested Prayer for Today

Heavenly Father, I confess to You that my heart has not always been in my prayers. I confess to You, Lord, that I have failed to come to You regularly and consistently as You desire for me to do. You gave Your life for me on the cross that I might have life. I will never cease to be thankful for what You did for me. I have life, but sometimes I even suck the very life out of _____ by the thoughtless words that come out of my mouth. I ask You to forgive me. I ask You, Lord, to give me the courage and the honesty to go to _____ and tell her/him that I am sorry and to ask for forgiveness. Help me, dear Lord, to be patient and understanding so that I don't cause friction or stress for my beloved by my thoughtlessness. I thank You, almighty God, for Your promise that if I ask You will hear. I pray in the precious Name of Jesus. Amen.

48

Peace through Prayer

Come unto me, all ye that labour and are heavy laden, and I will give you rest.

Matthew 11:28

Fred

Are you discouraged? Are you disappointed? Are you disillusioned? Has your marriage not turned out to be the enriching experience you had hoped and expected it would be? Have you been looking at your mate and seeing the areas where he or she is falling short of your expectations, hopes, and dreams?

It is so easy for each one of us to look at the other as the source of all our troubles. When ministering to couples struggling in their relationships, so many times we have heard one say about the other, "There's nothing wrong with me. If only she'd shape up and be what she's supposed to be we would get along just fine! . . . (or "If only he'd shape up . . .").

Our own wedding and marriage, which started out with what we thought was an auspicious beginning (a five-page spread in *Life* magazine's May 18, 1953 edition), went steadily downhill! We didn't understand each other. We had such a confused focus. Instead of looking at our own characters, personalities, and natures to see what might be interfering with the life we had expected, we did the obvious thing, what virtually every other young couple does: We looked at the flaws in each other. And . . . they weren't hard to find!

Instead of focusing on what had attracted us to each other, we both began to try to change the things in each other that we considered to be imperfect, offensive, or disruptive. The momentary high slowly and insidiously began to slide into what twenty years later was a deep abyss that we had created for ourselves. The fact that we have been able to come out of that crater and rise high above it to the relationship that God designed and intended for husband and wife to enjoy should give you encouragement that God has something even richer and deeper in store for you!

We labored to make our marriage successful, but after two decades of frustration we were each carrying so many burdens we were, indeed, "heavy laden." It might have seemed much easier to stop, make a new start with someone else, and try all over again. Fortunately, separation and divorce were not in the Lord's plans for us. Finally, I began to face the deep issues of hurt that were in me until I learned their source and then began in 1987 to come to the Lord daily in prayer. Although it didn't happen overnight, true to His promise in the verse shared on the previous page, He has brought that complete, emotional rest into our life together.

When I was willing to prayerfully look at myself for change instead of at Florence, I began to change. For some time she could not even trust the changes that were slowly taking place. She had seen too many previously good intentions go up in smoke. This made it additionally difficult for me. I had to pray for patience as my wife was learning to rebuild the emotional trust I had destroyed. But with God's help we both persevered, and the emotional walls of protection that separated us began to crumble. Now we can live, act, and think as one while still retaining our separate and distinct personalities.

It was worth it! Had we followed the path the enemy had plotted out for us, we would have both missed the "abundant life" the Lord Jesus has for us and promises to each one of us.

Prayer changed my life. Prayed healed our marriage. In prayer I was able to confess daily to my Father in Heaven the things I had done or said that had hurt my wife. I prayed, and I confessed until the time came that I rarely said or did those offending things any longer. Our Lord Jesus promised us that if we would come to Him and keep coming to Him again and again, day after day, He would not only hear us but He would give each one of us rest for our weary souls.

How about You?

Are you discouraged? Are you disappointed? Are you disillusioned? Are there areas in your marriage in which you would like to see changes and growth? Jesus said, "Come unto me." The most direct way to come to Him is in prayer. This is a conditional promise. He will do His part if we are willing to do our part! Begin today. Together and individually take that first step toward perfect peace and rest by coming to Him in prayer.

Suggested Prayer for Today

Dear God and Heavenly Father, I confess to You that I have been negligent in coming to You. Yes, Lord, I am burdened. I am heavily burdened. Can You really remove these burdens that I am carrying? So often I feel I am alone and no one understands my needs and my hurts. Because You have promised rest to my weary soul, I am coming to You today to ask You to heal my hurts and remove these heavy weights I am carrying. I ask You, Lord Jesus, to carry them with me, to share the load until they are gone, until they evaporate into the atmosphere of peace and contentment. Lord, this is my desire. I want that perfect peace. I commit to You today that I am willing to work for it. I will do whatever You tell me to do. I will work at it until it is done. Your Word tells me You will perfect the work that You have begun in me. Lord Jesus, I ask You to transform my mind, my spirit, and my emotions. Help me to see my mate with the same loving and patient eyes with which You see him/her. Thank You, Lord, for hearing my prayer today. I ask in Your precious Name. Amen

49

Your Inner Room

But you, when you pray, [you] go into your inner room, and when you have shut your door, [you] pray to your Father who is in secret, and your Father who sees in secret will repay you.

Matthew 6:6

Fred

Look carefully, and you will see that the word *you* appears four times in this verse and is implied two more times for a total of six. Is that clear enough? To whom is this verse directed?

For many years I had no inner room, no prayer closet. I had all but given up on having a personal prayer time. I found it hard to do, ineffectual, and too often unsatisfying. My mind would wander, or I would doze off; those two barriers kept interfering. It was easier not to bother than to struggle and feel guilty. The enemy was winning, and I didn't even realize it!

I have learned that countless Christians similarly struggle. When I ask the question "How many of you have the same struggles?" in a large group, 80 percent of the hands go up every time!

No longer do I struggle. No longer do I feel my prayer life is meaningless. Now I know the Lord hears me as He said He would. As a result I have seen the changes in my life, my marriage, and in the ministry to which He has called me.

How did I get so excited and enthused over prayer? In August 1987, the Lord spoke to me directly and told me to start WRITING MY PRAYERS. Since that time I have been "praying in writing" consistently. I have a daily personal communion with my Lord that has revolutionized not only my prayer life but my whole relationship with the Lord, virtually every aspect of my life.

No longer does my mind wander. Almost never do I doze off, and then it is only momentary. Writing my prayers enables me to keep my focus on the Lord without wavering or wandering! "Thou wilt keep him in perfect peace, whose mind is stayed on thee."[1] I have that peace that I never had before. Now my mind stays focused on Him. I look forward now to my special and personal daily time with the Lord in my inner room, my secret prayer closet.

For the first seven years I filled thirteen large spiral notebooks, naturally (being part Melancholy) writing on both sides! For the past three years I have been using my notebook computer. It is just as effective and enables me to "write" even faster.

You cannot imagine the joy and intimacy you will experience until you begin writing to the Lord each day. I do not suggest you try it; I urge you to DO it! David wrote his prayers, and they account for half of the Book of Psalms. In Jeremiah God instructs us, "Write thee all the words that I have spoken to thee in a book."[2] In Habakkuk we are further told, "Write down the revelation and make it plain on tablets."[3]

One morning several years ago after writing my prayers for about an hour and twenty minutes, I decided to read what I had just written. How long do you think it took me to read those pages? Only about four minutes. I heard a voice speak to me that I shall never forget: *You're wasting your time writing your prayers. Think of how many more people you could pray for if you prayed orally.* It sounded so logical. But then immediately I heard another voice clearly say to me, *No! I want you to continue to write your prayers, for all the time you are writing your mind is stayed on Me!*

Who was the first voice? Obviously it was satan. And there will never be any question that it was the Lord Himself who told me to continue. And I have done so ever since.

How about You?

Why should you wait? Find a time and get out your pen and notebook and begin a life-changing practice that you will never want to give up. Go into your inner room, and your Father who hears in secret will bless and reward you openly. Because you are tuned in to the Lord, because you are focused on Him, you will learn to hear exact words of answers, instructions, and guidance that He has for you.

Suggested Prayer for Today

I confess, Lord Jesus, that I, too, have struggled with prayer. Today I am determining that will end. I want You to think of me as one who is not shy about coming to You in private or in public. I ask You, Father, to confirm in my mind and indelibly inscribe on my heart this commitment that I make to You today, that I will now put into practice these things that You have taught me and directed me to do. Teach me, O Lord, to pray. Teach me, Lord, to be disciplined. Teach me to resist the devil, who I know will try to interfere. Deepen my faith, enlarge my spiritual horizons, and make my life a sweet-smelling savor unto You. Finally I pray that my family, and especially my mate, will begin to see changes in me. I thank You, my Lord and my God. I pray in Your Holy Name. Amen.

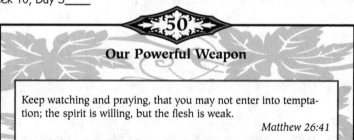

Our Powerful Weapon

> Keep watching and praying, that you may not enter into temptation; the spirit is willing, but the flesh is weak.
>
> *Matthew 26:41*

Fred

The enemy disguises himself as an angel of light, and the Bible tells us he "prowls about like a roaring lion, seeking someone to devour."[1] He will infiltrate our minds and our emotions at every opportunity where his way is not blocked. He will do whatever he can do to destroy, demolish, or devastate your marital relationship. He will interfere in your mutual trust and love for each other. He will keep your mind focused on what you are getting from your partner instead of what you are giving. He loves to make you self-centered. Be not deceived! This is his function. It is the unwary, the undiscerning who are most easily caught up in the devil's snares.

How then do we become wary and discerning? How can we recognize when the enemy is attacking us, trying his best to put a wedge between us? Our first line of defense is daily communion with our Father in Heaven. That we will be tempted, each and every one of us, is not only a foregone conclusion, it is a biblical certainty. Therefore we must be equally certain that we are well-armed and prepared with the spiritual weapons that our Gracious Father in Heaven has already made available to us. Unused weapons get rusty and dull. Ours must ever be handy, sharp, and well-used, readily available at the first sign of the enemies incursions into our spiritual defense perimeters.

Our adversary is sly and wily. We must be alert, on guard. Would a military opponent attack your armed forces where they were strongest and where you had the heaviest concentration of arms and weapons? Only a fool would do that. And our enemy is no fool. He only attacks in our areas of weakness, as any good general would do. He seeks out our areas of vulnerability. Each one of us has areas of strength, but we also have areas of weakness. This is precisely where he attacks, in our areas of weakness and he probably knows them better than we know them ourselves!

What are your areas of weakness or vulnerability where You might be more easily tempted? For us men it might be anger, lust of the eye, busyness, or self-righteousness. For wives it might be loneliness, depression, jealousy or coveting, or discontentment. Each of you now, make a list of four or five things that you feel are missing from your life or marriage. If you can share them with each other and talk about them all the better. If they are too sensitive at this point, keep them private for now, but make your list nevertheless. These are most likely to be your areas of vulnerability, areas where satan knows he can easily get to you. Our Lord Jesus admonished us to keep watching and praying, to be alert, to stand guard, that we might not enter into temptation. When our defenses are down, our flesh is weak and satan gains easy access.

What is the solution then? We are to keep on watching. We are to keep on praying. Prayer is our best weapon in our arsenal to use against these infiltrations of the enemy. There is no substitute for daily consistent times spent in our prayer closet. It is so important to me that I keep a daily record of the number of consecutive days that I have spent specifically in written prayer. It is my personal form of self-discipline. One of the things that the devil would surely like to interrupt is my dependence on my Lord!

How about You?

Reinforce that personal commitment to spend time with the Lord each and every day. Keep watching and praying. You will be fully armed and prepared to stand against the efforts of the enemy to bring destructive temptations into your life and your marriage.

Suggested Prayer for Today

Dear God and Heavenly Father, I confess to You that I have been weak in my resistance to the efforts and temptations of the devil to bring discomfort to me and disobedience to You in my life. I have failed to be the husband/wife that I know that I should be. I have said things I wished I had not. I have gotten angry when I felt offended or threatened. I have not been much like You lately. Your presence has not been sufficiently evident in my life. I want to have that mind and that attitude which was also in Christ Jesus. I want to be selfless, gentle, and compassionate. These are your qualities and I want them in my life. Help me, O Lord, to be alert to recognizing the times when I stumble. Help me to confess to You and to my family as well. Lord help me in the place where I am best known, my home, to exemplify these loving characteristics of tenderness, selflessness, and patience. In the Glorious Name of Jesus I pray. Amen.

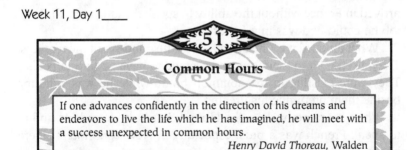

Common Hours

> If one advances confidently in the direction of his dreams and endeavors to live the life which he has imagined, he will meet with a success unexpected in common hours.
>
> *Henry David Thoreau*, Walden

Florence

When I first read this quote challenging us to prepare for the dream we might imagine, I was struck by the term "common hours." I began to wonder how much of my life was spent in common hours, times when my thoughts were wasted on daily routines, when my focus was on getting through a certain task, when I spent days without lifting my thoughts above the ordinary. How much of our lives pass by like a parade with no music as we keep step with our friends who have no goals.

Not all of life can be a mountaintop experience, but should we exist, even be satisfied, with nothing more than a series of common hours? It's been said that if you don't care where you're going any road will take you there. What about those of us who do care? Who wants to make the common hours a thing of the past?

Thoreau, a memorable American writer, was never content to be ordinary even though he lived a simple life. He knew the necessity of preparing the dream in order to be a success. If there is no dream, if we have imagined nothing beyond the level of today, we won't suddenly rise like a bird and soar to success. Yet, if we can project where we want to be and advance confidently in that direction, even we will be surprised with our results.

I talked with the concierge of a luxury hotel and asked how he had achieved this level at such a young age. He replied quickly, "I spent a year working in a factory." He explained that he had wanted to learn a foreign language and decided that spending a year abroad with the people would help him achieve that goal. When he arrived in France without the ability to speak the language, the only job he could find was in a factory.

"What amazed me," he added, "was the mind-set of the workers. They'd settled into their jobs and seemed to have no further goals." They were existing in the common hours while he was standing beside them preparing his dreams.

When he came back to the United States, he found his ability to speak French was a plus, especially in New York hotels where he started work as a waiter. Women loved his accent and assumed he was French. His evaluations from the patrons were so high that he rapidly became the concierge and wore a tuxedo each day. What a far cry from the factory! And what a difference in attitude from the other workers who were content to exist in the common hours.

I remember the summer I spent in a factory during World War II gluing labels on cases being sent to the Air Force. As a patriotic teenager I was doing my bit for the war effort. I stuck to my job—literally—until the end of August, but each day I vowed that I would go to college and never come back to those less-than-common hours.

Often months of hard labor tend to give us a passion to move on confidently in the direction of our dreams.

How about You?

Are your days spent plodding through common hours? Imagining the best and starting with where you are, what steps do you need to take to move ahead? Do you need to raise your eyes off the TV and lift them up to a bigger picture? Begin today to make a plan for your personal and family future so that you can meet with a success unexpected in common hours.

A hardy summer of heavy work might not hurt the children who these days seem to think the world owes them a living. I'm glad I learned that we don't start out as CEO but we can prepare our dreams even in drudgery so we can minimize those common hours and move on.

Together make a chart for one average week and then score each hour at the end of each day:

N   for negative times of stress, argument, worry, depression.

C   for those common neutral hours of getting nowhere, watching TV, biding time.

A   for average hours, work, housework, caring for children, eating, visiting.

AA for above-average hours when you have time to think creatively, set goals, plan for the future. This is time when you read good books, study, write letters, watch educational TV programs, converse with the family, call lonely relatives or friends, give time to charity. Try to do things that are beyond your common hours, things that will help others. In Luke we are told that those of us who have received much (ability, drive, money, talent) are required of God to do something special with our lives. Chart out your week—make sure your time is not all spent in common hours.

Suggested Prayer for Today

Lord Jesus, we know You expect more of us than we have so far achieved. We've had too many common hours, time we've wasted when we could have been learning. We know the harvest is ripe and the laborers are few, but we haven't thought much about this before. We've been content to move on at our own pace and not think beyond today. Lord, lift our eyes to horizons we can't even imagine at this time. Give us the desire to dream and then move in the right direction. We pray for wisdom in the Name of Jesus. Amen.

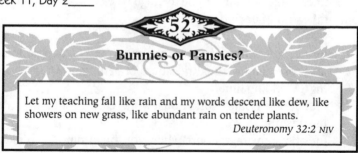

52

Bunnies or Pansies?

Let my teaching fall like rain and my words descend like dew, like showers on new grass, like abundant rain on tender plants.

Deuteronomy 32:2 NIV

Florence

When I first found this verse, I read it over and over. I liked the feel of it, the cool touch of a gentle rain, delicious refreshment on a thirsty day. Fred and I live in the desert of Southern California, and we seldom see rain. The only water in our air is from the irrigation system on the golf course stretching out before us.

In early spring new grass is being planted and much water is needed. Fred planted pansies by our front walk, precious little faces smiling as we enter, but we have an abundance of baby bunnies who have precious faces also. They hop right up to our glass doors and look in like little friends, pets that we don't need to care for or feed.

Yet, in a way, we do feed them, for they love Fred's pansies, the tender plants. They aren't interested in the passé pansies, yesterday's blossoms now faded by the heat. They are discriminating. They only eat the tender shoots full of moisture. In fact they eat the buds just before they open their faces. Our front walk has lost its welcoming pansies. The plants are still there, the lonely stems are erect, but the blossoms are pruned off each day.

Fred and I have different attitudes about these feats of nature. To Fred these rabbits are pests who eat what he has taken the time to plant. For me, even though I like the pansy faces, I prefer the bunnies. They're alive; they come to see me. They make me smile and sometimes even laugh. They are not pretty, white, fluffy Easter bunnies; they are the color of the sand, and their tails look like a flat piece of glued-on cotton. Because they are jack rabbits, their back legs are longer than the front ones so they are forever heading downhill. Sometimes when they're little and take a big hop, they crash their little faces on our cement patio. When they appear at breakfast time, I exclaim, "Oh, my good little friendly bunnies are here!"

Fred looks up, "The bad rabbits who eat my flowers."

God created both the bunnies and the pansies, the sunshine and the rain, the heat and the cold. What an awesome God to put all these opposites together and yet to speak to us through each natural element so that we all hear, see, and respond in our own way.

How about You?

Our verse today is not one of instruction but of beauty. It is a verse to make us pause and think of the rain, the dew, the showers, the grass, the tender plants—and even the bunnies who eat them. A verse to remind us of our amazing God, who from nothing created a world, planted a garden full of fruit and flowers, caused the rain to fall upon it, made little bunnies to hop about for fun, and then made us to take care of His creations.

Fred likes the bunnies; he just liked the pansies better because he had creatively planted them. Share with each other today what animals, flowers, and fruit you like best. It's good now and then in our busy lives to stop and smell the roses, to discuss something so subjective that you can't possibly argue about it.

Look around your house today. Are there pretty things that give you pleasure when you see them? Do you have something growing in your yard where your children can learn the process of growth, the change of the seasons? Do you ever talk to them about the beauty of God's creations? Ask them tonight what are their favorite flowers, trees, animals, tender plants. What are your favorites? God doesn't care whether you prefer poppies or petunias, just that you remember He made them all and that His Word is a refreshment to us, dropping as the gentle rains from Heaven.

Suggested Prayer for Today

Dear Father God, Creator of the world and all that's in it, we pause today to thank You for making us in Your image and for creating natural beauty for us to drink in and enjoy. You revive our spirits and give us cool water to drink in a dry, thirsty land. Give us the moments today to look upon Your world with a new appreciation and reverence for Your eternal creativity. We praise You and thank You, and in the Name of Jesus we pray. Amen.

53

The Tent Test

> May never was the month of love
> For May is full of flowers;
> But rather April, wet by kind,
> For love is full of showers."
> *Robert Southwell (1500s)*

Florence

When our two daughters began dating, I wanted to bring a touch of reality to their romantic ideals. The day after a date with some football star, they would share how great he was and assure me he was "the one."

I would then ask, "Could you spend two weeks alone in a tent in the rain with him?"

"With no TV?" Lauren asked.

"With no phone?" Marita wondered.

"Just you two alone, in a tent, in the rain."

Amazingly the thought curbed some budding romances and ended others. We named this query "the tent test," and often after a date one of them would come in and say, "He flunked the tent test."

They began to understand that any jock can be appealing on the field, conversant at parties, and dashing when dressed for the prom, but how would he be with no entertainment for two weeks in a tent in the rain?

One day Marita asked me, "Why did you come up with this tent idea in the first place?"

I explained, "Because married life isn't parties, movies, proms, and long-stemmed roses. It's day upon day without exciting external stimulation. Just you and him, and perhaps a screaming baby, alone in the tent in the rain."

For Lauren, who was very popular with the football set, no one passed the tent test. While she was in and out of love with one boy after another, her Phlegmatic friend Randy sat around our house waiting for her to come in. For three years he and I "went steady" until the day Lauren realized Randy passed the test. He'd seen her at her worst, listened to the tales of her dates, and never gotten angry over being slighted. She'd already spent time with him in the rain, and he had been faithful.

He's been faithful ever since, and while their marriage has been more sunshine than rain, they know they can pass the tent test. They have a commitment to each other that keeps them from even thinking of a brighter horizon somewhere else.

We do a disservice to young romantics today by playing up the pleasures of life without giving them an umbrella, for as the poet says, "Love is full of showers."

Fred and I didn't take a tent test. We got married in the Happy Days of the fifties, and we knew we would live happily ever after. Our personality differences became apparent on our honeymoon, but I was the typical June Cleaver and adjusted my behavior to fit Fred's standards. Because he was successful in business and we had the big house, the Lincoln, and the fur coats, I was able to stay content. With my poverty background, the affluence was fairy-tale stuff for me, and with my Sanguine nature I was having fun. I was a socialite of sorts, and my Choleric personality loved being chair-man of charity events and president of all the clubs.

In retrospect we didn't know what love really was, but we were functioning in high gear and we were committed to each other. As we lived in the sunshine we weren't prepared for rain, so when we had two sons, one after another, who were born with a degenerative brain disease, we almost drowned. We had to face years in a tent in a downpour. How did we do it? How did we live through double death without our marriage falling apart?

Our marriage survived for three reasons: One—we had a commitment to each other that transcended lack of passionate love and those agonizing days in the tent. Second—in our misery and constant state of numbing shock, we came to the end of our ability to control our circumstances. We were open to hear the plan of salvation when it was presented. Third—it was at this point that we started our study of the personalities and began to really understand our differences for the first time. As we saw there was an explanation for our personalities we drew closer together. We began to teach other couples who were in the "rain," and God used us to spread His sunlight on those in need.

How about You?

Were you prepared for the rain when you got married? Had you thought ahead of any problems you might have? Did either of you take the tent test? What was the first thing in your marriage that signaled to either of you that some rain was going to fall? How have you weathered the storm?

We reconfirmed our commitment to each other, dedicated our lives to the Lord Jesus, and began to study the personalities so we could love each other without being judgmental. We hope that wherever you are standing today, perhaps in a tent in the rain, that you will learn from our example what we have done to stay together for forty-five years even though "love is full of showers."

Suggested Prayer for Today

Dear Father God who loves us and who protects us from the rain, give us Your big umbrella and help us out of the negative feelings we have about each other sometimes. As I read this section today I thought of a time in the rain. It was when . . . (each of you complete the sentence). Thank You for always being there for us and for helping us to bring sunshine into each other's lives and then into the lives of our children and our friends who are standing in damp places. I think of . . . (name a friend or two in difficulties). Bless them in a special way. Bring a healing touch to their pain. Thank You, thank You, Lord. In Jesus' Name. Amen.

54

Showers of Blessing

I will bless them and the places surrounding my hill. I will send
down showers in season; there will be showers of blessing.

Ezekiel 34:26 NIV

Florence

We all know the expression "Don't rain on my parade," but can
rain sometimes be a blessing? When rain interferes with our social
plans is there ever a way to redeem the circumstance? Can there be
showers of blessing?

One summer evening Elaine was scheduled to share her testimony at a friend's poolside supper party. As the guests arrived the
skies parted, and rain poured onto the patio. Tables and chairs
were quickly dragged into the small living room, which was so filled
with furniture there was no room for the people.

The resourceful hostess, seeing no change in the weather, decided
to move the party and Elaine's performance into the garage. "This
was no finished room," Elaine explained, wide-eyed. "It was just a
dirty old garage with a wheelless Dodge up on jacks. Water was
pouring in under the doors and rising up against the far wall. It
began to look like an oil-laden swamp."

Elaine stood at a podium that was placed over the drain in the
garage floor and told her life story to a sad-looking group who well
may have wondered what they were doing listening to Bible verses
in a garage with water swirling around their feet.

At the conclusion, the hostess, seemingly oblivious to the damp-
ened spirits and wet shoes, asked all the guests to take off their limp
name tags, put an X on them if they had asked the Lord into their
lives, and then leave them behind on the table. After the guests
"swam" out to their cars, Elaine was too embarrassed to look at the
tags, but the hostess counted the decisions and found that despite

the rain twelve people had met the Lord.

Because Elaine had been obedient in a bizarre set of circumstances, twelve searching people found God in a garage in the rain.

When Fred and I lived at the Campus Crusade for Christ headquarters in Arrowhead Springs, California, we were in charge of feeding what seemed like "the five thousand." Actually during the summer, we did have about twelve hundred people for three meals a day, seven days a week. The line never seemed to end. One summer at the conclusion of staff training, Fred planned a special banquet on the lawn. He rented tables and chairs and covered the tables with white paper tablecloths. As time neared for the celebration, the waiters put the salads and the glasses of iced tea on the tables.

As the guests were gathering in the hotel the sky turned dark, and rain deluged the tables. Even if we'd had waiters with wings, there was no way that over a thousand salads could be retrieved. We just stood, dumbfounded, as it "rained on our parade." Within minutes the storm passed by, and we were left to feed these people salads floating in water as they sat on wet chairs with the paper tablecloths dripping and drooping into their laps. What's a person to do?

I went quickly to the storeroom and brought out cases of paper towels. As the guests walked to the lawn in their groups, Fred gave a roll of towels to one person from each table. It was his or her job to drain the water from each salad and give out enough towels for each person to wipe up his own chair. The paper-towel chairmen instantly rose to this occasion, took charge of their damp domain, and turned it into one big game. People made humorous comments about how Noah must have felt when eating on the ark and every joke anyone could remember about rain was sprinkled over the table.

We may have served better banquets during our time at Crusade, but not one was so memorable as the deluge. Thirty years later we still meet people who say, "Remember the time when we had the salads full of water?"

Some rain can be showers of blessing!

How about You?

Have there been showers in your life? Physical showers that changed your plans or emotional dampness that held you down? Have you let the rain ruin your life? Discuss some of the damp times in your past, identifying when, where, even why those times occurred. Did either of you overreact at the time? What did you learn from the situation? In retrospect, what could you have done differently that would have made the outcome more positive? Have there been any negative situations that, when all was known, became showers of blessings? Many times if we stay calm in the deluge, we'll have nothing to mop up but a few plates of drowning salad.

Suggested Prayer for Today

Lord Jesus, You can work in the showers as well as the sunshine, but how often we panic at the first drop of rain. Please give us a quiet spirit and let us be creative in dealing with the damp days ahead that we can trust in You and find showers of blessing in every storm. In Jesus' Name. Amen.

55

Commitment

Commit your way to the LORD; trust in Him and He will do [much].

Psalm 37:5 NIV

Florence

Larry was an extremely attractive businessman who conducted seminars on success. He invited me to one of his groups that met once a month to teach them about information I'd recently gathered into a book, *Personality Plus.*

Before I spoke, he gave the members their "word of the month." He explained they should write down the word commitment, read it every morning, and use it often in conversation. As they focused on this word, he said, they would begin to understand "commitment." They all listened to his instructions and dutifully wrote down their "word of the month."

The next morning Larry called me and said he had to talk with me: Would I go out to lunch with him and his wife? As we sat in a corner booth, Larry looked me in the eye and asked, "How do you find God?" For a moment I was stunned; I'd never been questioned quite so bluntly or quickly.

He continued, "I've always been a good person; but my wife just had a mastectomy, and while she was in the hospital and I was faced with the fact that she might die, I had nowhere to turn. I realized I didn't know God. How do you find Him?"

By then I had regained my composure, and I started with his teaching of the night before. "Remember how you told everyone to concentrate on the word *commitment?* Commitment to what?"

He hesitated and then answered, "Commitment in general."

"You'll find God when your commitment is specific. A general commitment is an intellectual exercise, but when you commit your life to Jesus, you will come face to face with God."

"I've been committed to good works," he replied, "but somehow when the chips are down, that's not enough."

I then explained that good works are commendable, but they don't bring you into a personal relationship with the Lord. I shared a verse from Ephesians: "For by grace [God's gift] are ye saved through faith [belief, commitment]; and that not of yourselves [not from your earnings and strivings]: it is the gift of God: Not of works [no matter how impressive yours may have been], lest any man should boast [or take the credit]."[1]

"But I'm a self-made man who's committed to excellence," Larry insisted.

"There's nothing wrong with good motives, but you won't find the peace of God until your commitment is to Jesus. You have to give up your own will and present yourself as a living sacrifice to the Lord." I had to assure Larry that a commitment to Jesus was not a weak thing to do, but that it took a strong man to recognize he needed a power beyond himself. I explained that Paul, a man's man, was not ashamed of being a Christian. "I know whom I have believed, and am persuaded that He is able to keep that which I have committed unto Him against that day."[2]

"He'll only keep that which you have committed, Larry. Can you sacrifice your will and commit your life to Jesus?"

Larry was looking for success in life in a word; that day he found meaning to life in the Word!

Perhaps this would be a good time to ask yourself whether you have actually had a moment when you said to the Lord, "Jesus, I can't handle life as it is. I give myself to You. I commit my way to You. I trust in You."

Fred and I, two very strong people, got to the point where we gave up on ourselves. We had one son who'd died and one who was dying. We could do nothing to change our circumstances, and we made our commitment to the Lord. He didn't revive our sons, but He did change the direction of our lives. Why did we have to wait until tragedy struck to commit our ways to the Lord? Why did

Larry have to wait until his wife had cancer to think of eternal life and wonder how to get it? Why do so many wait until a crisis arises before going to the Lord in a sincere and meaningful way?

Somehow we want to do it all alone. We want to show ourselves our power. We hope others will notice our achievements, but when we face something beyond our control, we look for spiritual help.

How about You?

Each of you ask yourself if you have ever committed your life to Jesus. This doesn't mean, "Are you a good person or do you go to church?" This question is one of turning your life, the control and direction or it, over to someone you can't see, in faith believing that Jesus is there and you can trust Him to lead you from here on. It takes a strong person to be willing to give control over to the Lord. Are you ready?

You may say, "Well, I think I did that once." If you're not sure, you probably didn't, because when the Lord Jesus gives you new excitement in your life, you know it. If you've had difficulty answering some of these daily questions in front of your spouse, perhaps you are still functioning in your own strength and get easily embarrassed. Some of you may not be sure you even want your marriage to work, and you're sick of trying.

No matter where you are in your personal opinions and emotions, commit your life to the Lord Jesus today. You may pray to Him in any way you want, but here is a sample you can follow.

Suggested Prayer for Today

Lord Jesus, I need You. I've tried to do everything my own way, and it hasn't worked out right. I ask You to come into my life and change me into what You want me to be. I commit my life to You. "I know whom I have believed, and am persuaded that He is able to keep that which I have committed unto Him against that day." Today is my day, and I commit my life to You in thanksgiving and anticipation. In the Name of Jesus. Amen.

Barriers to Communication:
Interrupting

> If anyone considers himself religious and yet does not keep a tight rein on his tongue, he deceives himself and his religion is worthless.
>
> *James 1:26 NIV*

Fred

Robert Frost once wrote, "Something there is that does not love a wall."

In marriage no one loves a wall. Nevertheless, many of us are as busy as beavers building barriers that effectively block our communication. We find an abundance of building materials we use to construct an emotional barrier in our lives as effective as the old-fashioned bundling boards were for the Puritans, who stuck them between courting couples so their bodies never touched! Similarly, something has come between many couples today. They may be in touch physically but their minds never meet.

In the next few days we will look to see what walls may have gone up in your marriage that are keeping you from communicating on the same wavelength.

What happens when someone you are trying to explain something to never lets you finish? What happens to you if that person jumps in and finishes your sentence for you, as if you didn't have brains enough to say it yourself? Let us suppose that interruption is accompanied by a burst of anger or denial. Do you resolve then and there to keep your mouth shut? Why even bother to talk if the other person is never going to listen? Why try to express your feelings if he or she doesn't care enough about you to let you finish? Shutting down when someone else continually interrupts you is only natural. We all have done it to some extent. The only problem is that when we shut down, we add another block to the wall between us. When these walls go up within a marriage, the consequences can be devastating.

In fact, the person who interrupts may be doing it for that very purpose—to build a wall. People may become constant interrupters to keep others from saying anything that might hurt them, offend them, or let others get too close to areas they want to keep hidden away. No matter why it occurs, perpetual interrupting eventually turns off the flow of ideas, thoughts, and emotions that must be shared if a marriage relationship is to be healthy and fulfilling.

Some think God made a mistake when He said, "It is not good for the man to be alone. I will make a helper suitable for him."[1] But, no, God never makes mistakes! No, it is not good for man or woman to be alone in the marriage. Many husbands and wives are living together, but they are still living apart. They are living as two in one house. The only thing that is common between them is the roof over their heads. What happened to the plans and the dreams they had when they both said "I do" and "I will"? Somehow, over the course of living together, they have built these walls. They probably built them to protect themselves, but now they are effectively keeping the husband and wife apart.

How about You?

Interrupting is the cornerstone of the walls many people have built around them. Can you resolve together to help each other see when one of you interrupts? When one has a tendency or habit of interrupting, the other frequently will as well. Make an agreement now to remove this block from whatever wall may exist between you. Give your mate permission to lovingly say to you, "Excuse me, honey. I wasn't finished; I was interrupted." When permission has been agreed on in advance and the reminder is given in a nonthreatening manner, the one who interrupted is usually not even offended. Instead he or she is more likely to say thank you and then apologize! That would be a switch, wouldn't it? Try it. You will see that it works. The first thing you must do is agree that you want to help each other and then be willing to "hear" what comes out of your own mouth.

To be successful and enjoyable, any game has to have ground rules and people who are willing to enforce them. Baseball has its men in black. Football has its zebras. Basketball has its whistle-blowers. All these games' rules were made in advance by agreement for the good of the game. They were also made over a period of time based on need and experience as the game developed. Marriages develop over time too. We need to make ground rules by agreement, not by decree! Make one today that you each have the right to remind the other when he or she interrupts.

Suggested Prayer for Today

(Over the past weeks you have both read aloud many suggested prayers. Today let us make a different suggestion. Each of you, quietly in your own heart, ask the Lord to guide you in a prayer that your mate will hear. Then, each of you in turn pray aloud what God has put on your heart regarding your tendency to interrupt. This is what the Bible refers to as praying in the Spirit, praying as the Spirit of God leads you.)

57

Barriers to Communication: Anger

Do not let the sun go down on your anger, and do not give the devil an opportunity.

Ephesians 4:26–27

Fred

"Don't you ever say that again. You know that makes me furious!"

If you didn't know before, you know it now. You have probably heard it before, but you tried one more time. It didn't work. Inwardly you resolved, *Never again. I don't need that!* No one wants to stir up anger in another person. Worse, however, is to be the target of another's attack. Those words sting and hurt. Angry persons know that. They put themselves in a strong position to weed out any topics they don't want sprouting up around them. Angry people use their anger to manipulate others.

After demonstrating their volatile temper, they let you know you had better take no chances with them in the future. And you know you'll pay if you do. After a while the angry person doesn't even have to blow up; he or she only has to threaten, knowing by experience you will back off. You hoped to discuss something with your spouse about next weekend and your parents' visit? You know you can forget it. Your husband (or wife) has already laid his or her own ground rules: It's my way or the highway!

Muriel and Daryl are two such people. They both came into marriage from deeply troubled backgrounds. Both have valid reasons for the boiling kettle of anger they carry inside themselves. They both can be as "sweet as can be" to the other when they want to or when they are not feeling threatened. They are two hurting people who were attracted to each other out of a sense of need and are trying to build a marriage. They have no children at home, and both work full time. Everything they earn seems to go to pay their current household expenses.

Daryl also has experienced some severe illness and surgery, and he demands that Muriel take care of his every need while refusing to do anything around the house to help with the load. His free time is spent on the golf course with his friends. If Muriel should momentarily lose her head and try to suggest something other than what he wants to do, he screams at her and threatens to leave. The sad truth is that neither of them can really leave, for neither one could get along without the other's income! Hardly a sound basis for a healthy relationship.

This description is not meant to paint Daryl as all bad; he can at times be charming. Muriel occasionally has some special needs, and Daryl is very gracious about taking care of her or doing what she needs. Is this a hopeless marriage? Not at all. Is this a happy marriage? Not at all! Because Daryl is the more forceful of the two personalities, when his anger erupts Muriel has no choice but to suppress her feelings and slip emotionally out of sight. When Muriel's anger comes up, Daryl's response to her is, "Stuff it! You know I hate to deal with your anger!"

Do they communicate? Well, they say things like, "Have you paid the mortgage yet?" If this is communicating, the answer is yes. Can they talk about their feelings with each other. The answer is no. To friends outside the home their marriage might appear normal and healthy when in reality they are both only tolerating each other. We know them both quite well. We know the truth of their life together, because we are helping them deal with the roots of their anger. Because they are both sincere, we know that the Lord will eventually bring them to the point of healing and cleansing of their hurts and their anger. Until that time there is little hope that they will be able to communicate with each other. Their anger stifles them every time the truth penetrates or becomes threatening.

While anger is the loudest block to communication and definitely promotes disagreements, the person who uses this tool is ultimately unloved and unaccepted and therefore lonely. His or her mate and children will always be looking for some way of escape, some haven to run to, some way to come in from the rain of torrential tirades and temper tantrums.

How about You?

For those who may have struggled for much of your life with an anger similar to that which has plagued Muriel and Daryl, we would urge you to carefully and prayerfully read and work through these two books: *Freeing Your Mind from Memories That Bind* and *The Promise of Healing*. Both books deal with the single cause of 95 percent of all long-term and volatile anger. All the resources and classes on communications and anger management will be of limited use until the roots of your anger are dug up and cleansed away.

Suggested Prayer for Today

Lord Jesus, as I read Galatians 5:22 I do not find "anger" listed as one of the fruits of the Spirit. Yet I confess that there is anger in me. I have always thought my partner caused it. Now I am beginning to see that he/she only stirred up the anger that was already inside me. I should have seen this earlier, Lord, for I realize now that I have been an angry person for years, even before we ever were married. Dear God, I don't want to live like this any longer. I know I am pushing my partner away from me. I need love and acceptance, and now all I seem to get is more rejection and loneliness. Help me, O Lord, to be willing to look at myself and not to blame my mate when the anger flares up. I want to wash away this anger that is keeping us from communicating with one another. Your Word tells me we should be able to do that. This is what I desire, Lord Jesus. Thank You for listening to me today. In your Name I pray. Amen.

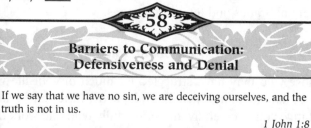

58

Barriers to Communication: Defensiveness and Denial

If we say that we have no sin, we are deceiving ourselves, and the truth is not in us.

1 John 1:8

Fred

Some people have minds like lawyers. They have a case ready for the first person who tries to get close to their heart. You never ask them the *why* of anything, because they will give you more than you ever wanted to hear. Whatever happened, it wasn't their fault. If you question their judgment they will attack you with a string of statistics that make you look stupid. They build strong walls or barriers around themselves that will resist any outside intrusion. Then they wonder why they're standing alone in the court.

Do you know any such person? Are you living with a person whose mind thinks that way? There is nothing wrong with gathering statistics and facts to weigh before you make a decision together. In fact the Bible instructs us to count the cost before proceeding. It is when the facts and statistics are the only weights that are permitted to be put on the scale that the beam becomes lopsided.

We men tend to think this way more than women. Women are more intuitive while men tend to function more in the intellectual. Men tend to think that their perception is the only valid one; too often we tend to look with disrespect and to discount our wives' opinions.

In order to have meaningful and honest communication both husband and wife need to listen to the other's point of view and perspective. When one becomes defensive all hope of coming to a harmonious and valid solution to any question is virtually lost. I used to do that to Florence. With my Melancholy nature, I always figured everything out and developed excellent projected figures of what we might expect. What I too often failed to do was develop figures that would show the result if things didn't go as expected! What I also failed to do was listen to Florence's intuition. Instead I pressured her into agreeing with my decision. Then I was the deluded one, thinking that we had come to a mutual conclusion. In fact, all I had done by my defensive attitude was to shut down her ability to communicate with me. She felt she had been coerced into agreement.

Equally damaging as a defensive attitude to marital communications is denial. People who are in denial don't even think there is a problem. If the existence of a problem is proven to them, they neatly get around it by a carefully woven case that completely exonerates themselves. That leaves only one other person who could be at fault: You! It has been well said, "There is nothing harder to open than a closed mind." Denying that you could be any part of the problem is a sure way to completely shut down a free and healthy exchange between you and your spouse. When a husband shuts his wife down he loses! He loses all the benefits of her God-given wisdom and insight.

God created our wives to be our helpers, to be an important part of the team. He gave them understanding and perception that we husbands frequently do not have. Women can see things we don't see. We are foolish to cut them out of the decision-making process. We need the gifts God has given to them. If we are defensive to their opinions or ideas, if we deny reality when they are trying to make us see, if we are so assured of our own rightness that we do not listen, we have effectively dropped a barrier into our communications, not only now but in the future as well. Rarely will a person try again after he or she has already been kicked down too many times before.

How about You?

If we, either men or women say that we have no sin, no defensiveness or denial, when in fact we do, we deceive only ourselves, "and the truth is not in us." Take a few moments now together and grant to one other the uninterrupted opportunity to express if he or she thinks that defensiveness or denial is shutting down your ability as a couple to share openly and honestly with each other.

Suggested Prayer for Today

Heavenly Father, I do not want to be in denial; I do not want to be defensive. Nor do I want to be deceived, Lord. That is the devil's playground. I do not want to give him any blind spot in me that will make it easier for him to intrude into my life or into our marriage. Lord, if I have been guilty in the past of one of these barriers to communicating with my partner, I ask you to open my eyes that I might see. I ask You to shine your light of truth into the darkness of my mind that I may be free of these things that are a stumbling block to our life together. Lord, I ask You to give me an open mind so that when my mate tries to tell me something that I need to be aware of I will listen and take heed. I am so thankful to You, Lord, that You are showing me a better way. I am so thankful, Lord, that Your ears are always open to my prayers. Lord, I am feeling so encouraged. I now know, I don't just think, that there is hope. I ask You to start the transformation process within me! I thank You and praise You in the Name of the Lord Jesus Christ. Amen.

Barriers to Communication:
Spiritualizing

Not that we are sufficient of ourselves . . . our sufficiency is of God; who also hath made us ministers . . . not of the letter, but of the spirit; for the letter killeth, but the spirit giveth life.

2 Corinthians 3:5–6 KJV

Fred

Many a discouraged wife has said, "My husband tells me he is the head of the house and that God speaks to men and the wife must obey. Then he quotes a verse to justify what I think is a bad decision. When he throws a scripture at me, there isn't anything I can say. He stops me cold. He shows me I am wrong because the Bible says so. What can I do? I think he is just using Scripture to justify what he wants to do. I know in my heart that he's wrong, but how can I argue with the Bible?"

Sound familiar? This is what is called spiritualizing, a most effective barrier to communication in the Christian home. This is one complaint you'll probably never hear from an atheistic couple! They don't know the Bible, so they don't have Scripture to use as a support weapon to their impulsive or foolish purposes. This is a uniquely Christian barrier! It is using the letter of the law without the Spirit, and without the Spirit there is no life!

Think for a moment of some of the "works of the flesh" described in Galatians 5:20: strife, jealousy, outbursts of anger, disputes, dissensions, and factions. Are these not typical of the one who lives by the letter of the law and not of the Spirit? They also sound like perfect examples of additional barriers to communication!

If our marriage is to be a ONEness in Christ, "to be of the same mind with one another . . . that with one accord you may with one voice glorify . . . God,"[1] we must learn to live by the Spirit. Let the fruit of the Spirit be made manifest in your lives. You know the characteristics that abound when the Spirit of the living God is empowering your relationship: love, joy, peace . . . Need more? Let's continue then: patience, kindness, goodness, faithfulness, gentleness, self-control.[2]

How about You?

If you decide to sell a home you have owned for many years, you probably have enjoyed a significant rise in market value. Before pricing the home and putting it on the market, what is the wise thing to do? Call in an appraiser who has an objective view of the worth of homes in your area and can give you a fair market value. Would you like to try to be an objective appraiser of the current status of your marriage? Place a check mark on the blank lines below that describe each quality you think is regularly recognized in you both by your family members as well as outside your family. Mark both columns. One of you can use ink and the other pencil to differentiate your separate evaluations.

	Husband	Wife		Husband	Wife
1. Love	_____	_____	6. Goodness	_____	_____
2. Peace	_____	_____	7. Faithfulness	_____	_____
3. Joy	_____	_____	8. Gentleness	_____	_____
4. Patience	_____	_____	9. Self-control	_____	_____
5. Kindness	_____	_____			

Are there many check marks in both columns? Or are there only a few? Have you both checked more or less the same lines and left more or less the same lines blank? This will give you an idea of how well you understand where your marriage is, that is, if you have been honest and objective in your appraisal!

If few lines are checked in either or both columns, there is a good chance that one or both of you may be using spiritualizing to block your ability to share with one another what is important to you. Remember the expression, "If life is a journey it's a shame not to have enjoyed the trip"? If you have seen this barrier in your home, will you resolve today together to start tearing down this part of the wall that has risen up between you? If you will ask the Lord, He stands ready to help you. He is never too busy when you call to Him. You will never get a busy signal when you dial His number. Incidentally, do you know His phone number? It's 537-3303, that's JER 33:03! See for yourself!

Suggested Prayer for Today

Dear Father in Heaven, I call upon You today. Show me great and mighty things that I know not, that I have never seen before. I have seen some things in me I don't like! There are some qualities missing from my life, and I need help in resolving these issues. I need to be transformed by the renewing of my mind. I ask You to give me a sound mind, a new mind, the mind of Christ. I truly desire, Lord, that when my family looks at me they would see the clear evidence of the fruit of the Spirit in me. I cannot do it alone. I have tried, but I have never succeeded. Now, Lord, I am willing to give up living by the letter of the law and turn to living by the Spirit, by Your Spirit. I ask you to set me free from the sin of spiritualizing and controlling my loved ones. I don't want anyone to control me, nor do I any longer want to be a controller. Set me free, Lord, from this bondage that is engulfing me. Teach me to pray, Lord, as I have never prayed before. I thank You, blessed Lord Jesus. Amen.

Barriers to Communication: Silence

> There is a time for everything, . . . for every activity under heaven:
> . . . a time to be silent and a time to speak.
>
> *Ecclesiastes 3:1, 7 NIV*

Fred

How do you handle silence? It's impossible to fight; it just won't sit up and respond. How can you talk with a statue? How can you exchange ideas with a wife who suddenly became a deaf-mute? How can you converse with a husband who's encased in a sound-proof newspaper? Silence is one of the greatest barriers to communication. It seems so inoffensive, but it effectively halts any two-way dialogue.

When this kind of silence exists in the home, the silence itself is actually saying something. What it is trying to project to the partner is:

"I can't take any more of your abuse."

"I'm sick and tired of your anger, and I'm not going to allow you to subject me to it anymore."

"I don't need you telling me once more that it's all my problem."

"I'm tired of being interrupted all the time. You never listen to what I have to say!"

"You keep digging up the past. I don't want to hear any more about it."

"You have hurt me enough. I've drawn the line, and that's it!"

Silence is therefore a defensive mechanism to eliminate any chance of feeling victimized again. Because the hurt is so deep and pervasive, silence is the most difficult barrier to overcome, the most difficult wall to dismantle. It results from not only the perceived attacks of the partner, but it also cuts down into the deeply embedded resistance to vulnerability of the one who is being silent. To communicate, to listen to the feelings of another, to be open and not feel threatened requires a willingness to be vulnerable. Some people simply are not able to do this.

If your mate refuses to talk, it may be that he or she is simply not able to. Don't write the situation off as hopeless. Don't give up on your husband or wife. This person is in desperate need, or he or she wouldn't put up the cold silent front. People who resort to this kind of defense have been hurt so much in the past they cannot risk another painful experience.

You may not be the cause of the deep hurt. You may be only triggering what is already inside your silent mate. You may, however, be exacerbating the problem by a lack of understanding or compassion for his or her need; you may even be unaware of what you are doing yourself to make the situation worse.

I was one who built a wall of silence. Unaware that I even had any deep hurts, nevertheless, I brought them with me into our marriage. What I did know was that Florence hurt me too many times with what she thought were cute comments, so eventually I clammed up. I couldn't or wouldn't take it anymore. I would grit my teeth and not say a word, fearing that if I opened my mouth I'd say what I was feeling and deeply regret it later.

Now I know it wasn't Florence at all causing the problem. It was what was inside of me. That old rubbish, the hurt and the fears of being hurt, has all been finally washed away. It took time. It was a journey and not necessarily an easy one. But it was worth it. It will be worth it for you as well. Now the barrier of silence is gone between Florence and me! We now can talk openly of anything at all! Yes, it is worth working for.

How about You?

What can you do if you are facing this problem in your marriage? Here are two possible solutions:

1. Carefully and patiently let your partner know that you want to be able to understand his or her unwillingness to talk with you. Confess that you are sure it is something you have done. But unless he or she is willing to share with you what it is causing the trouble, how can you improve? Convince your mate if you can, gently and tenderly persuading him or her that you really want to change. Let your spouse know that it is your heart's desire to do everything you can to please him or her. At this point, don't lie! If it isn't your heart's desire, pray again and again until the Lord does give you that desire.

2. Recognize that your husband or wife's silence may date back to something or some conditions in his life long before he or she ever met you. This baggage of hurts came along, unseen, into your marriage, even though he or she may not have ever been aware that it even existed. Help your mate to try to be willing to see where or when the roots of these hurts were planted. Scripture teaches us that, "Every plant that my Heavenly Father has not planted will be pulled up by the roots."[1] There are numerous valuable resources that will help you both to find and identify these roots. Some will be listed at the back of this book.

Suggested Prayer for Today

Lord Jesus, is it really possible to be rid of all these hurts and fears? Is it possible that someday I could entrust my emotions to my wife/husband without the fear that I would be made to feel stupid or worthless? Is this something You, Lord, can do for me? Is there a way I can tear down this wall of silence? I confess to You, Lord, that I do raise it sometimes when I just can't deal one more time with the challenges and attacks. Lord, if what I have read today is possible, I ask You to begin this work in me. Did You not say, "He who began a good work in you will perfect it until the day of Christ Jesus"?[2] I have heard that, but now I ask You to make it a reality in my life. I am willing, Lord, to take a chance and take down the barrier of silence. I will do whatever You ask me to do to be free of these hurts I have been sheltering inside myself. I thank You, my Lord and my God. I pray in your glorious Name. Amen.

Different Isn't Wrong

Search me, O God, and know my heart; test me and know my anxious thoughts. See if there is any offensive way in me, and lead me in the way everlasting.

Psalm 139:23–24 NIV

Florence

It was after fifteen years of an uninspiring marriage that Fred and I began to study the four basic personalities. Right from the beginning of our marriage I had hoped he'd loosen up and become fun, and he had worked hard to get me on a schedule and to organize my life.

As many couples do, we had fallen in love with opposite strengths and gone home to live with opposite weaknesses. Before we were even engaged we had noticed our differences, but they seemed positive rather than negative. Fred told his mother we were like two cogs that turned and meshed together. But after we were married Fred no longer thought my stories were funny, and he corrected my creative statistics. I wasn't used to being corrected, and I hated all the charts he made me check to get me in line and keep me on time.

After struggling with these differences for years and learning to get along politely with each other, we began to read Tim LaHaye's book, *Spirit-Controlled Temperament*. We were new believers, and we wanted to be Spirit-controlled. In looking for spiritual guidance we found some personal information we hadn't expected. We came to see that we were born with opposite personalities; we suddenly realized it wasn't our fault and being different isn't wrong. I got excited when I found I was a Sanguine, the "Popular Personality" who wants to have fun. I began to realize that I was only myself when I was not with Fred. Out with my friends, presiding at meetings, directing musicals, I was at my best. People loved me. I was charming and exciting, but when I was at home I was different. I'd walk in the door and say to myself, *Wipe that smile off your face and get down to business.* I'd get serious and try to be the perfect wife Fred wanted, but I was never perfect enough.

How about You?

Does this sound familiar to you? Is it possible you are at your best when you are apart? Discuss your differences. Are they positive or negative? How have you each changed since you got married? Are these positive changes or due to willful control? Do you ever wish you could be what you used to be?

As I studied further, I learned that the reason Fred was not like me is that he was born a Melancholy, the "Perfect Personality," and by nature he desired all of life to be in order. He wasn't out to get me; he wasn't being so disciplined just to show me up. What a revelation! As we accepted our differences and stopped hoping for the other one to change, we were both encouraged. Maybe we could enjoy each other after all. Then I read further and found we were not only opposites but we were also both Choleric, the "Powerful Personality," and therefore we each wanted to be in charge. That explained why we both did better apart than together. We could always find others who would do things our way, but when we were at home each one of us was bucking for control. Since he was the man and bigger than me, he took charge, but I was a reluctant follower and was frustrated that I couldn't get my way.

We didn't hate each other; we just did much better when we weren't together. As we have helped thousands of couples over the years we have found the majority to be like us. "We don't hate each other," one adorable Sanguine told me. "We just can't stand to be together." I understand. So many of us bring out the worst in each other.

Understanding the personalities is not a cure-all for marriage problems, but it surely started us in the right direction. Over the years we have received letters that say what a help this concept has been for them. "Life-changing!" "It set us free to be real," "Wish I'd known this years ago," the letters say.

Suggested Prayer for Today

(For our prayer today, let's use the verses in
Psalm 139 and pray from them:)

Father God, what a future we have as we begin to search ourselves and look for the good in each other. We ask You to search us and know our hearts—who we really are inside. We're not sure who we are. Show us, try us, and test us, and let us see how we appear to others, for Father, if there is any offensive way in us that is causing us problems and keeping others from wanting to be Christians like us, we want to change. Give us the tools to use to build an exemplary marriage. We are open and ready for Your instructions, Lord Jesus. Praise Your holy Name and lead us in the way everlasting. Amen.

Mongrel Christians

For you created my inmost being; you knit me together in my mother's womb. I praise You because I am fearfully and wonderfully made; your works are wonderful, I know that full well.

Psalm 139:13–14 NIV

Florence

Dear God, our Heavenly Father, what a blessing it is to know that You created each one of us, that You knit us together in our mothers' wombs. You had a separate pattern of knitting instructions for each one of us. We're different sizes, shapes, colors. We're each unique. I know that I am fearfully, wonderfully, awesomely, amazingly made like no one else. I know that full well. Amen and Amen!

Isn't it exciting to know we are not ordinary people and that, without bragging, we can accept the fact that God knit us together and that His works are wonderful! We are each originals. Now that we know this, what are we going to do with this awesome news?

As Fred and I started our new life as believing Christians, we studied God's Word and took action on our personalities. We hardly understood ourselves, and we were teaching Scripture and showing others how to accept their mates and not try to remake the other one. As we held classes in our home, we saw marriages changed and families re-energized. Once husbands and wives saw their mates were not out to get them but they were just different— and different isn't wrong—they began to relax and not be so defensive. We all learned together.

That was thirty years ago, and since that time we have taught thousands of individuals how to understand their own strengths and function in them and how to accept their mates and not waste emotional energy trying to change them. We taught that even if you succeed in remaking someone, what you have on your hands is a phony person, a robot, a mongrel. It's as if you crossed a schnauzer with a poodle. You'd produce a cute little puppy, but what is it?

We have too many mongrel Christians who started out as one type of personality and then had a parent or a mate or both who wouldn't accept them as God made them. With tremendous effort that person chipped away at them until ultimately the real personality was gone and a new but unreal one replaced it. This is doubly hurtful; it hurts the one who is redone, and it causes the one doing the work to live with a phony. No one really likes people who aren't being themselves.

How about You?

Do you know anyone who has been through this scenario? This story has been told to me over and over. A Melancholy man marries a Sanguine woman. He is attracted to her vivacious personality and her ability to fit in anywhere. As soon as they're married he sees her as scatterbrained, too loud, and self-centered. "Why do you always have to be the life of the party?" he frequently asks.

He begins to tone her down, ridicule her in front of others, and wipe the joy and spontaneity out of her. She tries to please and soon doesn't know who she is. A few years go by. She is now on a chart, she doesn't tell any stories while he's around, and she's frequently depressed. One night he comes home and announces, "You are not the girl I married. You're no fun anymore." No wonder she's no fun. He has erased her personality and left her an empty shell of a woman. Often he then adds, "But I've found someone who is like you used to be." Another Sanguine who doesn't have a very bright future ahead of her.

Is one of you trying to remake the other to be what you perceive a real mate should be? If so, stop today and apologize for trying to recreate what God designed in the first place. I've never met a person who was secure in himself who was functioning outside of the God-given birth personality. To find your birth personality take the Personality Profile in the Addenda at the back of the book.

Suggested Prayer for Today

Dear God, once more we ask You to help us accept each other as we are and not as we might struggle to become. Let us be real and natural and not measured robots walking sadly through life. We want to be grateful for our differences and not upset over them. We praise You that we are wonderfully made, and we accept that as fact. In Your name we pray, dear Lord. Amen.

He Knows Us All

> O LORD, you have searched me and you know me. You know
> when I sit and when I rise; . . . You discern my going out and my
> lying down; you are familiar with all my ways. Before a word is on
> my tongue you know it completely. *Psalm 139:1–4 NIV*

Florence

Psalm 139 has become my very favorite psalm because it speaks to me personally. It assures me that I am made to be special and that God knit me together Himself. What an honor! It also tells me that the Father searches me and knows me inside and out and that He wants me to get rid of my offensive ways that hurt other people. Just accepting all this and acting on it is quite an assignment, but the first four verses we share today show me that the Lord observes all different personalities.

In verse one, He sees the deep and sensitive Melancholy who loves God and wants to be searched and to be known for who he or she really is way inside. What a blessing that God doesn't just skim the surface of our lives but enters into the very hearts of our being. Others may not understand us, but the Lord sees into our inner being. We can bleach our hair, wear a disguise, or even move out of town, and He is always there. We can't shake Him. He sees through the visible into the invisible; He knows all of us.

The Lord follows the busy Choleric around hour by hour. Verse two says He knows when the active person sits down and rises up and when he or she has hastened afar. He knows not only our depth and our heart, but He is aware of our every move. I remember our son, Fred, when he was three years old praying before bedtime. We were visiting my cousin for the weekend, and little Fred didn't want God to have trouble locating him. He prayed, "God if You don't know where I am, I'm in Georgetown."

Little Fred wanted to keep in touch and let the Lord know his whereabouts. This verse tells him the watchful Father already knows. Isn't that a comfort to know He's with you in the car, on planes, and even on vacation? He sees us from afar, even in Georgetown.

The peaceful Phlegmatic can take assurance that even when he or she is lying down, even asleep, the Father is discerning and understanding of his or her needs, even those that are physical. God is familiar with our ways, our habits, our patterns. He knows our quirks, our behavior, our responses to others. He knows we are not like other people. He doesn't overlook the Phlegmatic because he or she is quiet and undemanding; He knows us all, awake or asleep.

And how exciting it is for us chatty Sanguines to be assured, as verse 4 says, that the Lord knows our every word before it comes on to our tongues. Before those thoughts roll out, like colored gumballs jumping from the machine—in fact while they are milling around in our minds, God knows them. Even if we suddenly started speaking French, God could translate. He knows our words in any language before they are formed and on our tongues.

How about You?

Is it as exciting to you as to me that God is all-knowing? He knows our deep thoughts; He's searched us. He knows our positions, up or down, in or out of town. He knows where we are. He knows us when we are asleep or awake; He's familiar with our ways. He knows us completely. He knows what we're about to say even before we say it. Maybe we should monitor our thoughts from here on before they burst forth, because once they're out we can't stuff them back inside.

God could have made us all the same. He could have created us with all strengths and no weaknesses. But instead He gave us different personalities, different talents, even different degrees of intelligence. By studying the personalities we can see that we're not all the same and that different isn't wrong. God didn't take the easy route; instead He has worked creatively on each one of us.

What an awesome, inclusive, omnipotent, and omnipresent God we have!

Suggested Prayer for Today

(Each one of you pray this separately.)

Dear all-knowing God, what is there for me to say? You know it all already. You know what I'm thinking and saying, where I am and where I'm going, when I'm asleep and when I'm awake. I don't know that much about my mate or my children. I thought I had eyes in the back of my head, but Your sweep of vision is way beyond my best observations. Today I am in total awe of a God so far-knowing and far-reaching. I have a new respect for Your length and breadth, Your ups and downs, Your ins and Your outs. You're with me at all times. I need You with me. I need Your constant guidance. Keep me from being in the wrong place and saying the wrong thing. I ask for Your control and Your understanding. Make me the person You want me to be. Amen.

Embroidered with Various Colors

My frame was not hidden from You when I was being formed in secret [and] intricately and curiously wrought [as if embroidered with various colors] in the depths of the earth [a region of darkness and mystery]. *Psalm 139:15 AMP*

Florence

Have you ever thought about how you were created? That out of something the eye couldn't even see you were formed. Have you ever stopped to realize that even though your parents may have wanted you more than anything in the world, even they didn't see the actual conception? You were started in a secret place, hidden away from any snooping eyes, watched over by God Himself. Even atheists are often in awe of the miracle of conception. How can the sperm and egg find each other? How can they hold within them the determination of sex, intelligence, eye color, hair color, body shape, and even personality?

I never thought much about my own conception, and in the fifties and early sixties when I gave birth to my children, I took the whole process for granted. Women got married, stayed home, and had babies; that was just the way things happened. I don't think I was really in awe of the birth process until I saw my grandchildren within minutes of each one's birth. There's an amazing tug on your heart when you realize that you are being passed on. Part of you is going to continue into succeeding generations.

In my grandchildren, I realized that each child, even with the same parents, was uniquely created. Each had some family similarities, all light hair and blue eyes, but there are now so many differences. Randy, now nineteen and over six feet tall, has a similar build, the same body shape and facial features of his grandfather Fred—a Melancholy personality with musical ability, he's a saxophonist in a traveling band.

Jonathan, almost sixteen, is such an image of his father that their baby pictures look like the same person. Their body structure is the same, along with the sandy hair color and freckles. Jonathan is Sanguine, also musical, plays trumpet in the jazz band, and keyboard in the high school marching band.

Bryan is now eleven and is the Choleric controller. He moves quickly and constantly, always sensing adventure and leading the pack. He's musical, plays the piano, and looks more like Macaulay Culkin than like the rest of us.

When I review these three children, I see similarities in looks and talents but differences in personality and lifetime goals. Even with sonograms to view the little ones in that secret place, we can't predict their looks, talent, or personality. But God already knows them.

How about You?

Have you ever reviewed your own children for their similarities and their differences? Why not make this analysis a family project? Ask your children what they see as the things that are the same and different in each of them. From your children's grandparents on each side teach them about God's creation of each one of them—not our way but God's way. Show them the verses from Psalm 139 that tell them they were knit together in their mother's womb, fearfully and awesomely made, and as the Amplified Bible states, intricately, curiously wrought as if embroidered with various colors, in darkness and in mystery.

Teach them in a practical way to see God's hand on all creation, to see how God made each one of us with family similarities but individual differences, to see that we were made in color, not black and white, embroidered with bright and beautiful threads. Yes, there is a mystery to each one of us: How will we all turn out?

Suggested Prayer for Today

Dear Heavenly Father and our Creator, how exciting it is to know that we are Your projects. You could have made us any way You wanted, and You chose to create us as we are. We haven't always realized how awesome the birth process is, and we haven't always taken care of our bodies in relation to the wonder of their creation. Father, thank You for knitting us and then embroidering us in color. We praise You and stand in awe of You. In the Names of the Father, the Son, and the Holy Spirit. Amen.

The Overflow of the Heart

How precious to me are your thoughts, O God! How vast is the sum of them! Were I to count them they would outnumber the grains of sand.

Psalm 139:17–18 NIV

Florence

If you were to start right now making a list of all the good qualities about your mate, would they be as many as the grains of sand by the sea?

If you did the same thing for yourself would you come up with many more? How about your children? Your in-laws?

Isn't it amazing how fast we run out of positive words about anyone, even ourselves? We think we are uplifting Christians, meditating on precious thoughts, but when we put ourselves to the test we come up with negatives and have to strain to speak in glowing terms about anyone. Why is this?

Jesus says, "For out of the overflow of the heart the mouth speaks. The good man brings good things out of the good stored up in him, and the evil man brings evil things out of the evil stored up in him."[1]

During the first two decades of our marriage Fred and I gave our negatives to each other in different ways. He did the constant reprimand in the guise of needed instruction. Everything he said was correct. He never taught me faulty information, and I did learn much from him. It was difficult to discuss his positive instruction as a negative because he meant so well, but it was the continuous flow of correction that wore me down. After a while I felt I couldn't do anything right, and I varied between trying my best and giving up on ever pleasing him.

Because I couldn't win in any discussion and he could always prove me wrong, I resorted to sarcastic comments that would cut him down. Other people thought I was funny, and when he went in a sulk over some quick barb I had loosed, I would show him he didn't have a sense of humor.

Can you see how we both were focusing on negatives while pretending to be positive people? Fred was just giving instructions, and I was just trying to be funny, but our overflow was flowing over. Thank God, we can now talk about our negatives and not stuff them until they explode.

How about You?

Is it possible that some of you have a "negative streak" in you as Fred and I did? A streak that overflows from the heart to the mouth? Where did this come from? Start by asking your mate if he or she sees or hears any evidence of negatives or nastiness in you. Don't be defensive, for you need to know. How can you have "precious thoughts" if there is an abundance of anger in your heart?

If your partner feels that there are some negative traits inside of you, ask him or her to name one area that seems to erupt frequently. Is it directed at a particular person? Who? Why? Talk it out together and find its source. Is it from abuse, negative upbringing, deprivations of your childhood? Get it out on the table and then pray and ask the Lord to take this negative thinking away from you. It's His will that you store up good attitudes within you. For what's in the heart will come out. It takes tremendous control to keep stuffing bad thoughts back down each time they start to emerge. Sooner or later that overflow really does flow over . . . onto your mate and your children, and sometimes it spills onto the dog!

Now reverse the process and tell your mate in a kindly manner one area in which he or she pours out negative words. Where do these thoughts come from? Current problems, dislike for people who don't agree with you, background pain and hurt, impatience with the dummies of life?

Are you trying to be tough and macho and you think vulgarities are positives? Any time a comment offends, puts down, or insults another person, the remark is an arrow into the heart of God. It doesn't matter how we look on Sunday if the overflow of the heart is evil in any way.

Jesus said to the Pharisees, religious men who were judging others, "Woe to you, teachers of the law and Pharisees, you hypocrites! You clean the outside of the cup and dish, but inside they are full of greed and self indulgence. Blind Pharisee! First clean the inside of the cup and dish, and then the outside also will be clean."[2]

What do you two have to clean up? Wash the inside, so the outside will be clean also. Purge whatever pain is stored in your heart so it will no longer overflow onto others. Begin to intentionally focus on positives, on "precious thoughts" from the Lord, so that your strengths will be beyond accounting, as many as the sands on the seashore. Now go back and reread this lesson one more time, discussing all the questions asked.

Suggested Prayer for Today

Dear Lord Jesus, we've heard from You today to clean up our lives, both in and out. Lord, I am now aware of some of my negatives that have been flowing over onto others. I confess the following destructive patterns:

_____

_____

_____

I know You will forgive me of my "wicked ways" and move me on to a new purity I've not thought about in the past. I don't want people to see me as a negative, put-down kind of person. Each time I hear myself say something insulting or hurtful, I will stop it before it comes out. I pledge this to You. From here on, I will focus on uplifting words and ask You to give me Your precious thoughts. In the perfect name of Jesus. Amen.

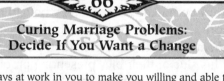

Curing Marriage Problems:
Decide If You Want a Change

> God is always at work in you to make you willing and able to obey his own purpose.
>
> *Philippians 2:13* TEV

Fred

We used to think that every couple with a problem wanted an answer. We assumed that if we offered them a solution they would run home with our wisdom tucked under their arm, eager to unroll the scroll and put it to work. We expected that if they promptly planted the seeds of change we had given them they would soon see little sprouts popping their friendly heads out of the soil to grow into strong and healthy plants.

The more we worked with real people with real problems, the more we began to see how few of them wanted to do something to improve their situation. Too often they just wanted to talk and have someone listen. We soon realized that if they were unwilling to take hold of the first step and decide to take action, there was no point in bothering with the rest of the steps at all.

Someone else could lay out the most brilliant plans for strengthening your marriage and eradicating the weeds from your relationship garden, but if you have no desire or commitment to move, the thoughts and the time would be wasted. All too often one person is unwilling to take the first step until he or she sees that his partner has already started down the journey of change.

Harold and Missy had come to us because they were miserable together. He was a meticulous nitpicker, and she was a casual housekeeper. He wanted everything perfect, but she couldn't care less. He not only lined up all his shoes in precise order in the closet, he tied all the laces into neat bows before he put the shoes away! Harold had wanted to marry a "long, sleek

Cadillac," but instead he found and purchased a "chubby little red Volkswagen."

Because they both liked animals, they bought a little farm and agreed to work it together even though they each had full-time jobs and at home couldn't even get along on the simplest of projects. Here's his side of their big "presenting problem": "How can you expect me to be romantically interested in her when she comes to bed at night straight from the barn, drops her overalls and smelly boots on the floor, and hops right into bed without taking a shower?"

Missy's retort: "I wouldn't get into bed dirty if he'd help me milk the cows. When I come in from the barn, he's lying there gorgeous and perfumed, and I get furious."

When we tell this story at a conference and ask, "What advice would you give this couple?" somebody invariably answers. "Sell the cows!" But are the cows their problem? Many of us, when faced with a problem, want to "sell the cows." It's always easier to run away than to face and address the difficulties. Too often we find ourselves dealing with the symptom rather than the source of the problem.

As the first step, we gave Harold and Missy the logical solution to the cows: Share the workload together. A few weeks later Florence met Missy and asked, "How's the overall game going?"

"Just the same," she answered. "He won't help milk the cows, so I won't take a shower." When neither side is willing there is little hope that a marriage problem can be erased. When one side is willing there is some hope. When both are willing, there is always real hope.

How about You?

Are there some "cows" in your marriage? Something you won't do to please your mate because he or she isn't willing to do what you are asking? Such foolish things as "the cows" may stymie any hope for real change in your relationship. Search your mind. Are there any things that are especially important to you that you feel need changing in your home? Share them with your mate. If you expect him or her to listen and agree, you must be equally willing to listen and agree to what your partner is asking of you.

Are there changes you desire? Decide today whether you are willing to do what you must do to bring about those changes that will lead to greater harmony and oneness.

Suggested Prayer for Today

Dear God and Heavenly Father, I confess that when I read about the cow story I realized that I have some cows too. There have been some things I haven't been willing to do for (wife)/(husband) whom You gave to me to love, to encourage, and to bond with. Lord, I do want us to have a better life together. I ask You now to give me a more caring and selfless attitude. I want these changes in my life and in my home. I am willing to work at achieving them. I am willing to become whatever You want me to be. Yes, Lord, I am willing to put aside my self-centered attitudes to try to become selfless, as You are. Help me, Lord Jesus, to become all that my mate desires me to be. Cleanse me and show me whenever I stumble. I ask in your precious Name. Amen.

Curing Marriage Problems:
Examine Yourself. Find Your Own Shortcomings

Examine and test and evaluate your own selves to see whether you are holding to your faith.

2 Corinthians 13:5 AMP

Fred

Why are people having so many conflicts? Why are so many people unhappy? Why do so many individuals and couples give up trying? Why do so many marriages end in divorce? Why are so many couples seeking the help of counselors and therapists? Why are so many people regularly taking pills to tranquilize, capsules to energize, or popping Prozac to get them through another day?

The Bible tells me if I say I have no sin I am deceiving myself, and the truth is not in me! Until I understood this verse, I always felt I was okay; I knew all the problems in our marriage were Florence's fault. How did I know? Two simple reasons: I knew myself, and I was happy with myself the way I was. I didn't give myself any trouble. Second, I worked hard at making our marriage a success. I wanted that more than anything else on earth. Over the years, however, it became quite obvious to me that Florence did not share my dedication and commitment. Instead of working to be the wife I needed she seemed to be pulling away from me emotionally.

One day in the fifteenth year of marriage, two years after we became Christians, a new friend handed us Tim LaHaye's book, *Spirit-Controlled Temperament*, which focused on the four basic temperaments, what we now call the four "personalities." The concept of the four different personalities has enabled us to examine ourselves; prior to that time we had always checked on each other to see if the other was measuring up. This concept has helped literally hundreds of thousands of couples examine themselves to understand their own strengths and weaknesses.

As the result of our in-depth study of the four temperaments, Florence has written numerous best-selling books on various aspects of the different personalities. In the back of this book, you will find many of these titles included in the list of valuable resources that can help you do what the Scripture commands us all to do: Examine ourselves and put ourselves to the test.

At one point, our marriage deteriorated to the point that I agreed to turn to outside help—for Florence, of course. The one time I went to see Florence's doctor, who had agreed to try to help us, I remember going eagerly. I had one thought on my mind, sharing with him the areas in which Florence was failing to be the wife I wanted and needed. I thought that somehow I had failed to communicate this need to her. I must have failed, I reasoned, for she seemed to be getting no better! So I went, hoping perhaps he could get through to her where I had not.

After my meeting with him, I remember eagerly waiting for the report of her next session with him. I was sure he would have straightened her out. Can you imagine my discouragement when all she told me was that the doctor said, "Fred is very immature"? What about Florence? What did he tell her to do? That was what I was waiting to hear!

It was many years later that I finally realized I was the main contributor to the dysfunction in the life we had so enthusiastically anticipated. I was the one who had to do most of the self-examining. I finally did what God asks all of us to do. I examined myself and learned to not oversee how well my wife was doing. I worked on me. I worked on becoming the man the Scripture says I should be and the husband that Florence needed and wanted. The results speak for themselves. Without them we could never have shared these truths with you.

How about You?

It is so much easier to place the blame for every conflict on the other. Florence and I were both experts at doing that. It takes the humility of one born of the Lord to be willing to look at himself or herself and admit that he or she might be the cause or the source of some of the struggles.

Are you now ready to obey God and examine and evaluate yourself only, to put yourself to the test?

Suggested Prayer for Today

Heavenly Father, I want to obey You more than anything else in this life. I want You to be able to look at me and say, "This is My daughter, this is My son, in whom I am well pleased." Lord, it is hard sometimes to be so selfless as to not think about how someone else is doing but to just look at ourselves. I ask You to help me. I ask You to remind me when I fall short. Remind me, O Lord, to confess to You and to my partner and even to my children when I cause them pain or hurt or grief—even in those times when I think they deserved it. Help me, Father, to become like the Lord Jesus. Help me to have His patience, His gentleness, His unconditional love. Thank You for hearing my prayer, which I ask in His Name. Amen.

68

Curing Marriage Problems: Confess Your Weaknesses

> I acknowledged my sin to you and did not cover up my iniquity. . . .
> I said, "I will confess . . . ,"—and you forgave the guilt of my sin.
>
> *Psalm 32:5 NIV*

Fred

Even though you are no doubt a very good person, is there anything about you that might be offensive to others? Is there any trait or habit of yours that is annoying or offensive to your mate? Are there some areas of your personality or character that might need improvement? Is there a habit you have not been able to break?

As you consider these questions, has something come to your mind? If not, take a moment and quietly think. If nothing comes to your mind, we can all ask one another, and we can always ask the Lord. If you have found something that is an offense to your mate, confess it to him or her and ask for forgiveness. Ask for help to gain victory over the issue. Ask for loving, tender help. The very best kind of help is praying together out loud to the Lord, asking Him, confessing to Him, and thanking Him.

Do not "help one another" by throwing back in the other's face the issue that has been confessed and for which help has been asked! This is not help. It is destructive and breaks down every trust you are trying to rebuild. In a tense situation, the devil loves to throw these harpoons, these flaming missiles, into the fray to pit you against each other. He is always working at counter purposes to what the Lord desires for You. Therefore we must do what the Bible tells us: Be vigilant, stand guard, and exercise the authority you have over him!

If you have found something in yourself that is not pleasing to the Lord, confess it to Him and ask His forgiveness. Don't hide it any longer—bring it out in the open to the Lord, and He will give you the peace that results from confession and the forgiveness that He always gives.

Ann met Florence for a brief reunion when Florence had an airport stopover. Ann had prayed with Florence five years before at a conference and asked the Lord Jesus into her life. At that time, Florence recalled that Ann proudly described her Christian activities and the ministry the Lord had given her with other women. But as Florence asked Ann about her relationship with her husband she winced, and Florence knew she had hit a nerve. Later she wrote to Florence:

"I had planned to say very little about myself but to listen to all about you and your exciting life. As you questioned me, my feet turned to clay, my heart to stone, my brain to putty.

"That night around 3:00 A.M. I awoke and knew I had to confess the hatred and resentment I had for my husband and ask for cleansing and removal of that burden. I have known all along that this area needed shaping up, but I just kept putting it aside. It was my pet grudge. All the time I was able to grow and grow and inspire others and have a terrific answered-prayer record. As long as I focused on others and not on myself, all was well.

"I did what I had to do. I know now that a healing is taking place. I feel no resentment, and I am able to reach out to my husband and treat him as I treat my Christian friends. That has been his request for some time. Thank You for caring and shepherding."

How about You?

What is there that is still keeping you in bondage to anger, to resentment, to _____? If we confess our sins, He promises us that He will not only forgive us but cleanse us from all unrighteousness. It starts with our willingness to confess.

Suggested Prayer for Today

Lord Jesus, I believe Your Word. I believe it is true. I believe the powers that are unleashed by my obedience can change my life. Yet

I confess that even though I have knowledge I have not always acted in accordance with what You want me to do. I ask You to forgive me. I ask You to give me a willingness to confess the things I have done or held out against my husband/wife. It takes courage, Lord, to confess to the one I have incorrectly blamed for the cause of my hurt. Now I know I am the cause of my hurt because I have been unwilling to confess. Lord Jesus, I ask You now to make me willing to seek forgiveness. Then I can be free of these emotional ropes that have kept me bound and far from the peace that I want so much to have. Thank You, Lord Jesus. Amen.

Curing Marriage Problems: Ask God to Remove Any Offensive Traits

If we ask anything according to His will, He hears us. . . . And we know that we have the requests which we have asked from Him.
1 John 5:14–15

Fred

Will you ask yourself today, What is there about me that my husband/wife finds difficult to live with? There was a popular book title several years ago that theorized, *I'm OK. You're OK.* If that were really true, most of the couples who have come to us for help over the past fifteen years would never have come! They weren't OK. We cannot remember anyone ever coming to us to say, "My husband is wonderful, but I can't stand to live with him any longer!" Or, "I have the greatest wife in the world, but I want out!"

One of the great advantages in studying the four personalities is that this knowledge helps us to see that God created us each with a set of specific and unique strengths and also allowed us to have certain weaknesses. In addition, through the course of life we usually pick up a number of character flaws as well as some emotions that make it difficult for our families to draw closely to us.

Florence used to tell me I had built such a wall around me that she couldn't get near me. She was right. I know that as a child I had so often been hurt that I effectively built a brick wall around my emotions so that no one could ever hurt me again. Florence never noticed the wall during our courting days, but it became obvious as our marriage progressed from bad to intolerable. No, my protective device did not serve me well in marriage.

Ironically, as the years went by and I began to see that I wasn't getting from my wife what I thought I needed, I added more bricks to the top of the wall. Instead of tearing it down, I strengthened it! That was just one of the things we allowed to interfere in the harmony that God designed for us in our life together. She had trouble loving my wall!

Finally I had to be willing to examine myself and see what there was about me that was offensive to my wife. Then I had to confess these things to the Lord. The next step was to ask the Lord to help me remove these traits that were such well-entrenched barriers to my wife's ability to love me and feel emotionally safe with me. Can you imagine how difficult this was for me at first when I had known (not thought!) that I was OK and that all the problems were Florence's? I believed if only she would change we could be happy.

How about You?

Are some of your natural personality weaknesses making it difficult for anyone to love you, to accept you, to be close to you? Do you have emotions that push people away from you rather than draw them close to you? In marriage we want to be close to each other, so close that we are one as the Bible says we should be. If you don't know whether these barriers exist in you, then ask. Ask the Lord. Ask your mate. Between the two of them they probably will be able to come up with a little list that you can use. Start now to ask the Lord to help you recognize these traits when they pop up. Then you can confess them to Him and ask Him to remove them. I have found this most effective to do in my daily written prayer when my Lord and I can talk together in secret about whatever is on my heart.

In James we read, "You do not have, because you do not ask. You ask and do not receive, because you ask with wrong motives."[1] Agree with God today to begin asking and ask with pure motives, to become the man, the woman, that God wants you to be, to please Him and to please each other.

Suggested Prayer for Today

Dear God and Heavenly Father, I commit to You today and to the mate You have given to me to love and cherish forever that I recognize and admit there are weaknesses and flaws in my human nature that need cleansing, correcting, and healing. I ask You now, Father, to help me recognize these things. I ask You to help me to be discerning so that I will become more conscious of them when their ugly little heads pop up. I ask You to help me overcome them so that I will be more of what my loved one desires of me and more the child of God that You want me to be.

I will continue to come to You, Father God, confessing and asking until I have become aware that these weaknesses have been erased. I do not ask in order that I may be happier; I ask in order that my partner may be freer, more relaxed in my presence, and better able to enjoy being with me. I thank You, Father, that I have the confidence according to Your Word that You are always there and that You always hear my prayers. This I ask in the life-changing Name of the Lord Jesus Christ. Amen.

Curing Marriage Problems:
Forgive Your Partner Silently and Apologize Orally

> If you forgive men [each other] for their transgressions, your heavenly Father will also forgive you. But if you do not forgive men [each other], then your Father will not forgive your transgressions.
> *Matthew 6:14–15*

Fred

Few of us enjoy forgiving others, because it implies that what they did wasn't so bad—when in fact it really was! It really upset us at the time. If we do truly forgive we might also forget the evidence, and what if we need it for proof in the future? Our minds function on such a selfish level that we don't like to let go of the bad examples of others, especially when that other person is our spouse, the one whose hurts we are often most reluctant to forgive.

Not only do we not want to forgive but we take pride in being able to repeat to others the tales of these grand mistakes. It shows that surely we are not guilty of any of these things ourselves. And second, putting someone else down makes us feel better about ourselves. Is it not true that if I have the discernment to see your mistakes, then mine (if there are any) must be pretty trivial? Finally, repeating your mistakes to you is often the best means of defense against the attacks you are trying to make on me. Oh, the games we have all played!

Florence now acknowledges: "I used to gather up Fred's faults with the fervor of a child picking berries. I had a whole shelf of overflowing baskets before the concept of God's forgiveness ever penetrated my mind. To be spiritual I plucked out a few of Fred's faults and forgave them, but I didn't want to clear the whole shelf. Where would I go for future reference material?

"God had to hit me over the head with my own bulging baskets before I was ready to forgive and willing to apologize. Even though I have learned and even taught this lesson, it was some time before

I was able to pick up a basket without starting to gather up some faults.

"Do you see how easy it was for me to find Fred's failures? They would jump right up and cling to me like lint on a blue suit. Does this sound familiar to You? Have you been out berry picking? Have you gathered in a bountiful harvest? Put it all in the trash today. Get rid of all bitterness, wrath, and anger."

How about You?

The acid of anger eats away only at the container. Do you have a basket or a mental container that is filled with rotten berries full of anger? That acid will gradually literally eat your insides out. There is no possible way you can build or rebuild a relationship between you and your spouse if you allow these hurts and pains the privilege of remaining in your consciousness or in your emotions. They must be dealt with quickly, surely, and with certainty. Do not wait. Empty that bucket of unforgiveness and anger now, and completely cleanse it with the scalding water of repentance and apology: Confess, ask, and forgive!

"Be kind to one another, tender-hearted, forgiving each other, just as God in Christ also has forgiven you."[1]

Suggested Prayer for Today

Blessed Lord Jesus, my Savior and my Redeemer, how could I have been so blind as to not see the container full of acid that I was storing in my soul? I confess to You, Lord Jesus, that I have reveled at times in my baskets of unforgiveness. I thought they made me feel better. Now I am beginning to see that this fault-finding was just one more device the evil one was using to keep me in bondage. Lord, there are times when I really feel that I don't want to give up what I have clung to so long. There are times when I don't want to forgive. How can I forgive when there is no apology in me, no repentance? Lord Jesus, I ask You now, because

I want to be obedient to You, that You give me first the desire to forgive and then the ability to forgive.

I commit to You today, my Lord and my God, that I will clean out that container and remove all bitterness and anger. Frankly Lord, I'm tired of dragging it through life with me, especially when You tell me that releasing it is my only hope and, in Your sight, my only option. I thank You, Lord Jesus. You have given new hope to me today. Amen.

(Now say aloud:) satan, in the Name of the Lord Jesus Christ, I bind you, I command you to leave me. You are not permitted to interfere in my life. In the Name of the Lord Jesus Christ, satan, I command you: Be gone!. . . Thank You, dear Lord Jesus. Amen.

Curing Marriage Problems:
Focus on the Good in Your Partner

> Whatever is true, whatever is honorable, whatever is right, whatever is pure, whatever is lovely, whatever is of good repute, if there is any excellence and if anything worthy of praise, let your mind dwell on these things. *Philippians 4:8*

Fred

"ANYTHING WORTHY OF PRAISE!" Capitalized! Accented! Underlined and italicized! Often after we have listened to a wife's terrible description of a husband who obviously appears to be an ogre, we ask the angry woman, "How did an intelligent lady like you ever get attracted to such a loser? What did you see in him in the first place?"

Usually her response is, "Well, he used to be different. When I married him he was handsome, witty, and generous."

Frequently, however she will respond defensively with, "Well, he's not all that bad!" as if it were our fault!

"What caused all this change?" we ask.

"Not everything's changed. He's actually still good-looking if he'd ever smile. He can be funny at parties, though he sometimes never says a word at home. He's generous with the kids, but he won't give me a nickel."

It's always easier for an objective outsider to see many good qualities in the one who is accused. It is also easier for the objective person to see that it invariably takes two to get them in the mess they are in. And most of the time it will take the two of them to get them out of it!

Somehow, some wives seem to bring out the worst in their husbands. Is he really as bad as she perceives him to be? What positive qualities does he still have? There are some very serious problems and issues in some marriages, and we in no way mean to belittle them or to say that there is a magic pill or an easy cure. However, we do stand on the fact that the truths of Scripture are true and effective if we will practice them.

Sometimes the problem is nothing deeper than two headstrong people each demanding to be right or to get their own way. Sometimes it is nothing more serious than an understanding of each other's personality differences. Sometimes the issue is simply bad habit patterns that have crept in over the years of the marriage, waiting for someone to go first to initiate the changes.

How about You?

Right now, before you forget, each of you make a list of ten things or traits that you like about the other. In doing this you will begin to obey Philippians 4:8, "Let your mind dwell on these things," things that are "worthy of praise." Secondly, when you have each listed ten things, and only ten, share your lists with each other.

You could start out by saying, "One of the things I really like about you, something that attracted me to you in the very beginning is . . ." Can you do that? Can you say that to him/her? (If one of you refuses or is unable, you know there are deep troubles in your relationship, and you may need objective and wise help, the sooner the better.)

Today, alternating back and forth, share and discuss the ten things you have listed. Do not start until both of you have a full ten items on the list. This can be the beginning of rebuilding those torn and damaged emotions that have sprung up because one or both were too often focusing on the negatives.

What is the natural reply for such an attack when one mate focuses on the negatives? Naturally, a counterattack! If I can hit her faster and harder than she hits me, I'll be protected and safe from her tongue.

Neither a counterattack nor the initial attack is ever God's way or His desire for the two of you. Remember: "A gentle answer turns away wrath, but a harsh word stirs up anger."[1]

Throughout this week, each of you make a special effort to tell the other each day at least one of those special qualities that you admire or appreciate each other. Before you retire each night, talk over together how you are doing. If one of you forgot for any reason to focus on the other's positive, do it at this time and apologize that you failed or forgot earlier. Remember: "Get a plan. Carry it through. You'll be amazed at what you [with God's help] can do!"

Suggested Prayer for Today

Gracious God and Heavenly Father, we are thankful that we have so many positive things in our marriage. We are thankful that we have a solid scriptural foundation and we know what to do. We know, Father, because You make it so plain to us. Your Word is clear. The problem is us. Each of us has spent too much time tearing down the other instead of focusing, as You tell us to do, on each other's positives. Too often we fail to see the strong and important things the other brings to our union. Too often we look at the shortcomings, the failures, and the broken promises.

Help us, O God, by reminding us to be mindful of Your words to us to think on those things that are good and right and positive. I pray, Lord, that You will help both of us to see any negative spirit that either of us has so that we can immediately confess it to each other and to You, Lord. Thank You, blessed Lord Jesus. Amen.

72

Curing Marriage Problems: Avoid Digging Up the Past

The one thing I do . . . is to forget what is behind me and do my best to reach what is ahead.

Philippians 3:13 TEV

Fred

Is there a marriage that would not be doomed forever if we continued to dig up past mistakes? Is there a marriage where there have been no errors, no misunderstandings? If we know how destructive it is to constantly flash reruns of our stumblings on the screen of life, why then do we all do it so much of the time?

A husband or wife might say, "I hate it when you do that to me. All I can do is strike back or go crawl in a hole and isolate myself so I can't hear. If I hate it so much, I guess you must hate it just as much when I do it back to you or when I shut down and crawl away. That way I don't have to face you. I feel so defeated so much of the time, I just get to the point that I don't care, or I decide it's just not worth it."

Have you heard this dialogue in your home? Have you heard yourself saying these words or something very close to them? For a couple who is conscientiously trying to rebuild or to strengthen a teetering relationship, hurling these failures into each other's face may cause all your rebuilding to tumble and make starting afresh and anew all but impossible. No one wants to get smacked the second time. We tend to learn from our past hurts and defeats, we resolve, "I will never again allow myself to get into such a vulnerable position." How then can we rebuild when tearing down seems to happen so often, to come so naturally?

What is our answer? As Christians our answer is always in one of two places, in the Scripture or in the person of the Lord Jesus Christ. We often ask ourselves the question, *What would Jesus do?*

How would He handle this situation? Philippians 2:5 clearly tells us to "Have this attitude [or mind] in yourselves which was also in Christ Jesus."

What then would Jesus do? Would He give up? He knew that He had to drink the cup of the crucifixion. He also saw that the very ones that He poured His life and His ministry into, the twelve men He selected to proclaim the good news to the entire world, would desert and deny Him. Knowing that, did He quit? Did He crawl away and hide?

No, the Scriptures tell us He resolutely pointed His face toward Jerusalem. He completed the work for which He came. He never gave up. He is our example. Now we must go and do likewise.

How about You?

Yes, every single one of us will stumble. Only those who persevere to the end will be victorious. Do you think that Florence and I did not often think of throwing in the towel? Do you not think that each of us at different times felt like quitting? We did. It was only our faith that kept us going, knowing that with God all things are possible, and praying and believing there would be changes dramatic enough to enable us to become one.

As we studied and grew in knowledge and understanding of God's Word, one of the first things we realized was that we had to cease digging up the past and reliving all the hurts we had caused each other. Instead we began to put into practice the formulas for harmony we found in the Bible. Many years ago I wrote something in neat and tiny letters in Philippians 2:3, which says, "Let each of you regard one another as more important than himself." I personalized it to read, ". . . regard Florence as more important than myself." That said something to me, reminded me clearly of what I must do.

I didn't like it when she reminded me of my past failures, so instead I worked hard at not saying the same kinds of things to her that provoked those responses. Rather, I tried to build her up and let her know two things: One, how much I needed and appreciated her and two, how diligently and prayerfully I was striving to be the husband she wanted and needed. Forgetting all the past hurts and disappointments that were behind, I did my best to reach what was ahead. In time she began to notice changes without my telling her about them! In time God softened her heart as well. He will soften your hearts also if you ask and if you will let Him.

Suggested Prayer for Today

Lord, I ask You to take Your big eraser and wipe out all those hurts, those grudges, those disappointments I have been carrying with me. The load is getting too heavy to carry. I have been feeling like dropping by the wayside. I don't ask You, O Lord, to carry this load for me or to shoulder half of it for me. This is a load I need to get rid of. I need to throw it away, make it disappear, once and forever. Please, O Lord, help me to dump it so that I can stand upright, ready to press on and reach toward what is ahead. Now, in the Name of the Lord Jesus Christ, I cut the bonds that have been tying this load of negatives to me, and I throw them to the winds. I will cast them aside as many times as I need to until they are totally forgotten and gone. I thank You, Lord Jesus, that You have given me Your perfect example to follow. In Your Name I pray. Amen.

Curing Marriage Problems:
Believe That God Can Help You

> When you pray and ask for something, believe that you have received it. . . . And everything will be given you.
>
> *Mark 11:24 TEV*

Fred

Does God know You? Do you really believe that He knows you?

Do you believe He knew you before you were created in your mother's womb?

Do you believe He's numbered the hairs on your head?

Do you also believe He knows every day of your life?

Do you believe, as the Bible says, not a sparrow falls without His knowing?

Every January 1, millions of people around the world make "resolutions." We all solemnly and seriously resolve to make significant changes in the way we do things, the way we live, or in the kinds of things we say. I do not remember ever keeping any of my own commitments to change for more than a few weeks. Either I forgot what I vowed to do, or the old habit patterns simply took over and it was once again business as usual. I am convinced that all of our best intentions eventually go the way of the trash pile. As creatures of habit, on our own, we just don't seem to have the capacity within us to make significant changes. This is even truer in the emotional and relational areas of our lives.

What then can we do? Is there any hope? Is there any possibility that change can be effected in our lives and in the way we treat one another? Can you change the way you react to your mate when something unkind or cutting is said to you? I have tried, and I'm sure you have as well. Somehow on our own we are not able to control our own reactions to what we perceive to be hurtful negatives. Ah, but the Bible tells me I can do all things! Yes, we can do all things, but we must complete the verse: "I can do all things through Christ who strengthens me."[1]

There lies the answer. All my own resolutions will probably go for naught, but when I enlist the Lord Jesus to help me, to do what I cannot do on my own, amazing and rewarding changes can take place. We must not, however, forget the first part of that verse. It still says, "I can do all things." We are not directed to let Christ do it for us. We must do it ourselves but with Him, with His help.

Oswald Chambers wrote, "We cannot do what God does, and . . . God will not do what we can do. We cannot save ourselves nor sanctify ourselves, God does that; but God will not give us good habits, He will not give us character, He will not make us walk aright. We have to do all that ourselves, we have to work out the salvation God has worked in. We have to get into the habit of hearkening to God about everything, to form the habit of finding out what God says. If when a crisis comes, we instinctively turn to God, we know that the habit has been formed."[2]

How about You?

Throughout these pages we are sharing with you how you can develop the habit of instinctively turning to God, how we have done it. We have believed that with God all things are possible. We have come to Him in prayer when we stumbled and confessed our shortcomings and asked Him to help us to be discerning the next time a similar challenge comes. Will you do the same?

Your own faith will be strengthened as you see His hand working changes in you. Believe that He can and He will. "Ask in faith without any doubting, for the one who doubts is like the surf of the sea driven and tossed by the wind. . . . Let not that man expect he will receive anything from the Lord."[3]

Suggested Prayer for Today

Lord, I ask You to strengthen my faith. Help me, O Lord, to believe. Help me to trust You more with each passing day. Help me, Lord, I pray, to come to You with every need that is in my heart. Help me to remember to bring every hurt and issue to You before my tongue reacts to the feelings that are going on inside of me. Lord Jesus, give me self-control until all the pains and struggles are washed away into the sea of confession and forgiveness.

Lord, I don't want to rely any longer solely on my own abilities. I want to learn to rely on You. I want to become so Christ-centered that being and serving as You are or as You would serve comes naturally to me. I will try, Lord. I will do all that I am able, but I am grateful to You that I do not have to do it alone. Thank You, my Lord and my God. In Your Name I pray. Amen.

74

Sometimes Dogs Make Better Mates!

> A happy heart is good medicine and a cheerful mind works healing.
>
> *Proverbs 17:22* AMP

Fred

It is also said, "A laugh a day keeps the doctor away." One of the sometimes-forgotten gifts that our Father has given to us is laughter, a sense of humor. It is not true that seriousness is next to godliness. Have you ever met one of those Christians who look at you as if you've gone carnal if you laugh or have fun? One thing I have been "freed up" to do as a confirmed Melancholy-Choleric is to have fun! Sometimes we have so much fun together that Florence says to me, "I think you're a closet Sanguine!"

I quickly assure her, "No! No! One Sanguine in the family is enough. We need someone who knows what day it is!"

Even the Lord tells us in Psalms 126:2–3, "Our mouths were filled with laughter, our tongues with shouts of joy. Then it was said among the nations, 'The LORD has done great things for them. . . . And we are filled with joy.'"

Now, for today's thought, we interrupt the steady stream of inspiration, encouragement, and Scripture with nothing more significant than to give you a few laughs . . .

Do dogs sometimes make better mates? Well, let's think about it for a moment.

Dogs don't care if you use their shampoo.
Dogs love it when your friends come over.
Dogs like it when you leave lots of things on the floor.
Dogs never need to "examine this relationship."
Dogs don't expect you to call when you're running late.

In fact, the later you are, the more excited dogs are to see you!

A dog's parents never visit.

Dogs understand that you raise your voice in order to get your point across.

Dogs don't want to know about every other dog you've ever known.

You never have to wait for a dog . . . He or she is ready to go at a moment's notice.

Dogs have no use for flowers, cards, or jewelry.

Dogs don't let magazine articles dictate their decisions.

Dogs don't get upset if you forget their birthday.

Dogs don't borrow your toothpaste.

Dogs know that instincts are better than written directions.

Dogs never criticize.

Dogs never say, "Take it back; we can't afford it."

Dogs love long car trips.

Dogs don't get jealous if the neighbor's dog is "drop-dead gorgeous."

A dog's time in the bathroom is limited to a quick drink. And he doesn't lock the door when he's in there.

Dogs don't go shopping and "do lunch."

Dogs love the way you sing.

Dogs sitting in the backseat don't tell you how to drive.

Dogs are most content just sitting at your feet.[1]

Can we learn from man's best friend? Laugh and enjoy, but is there some truth in all these witticisms?

Suggested Prayer for Today

Everlasting Father, we give thanks today for Your gift of humor. O Father, how we all need to laugh a little more, especially in our homes. I pray, Father, that I might be able to see more joy and humor in this world and in the circumstances that I find myself in. Help me, O God, to keep my mind focused on the good, the positive, the pure, and the right. Help me to see these qualities in my wife/husband and in those I come in contact with today. Your Word tells me if I practice these things the God of Peace will be with me and that the peace of God, Your peace, shall guard our hearts and minds in Christ Jesus. This sounds good to me, O Lord. In Your Name I pray. Amen.

75

Curing Marriage Problems:
Be Ye Thankful

In everything give thanks: for this is the will of God in Christ Jesus concerning you.

1 Thessalonians 5:18 KJV

Fred

One of the key instructions we see in Scripture is to be thankful, to always be thankful. We see it over and over again. Today's verse directs us to be thankful in everything and for everything. One of the key verses on prayer, Colossians 4:2, tells us our prayers should always be with an attitude of thanksgiving. Ephesians 5:20 further repeats God's will to us by saying "always giving thanks for all things in the name of our Lord Jesus Christ." These are only a few samples of the many verses that tell us the same thing.

With such clear directives telling us to be thankful, why then are so many Christians discouraged, depressed, and demoralized? Is it simply because we are not doing and being what we already know God wants of us?

Could it be that the reason we get upset with one another is because we are not thankful for one another? Can we be thankful for and angry at each other at the same time?

Could I angrily complain to my wife that she is not ready on time when our friends have arrived to pick us up for our dinner out together and then at the same time say to her, "Darling, I surely don't mind that you are still fussing with your makeup, for I will be so thankful when I see the finished product. You will be so stunningly beautiful, and our friends won't mind waiting a little while longer."

Do anger and thankfulness mix? Do oil and water mix? It seems we have to make a choice. We can be upset, or we can be thankful. The Bible is clear. God's way is to always and "in everything be thankful." Which will you choose? Will you each make an effort together to be thankful for each other?

How about You?

Read the following questions aloud, and then each of you give your own answer to the other.

1. Will you commit today to each other, that you will DECIDE to do something about where you are and do whatever it takes to make your life together even better?

2. Will you each acknowledge that you need to begin to EXAMINE yourself and cease all judging of the other?

3. Do you agree to CONFESS first to your Lord and then to your mate the sins, weaknesses, and bad habits that your self-examination has revealed to You?

4. Will you ASK God daily in prayer to help you overcome these issues that have become a stumbling block in your marriage?

5. Will you FORGIVE your partner for the things that have bothered you in the past so they can be removed as points of contention between the two of you?

6. Will you commit today to each other and to the Lord that you will make a daily effort to FOCUS on the good, the positive, and that which is worthy of praise?

7. Will you agree to cease DIGGING up the past and look only forward to the prize of a deeper love for each other?

8. Will you BELIEVE that all of this is possible through Christ Jesus, who loved you enough to give His very life for you?

9. Will you then begin by being THANKFUL to God for each other and THANKFUL to each other for the hope that is in you and for the foundation of love for each other that God wants to build upon?

Remember, building a life together is a journey! It is not an event. It will take time, patience, tenderness, forgiveness . . . and a lot of TLC. You will stumble; you will fall. You will become discouraged; you will be disappointed. You may even want to quit. Certainly satan will do his best to interfere and to intrude. But you stand against him with the authority you have in the Name of the Lord Jesus Christ! Then you will see that you will blossom, and you will grow! Then you will see how happy you will be when you have put God's principles into practice.

Suggested Prayer for Today

Dear Heavenly Father, I am thankful that You are opening my eyes. You have shown me, Father God, that Your Word is true. You have shown me that I have been weak and even disobedient in following what You have so clearly outlined and instructed me to do. I commit to You, Lord, that I do not want to live a life that is defeated in any way whatsoever. I do not want to allow the enemy to have a foothold in any area of my life. I want to be fully victorious as You have already enabled me to be, Lord, knowing the work is up to me. I want to be the husband/wife that You created me to be and that will be pleasing to both You and the one You have given to me to nourish, cherish, and encourage. But, Lord I am weak and a creature of bad habits. I ask You to help me to break those bad habits and to remember to do what I already know You want me to do. Help me, O Lord! For I know I cannot succeed on my own. I need You, my Lord and my God. I give thanks unto You. I offer up to You my sacrifice of praise. I pray in the Name of Jesus, my Lord. Amen.

76

Strengths and Weaknesses

Personality is that peculiar, incalculable thing that is meant when we speak of ourselves as distinct from everyone else. Personality is like an island, we know nothing about the great depths underneath, consequently we cannot estimate ourselves.   *Oswald Chambers*

Florence

As Chambers says, personality is what makes us different from each other. Personality is not something you can put your finger on like the color of your hair or eyes. It's incalculable, unable to be counted. We can't really explain our personality to someone else—it's too big, too intangible. What people see is just the tip of the mountain, sticking up as an island in the sea. Who knows what's hidden underneath?

Would you like to have a tool for understanding personality that's simple to use, that doesn't require you to get a new college degree to comprehend it? Let's look at the four basic personalities that were first labeled by Hippocrates, a noted Greek philosopher and physician and author of the Hippocratic oath taken by the medical profession over the years. As he dealt with complex human problems, he felt it would help people to understand themselves if he could simplify their personality traits and label them. Using the fluids of the body as names for the different personality types, he said the Sanguine (blood) was the talker who wanted to have fun. The Choleric (yellow bile) was the worker who wanted to be in control. The Melancholy (black bile) was the thinker who wanted everything perfect. The Phlegmatic (phlegm) was the balance for life who wanted to keep peace and avoid conflict.

Personality is the outward display of the inner self. We are all born with a certain predisposition and set of responses. We are not little blank pages waiting for fate to write upon us. If I am born a Sanguine, all my life I will be optimistic and bounce back quickly from negative experiences. If I am born a Choleric, I will refuse to let bad times get me down and take immediate action after negative experiences. If I am born a Melancholy, I will always have the tendency to think everything over carefully, to be pessimistic, and to get depressed over negative experiences. If I am born a Phlegmatic, I will stay balanced, seldom show my feelings, and look the other way in negative experiences. Because our personalities are so closely tied to our responses, we get a clearer picture of ourselves from our reactions than from our cultivated behavior. Taking charm courses may improve our manners, but it doesn't alter our heredity.

Each one of us is born with a set of strengths, our God-given personality. Because of these strengths, we also have a tendency to certain weaknesses. In fact as we begin to think about ourselves, we see that our weaknesses are our strengths carried a little too far, perhaps to extremes.

Sanguines' greatest strength is their ability to talk anywhere at any time on any subject with or without information and be entertaining. Carried to an extreme, they are babbling constantly, interrupting others with no sensitivity to the interest level of the group, exaggerating everything beyond any truth, and not being entertaining at all. People tend to avoid the Sanguine in the extreme.

Melancholies are the opposites of the Sanguines. They stick to the facts, don't try to entertain, and only respond when they feel it's appropriate. They know how everything should be done properly and can spot imperfection from a distance. These are very special and sensitive people. Carried to extreme, however, Melancholies get easily depressed when life isn't perfect, become oversensitive thinking everyone's against them, and nitpick others who are trying to improve their behavior. People tend to avoid the Melancholy in extreme.

Cholerics are more similar to the Sanguine in that they are both outgoing and optimistic. The major difference is that while Sanguines are talking about the job at hand, the Cholerics are doing it. They waste no time in idle chatter but get straight down to business.

Their greatest strength is in accomplishment. They love work and can get twice as much done in a given day as anyone else. They are born leaders and can preside over any group whether or not they've been asked. This superhuman being is beyond compare, but when these strengths are carried to extreme, Cholerics become overbearing, bossy, and degrading to "the dummies of life." People tend to avoid the Choleric in extreme.

The Phlegmatics are the peaceful people who cause no trouble, avoid conflict or confrontation, take the middle road, and provide balance to the other, more volatile personalities. In a time of crisis the Phlegmatics keep their cool and act rationally while the Sanguines are screaming "What shall we do?" the Choleric is telling everyone what to do, and the Melancholy is sinking into a depression, wailing, "Oh, woe is me." The Phlegmatics are the most likable and balanced of all personalities, so how could they end up in extreme? Those of you who have lived with one know the problem is subtle. When you ask them to do something, they smile and say, "No problem." So where's the problem? They just don't do it. They avoid trouble so completely that, as one lady said about her Phlegmatic husband, "He's just a piece of furniture. I dust him once a week." People tend to avoid the Phlegmatic in extreme.

How about You?

Isn't it amazing we get along at all with anyone when we don't understand either ourselves or others? If you haven't yet taken the Personality Profile in the back of the book, do it today. If possible, have the whole family take it and then discuss your strengths and weaknesses together. Have each family member say what's best about the others. Then go around a second time and ask if this strength is ever carried to an extreme. How often? How is it shown to others? How could this person emphasize more of his or her strengths and fewer of the weaknesses? This could be the best time of communication your family has ever had.

Suggested Prayer for Today

(Husband and wife should each pray
this prayer separately and individually.)

Dear Lord Jesus, open my eyes to my own strengths and the possibility that I might be carrying some of them to extremes. Show me how to pull back so people don't avoid me. Give me an acceptance of my mate and children and not the urge to change them. Thank You for this simple tool to use on both myself and others. In Your precious Name, Lord Jesus. Amen.

77

Nature vs. Nurture

Train up a child in the way he should go: and when he is old, he will not depart from it.   *Proverbs 22:6 KJV*

Nurture: the outside coming in. Nature: the inside coming out.
                    Janice Burns

Florence

Back when Fred and I started studying the personalities in 1968, the subject of genetics was only discussed within the medical profession. Some of us had taken enough courses in college to know that brown eyes are dominant and blue eyes recessive. I even remembered some charts about the inherited traits in fruit flies, but none of this had any personal application to me.

Even the available information on the personalities had not been updated for two thousand years; however, in the last twenty years the discussion over nature versus nurture has become widespread, and as we reach the end of the century there is an acute interest in Who am I? and How did I turn out this way? I have a collection of magazines with cover stories about genetics, material that was beyond public interest or understanding back in 1968. Here's a sample of some of those articles:

Atlantic Monthly, September 1994:
    "Personality is inborn to a greater degree than was thought—How we become what we are"

Newsweek, October 24, 1994:
    "IQ—Is it destiny?"

Newsweek, December 6, 1993:
    "The hunt for the breast cancer gene"

Time, January 17, 1994:
    "Genetics: The future is now"

Time, January 20, 1992:
> "Why are men and women different? New studies show they were born that way"

New Yorker, August 7, 1995:
> "Double mystery: The science of why we are who we are"

U.S. News & World Report, August 22, 1994:
> "Heredity—Can it be changed?"

U.S. News & World Report, May 25, 1987:
> "Predicting Diseases: New genetic clues to heart disease, cancer, AIDS and other killers could save your life"

U.S. News & World Report, April 21, 1997:
> "Born Bad? How the politics of biology shapes opinion, policy, and our self-image"

Is there a simple way to know the difference between what we inherit—our genetics—and what we learn from our parents and our experiences? How do I know my nature from my nurture? There is no bold line drawn down the middle of us saying this half is nature and this nurture, but from the many studies done in the last twenty years, we can make enough distinctions to analyze ourselves and our children.

For example, it has been proven by the University of Minnesota studies "Twins Reared Apart" that identical twins separated at birth and brought together many years later have close to identical personalities. Their inherited nature is the same. If they live similar normal lives and are not abused in any way, their personalities should be the same at age sixty as they were at age six. We are born with a direction (nature) of social skills that should stay true. The old idea that you move a child from the slums to Park Avenue and thus change his or her outlook on life (nurture) has been superseded. One of our seminar attendants told me she had adopted twin girls from a poor family with low moral standards. She raised them in a beautiful home, doted on them, and gave them every possible advantage. They seemed to enjoy and benefit from their surroundings, but at age eighteen they packed their bags and disappeared. They returned to their roots and duplicated their birth mother's behavior. Nurture had not changed their nature.

In our own experience, after losing our two sons, Fred and I adopted a baby boy. His nature was already in him when we received him at three months of age; we had nothing to do with what he had inherited. His Melancholy nature was already there, and it was not our job to change it. Our assignment was to nurture him, to give him positive surroundings where he could grow up in the nurture and admonition of the Lord. We could help him set goals, teach him manners, keep him in the church, and show him how to get along with his sisters. We didn't change his nature; we nurtured it. Gratefully, our experience is a positive one, and our son is a well-adjusted, well-mannered successful Melancholy. We have accepted his nature with joy and have done our best to nurture him.

How about You?

What does this mean to you? It means that your children came into this world with an innate sense of who they are, with inborn personality traits, their natures. What you do with them in accepting their differences can keep them feeling good about themselves, but if you try to change their personalities to fit your plans you can harm their emotions and make them feel insecure as they grow up.

We need to accept their nature and nurture them to fit their specific personality even if it isn't what we wanted. Proverbs 22:6 tells us to "train up a child [nurture the child] in the way he should go [his or her nature]: and when he is old he will not depart from it." Twist it the other way, and you can raise an insecure child who doesn't know who he or she is.

How about your childhood? Did your parents accept you as you were, or did they try to make you over? Discuss this question for you and your mate. Can you see a point at which you gave up being yourself and acted the way they found acceptable? How has this influenced your feelings of self-worth? Are you perhaps doing the same thing with your children?

Remember, as Janice Burns said at one of our personality training seminars:

> Nurture is the outside coming in.
> Nature is the inside coming out.

Suggested Prayer for Today

Heavenly Father, give us all the ability to train up each child in the way he or she should go, not the way we think would be best. Help us to accept our children's different natures and nurture them all with Your love. Help us to be examples of the Christian walk for them to observe. We pray in gratitude for this knowledge and in the Name of Jesus. Amen.

Altering Our Dispositions

The moment you are willing that God should alter your disposition, His recreating forces will begin to work.
Oswald Chambers, My Utmost for His Highest, *July 1*

Florence

Are you willing for God to begin to work on you to make you a new creature in Christ? I'm sure we'd all say yes, we are ready, yet there are two reasons why some of us don't ever change. One is we have only given up part of ourselves to the Lord. We need to have some control.

Isn't it logical that we maintain our own power and stay in charge of our lives? Yes, it's logical, but as Oswald Chambers says, until I am willing to let God take control of my disposition I have not in fact given my life to Him. Until I submit ALL of myself, including my disposition, to Him I haven't given Him complete control over me. I've given Him an apartment but not the whole building. I need to get to a point in my Christian walk where I know who is holding the map even if I don't know where I'm going. I must get to a point where I am willing to be directed by the Lord and let Him change my disposition and bring my personality strengths and weaknesses in from the extremes. He promises that when I am willing, He is able.

The second reason I don't allow the Lord to remake me is that I can't put my finger on what's wrong with me. If I knew my exact problems, I'd be happy for them to improve. I know what my mate tells me is wrong with me, but I've learned to ignore those outbursts and move on. Fred told me right from the start that I talked too much and I lied. I knew I didn't lie; I'm an honest person. I just couldn't remember how things went, plus I wanted to entertain and the truth wasn't always funny. I still feel if someone tells me a story that has some merit but is relatively dull that I should dress it up before passing it on in the same boring way in which I received it. I believe the truth should never stand in the way of a good story! Fred calls this lying.

For a long time I did not take him seriously, because people responded to my humor. Instead of changing, I didn't talk when Fred was around. I avoided the issue and had fun amusing people the minute Fred was out of sight. As long as we can rationalize around the things in us our mates tell us need changing, we don't have to do anything about them.

How about You?

If any of this sounds familiar to you, let's figure out how to move on through this issue in a survivor's way. First, we need to realize God is in the regenerating business. He specializes in making new out of the old, good out of bad, but only to those who are willing to be remade. Jesus is a gentle Master. He is not going to walk up to you, grab you, and say, "You need help!" He waits until He sees your permission light turned on, and then He asks quietly (so quietly some of us busy people don't hear Him), "Could you use some help?"

He always gives us the ultimate choice of how far we wish to go. But sometimes we answer, "Thanks for asking, but I'm not ready to try. I have so much to do; however, since You're available, will You start on Fred? I wouldn't want You to waste Your time."

If I do realize Jesus is standing at the door and knocking and He is willing to remake me, do a plastic surgery of the personality, then I have to decide if I'm willing. If I don't see my problems and think if Fred shaped up I'd be happy, then I won't get any better. Yet the Lord promises me a makeover the moment I decide. He doesn't ask me to phone for an appointment; He'll do the surgery today! What a physician!

Using the personalities as a tool to see our own strengths and weaknesses is often an eye-opening experience. It's like a report card of our progress. I guess I do talk too much and exaggerate. I guess I do offend people who see me as bossy. I guess I do bother imperfect people because I get depressed when things aren't right. I guess I'm not dependable when I say I'll do something and never quite get around to doing it.

Let's start at the beginning. Do you believe God has recreating forces that would like to get hold of you? Have you ever actually given your total self to the Lord, holding nothing back? If you're not sure of your answers, stop right now and pray.

Suggested Prayer for Today

Dear Lord Jesus, I do recognize that You can change me and remake me into a new person; I know I must be willing to let You, but I've always held back. Somehow I've wanted that control position, and yet in reality my life is out of control in some areas. You can see the whole picture, and You know what reconstruction work needs to be done today. I give You permission to repair me. I give You control of all of my life, not just part of it. You tell me that when I am willing, You are able.

Lord Jesus, I am ready for You to alter my disposition and make me what You want me to be. You are the great surgeon. I am the patient. I await Your operating skills with joy. In the precious Name of Jesus. Amen.

79

The Errant Golf Balls

> Stern discipline awaits him who leaves the path; he who hates correction will die.
>
> *Proverbs 15:10 NIV*

Florence

Now that we know God alters our dispositions when we are willing to give up our own control, let's look at our individual personalities and see what needs to be changed. In working with couples all these years Fred and I have found that opposites do attract and get married. In God's plan this is a good arrangement, because opposite personalities fill in each other's weaknesses. But since we wives and husbands don't realize that's the reason for God's opposites-attract plan, instead of making the most of our mates' strengths and weaknesses, we start changing the other person to "be like me."

If we were to put all marriages in a big pot and pull them out by couples, one by one we would have primarily two kinds of combinations: the Sanguine married to the Melancholy and the Choleric married to the Phlegmatic.

Let's look at the Sanguine-Melancholy marriage. The best part is that the Sanguine loves fun and games, humor and activity, and also is spontaneous, creative, and optimistic. Since the Melancholy is serious, stable, organized, and often pessimistic, the two together fill in each other's lacks. If the couple understands this principle, they can have a harmonious marriage. The Melancholy plans the schedule but learns to be flexible. The Sanguine doesn't have to worry about the details but must work to stay closer to the plans and remember to check the time. The Sanguine can come up with fun activities, and the Melancholy has to be willing to participate. The Melancholy likes some quiet time, so the Sanguine has to learn not to talk when the Melancholy wants silence.

Our aim is not to change one personality to be like the other but to bring the two personalities' extremes under the control of the Lord. When we don't have a list to check off, we don't always know what we have to work on, and our tendency is to pull away from each other and decide this marriage isn't working, figuring, "I guess I'll find myself a new mate."

Also, when we don't understand that our mates were born to be different and it isn't their fault, we tend to think they are "out to get us." One Sanguine woman told me, "I think he stays awake nights plotting against me."

When I asked him about his "plots," he didn't think he had any. "It's just when she makes mistakes I show her how to do it better the next time." She frankly didn't want to know.

As I have explained to Fred when I have a problem that is not going to happen again, I don't need a lecture on it. But to withhold preventative instructions for me in such times seems wrong to him. *Don't you want to learn to do better?* he wonders. I've had to show him that if I keep walking in front of moving cars he should teach me not to, but when I have funny, one-of-a-kind accidents, I just want him to listen, to be glad I lived through it, and not preach.

For a recent example: We live on a golf course, although neither of us plays golf. We find golf balls at our doorstep and bring them in. Fred has several hundred golf balls in his closet for no good reason. One day as I was doing dishes and had placed two crystal goblets in the sink full of bubbles, I decided I'd take this set of balls from the ridge behind the sink, where they were waiting for Fred to scrub them clean, so I started to put them in a bag. They'd been there long enough. I picked up the first few balls one at a time, but then to speed up the process I picked up two with one hand. Somehow they slipped, dropped into the sink, and each one smashed a goblet. In my state of shock I screamed, and Fred came running to see what had happened.

Now, did I need a lecture on how not to drop golf balls on goblets? Did I need to review the adage "haste makes waste"? Chances are I'm not going to run this experience through a second time. Of course, if he hadn't left the balls there so long in the first place, I wouldn't have been moving them. Considering the proverb, "Stern discipline awaits him who leaves the path; he who hates correction will die," I don't have much longer to live! Gratefully, Fred was not angry over the goblets, and he even said to me, "It's all right; that's why I bought extra goblets."

He opened the cabinet and pointed to the top shelf, where he had six extra goblets in each size. I am so blessed that Melancholy Fred thought ahead about the possibility of Sanguine me smashing a few goblets with some golf balls. We do fill in each other's weaknesses!

How about You?

Does this scenario sound familiar? Is one of you the instructor in a lifelong improvement program? If so, learn to curb the word lesson and save it for repeat offenses of the worst kind, not for uniquely creative mistakes. Sanguines don't mind doing wrong things that can, in the retelling, get a laugh. For Sanguines, every bad experience is a good example.

Suggested Prayer for Today

Dear Lord, help us to realize that all petty mistakes are not tragedies. Help me, the Sanguine, to be more careful to think ahead and anticipate possible problems. Help me, the Melancholy, not to turn everything into a corrective sermon. Remind me to weigh my comments against eternal values. Lord Jesus, help us both to look at each other in love and not in corrections, so we can truly become one. In Your Name. Amen.

80

No Respect

It is better to dwell in the wilderness, than with a contentious and an angry woman.

Proverbs 21:19 KJV

Florence

Are married couples always opposites in personality? Not always but usually. Seldom do we find people married to the same personalities in a first marriage. Sometimes in second or third midlife marriages, where passion is not the attraction it was in youth and the partners tend to be looking for companionship, men and women are more apt to choose someone of similar personality.

Think of what would happen if two young persons with the same personality married:

Two Sanguines having fun and telling stories at the same time with no one to listen.

Two Melancholies both perfect and organized, sitting quietly, having no fun or sparkle in their lives.

Two Cholerics ready to tell everyone where to go and no one interested in going.

Two Phlegmatics, peaceful, no fuss or conflict, but too complacent to decide where to go for excitement.

When we look at the possibilities, we can see why we seldom marry someone just like us!

We said earlier that the most common opposites who end up married to each other are predominantly Sanguines married to those who feature Melancholy strengths, and those with Choleric strengths married to Phlegmatics. In yesterday's chapter we looked at some of the typical situations that come up in Sanguine-Melancholy marriages, so today we'll review the Choleric married to the Phlegmatic. They are attracted to each other because the

Phlegmatic wants someone who can make decisions for them, and the Choleric loves to make decisions whether or not they are asked for.

When the newlyweds don't understand the personalities, this combination sometimes drops into a boss-slave relationship. The fewer decisions the Phlegmatic makes, the more the Choleric takes control. When the Phlegmatic doesn't get up and move, the Choleric takes over the chores. What could be a positive relationship turns sour for one of two reasons: Either the aggressive Choleric thinks, *I'm doing all the work. What do I need him/her for?* or the Phlegmatic thinks, *My opinions don't count; I'm a nobody here. Why don't I find someplace where I'm respected?* It's easy to see how these two pull away from each other. Their initial strengths have been carried to extremes and become weaknesses. They're tired of trying to change the other one with no results, and soon they have little use for each other.

What can be done about this marriage problem? Obviously prevention is far easier than cure, but let's assume we have a ten- to fifteen-year marriage. At a network marketing convention a strong Choleric woman came up to me. "I'm so embarrassed," she said. "All the other men in the business are moving ahead, and my husband just doesn't get with the program. I push him and tell him what to do, but he still won't do anything. He won't speak up or say a word. You'd never think he knew anything!"

Immediately, the classic Choleric-Phlegmatic case rears its head! "Is he here?" I asked.

"Right over there." She pointed to a good-looking young man leaning against a marble column in the hotel lobby.

"Ask him to come over," I suggested.

She marched over to him and said, "The speaker wants to see you."

"What for?" he asked.

"I don't know," she stormed impatiently. "Just come!"

He dropped into the easy chair beside me and smiled an engaging smile. I could see why she'd been attracted to him in the first place. He had a lot more charm than she did. Choleric women are usually drawn to the cool look and reserved manner of the Phlegmatic man.

"Why did you get into this business?" I asked him.

She answered, "He has no idea."

No wonder he didn't talk much. She did it for him!

I repeated the question and looked at him while patting her knee to be quiet. "I like the people. The men are great, and I enjoy being with them."

"All he wants is the fellowship," she added. "He won't do a thing."

I ignored her and asked him again. "Do you want to stay in the business?"

"Yes, I like the meetings."

"Are you willing to go out a few times a month and share the plan?"

"I guess so."

"How many times would you estimate?"

While he was thinking, she said, "Don't believe whatever he says, because he won't do it."

"Maybe once a week," he said.

"Will you make a commitment to me and to your wife that if she'll stop nagging you, you'll go out without urging once a week?"

As he said, "She'll stop nagging? That'll be the day!" she fumed, "I don't nag him. If I didn't move him, he'd never get out of the chair."

I turned to her and said, "You must really be something to live with."

"What do you mean?"

"You don't even know me, and you keep interrupting me. What must you do with him?"

I looked back, and he had a smile on his face and a twinkle in his eye. "What are you feeling right now?" I asked.

"I can't believe you said what I've always wanted to say and didn't dare to!"

He will never forget my remark to his wife!

How about You?

If you were the counselor here, what would you do? Can you see the two sides clearly? She has to stop nagging him and realize they will probably not get to the top in this business. She has to be grateful for such a charming man, lower her expectations, and stop putting him down in public.

And what does he have to do? Decide whether he does want to be in this extra business and if so commit to spending some time and then following through.

What about your marriage? Does any of this sound familiar? If so, pretend you're a different couple, lay out your individual perspective, and then be your own marriage counselor. Start with one problem you don't agree on. State each side calmly and concisely without anger. What would an objective person say about each side? Is there an obvious compromise you could agree upon?

Suggested Prayer for Today

Dear Lord Jesus, why can't we all be objective about our situations and solve them before they become big issues? Other people's cases seem so simple, and yet we hold back until we're so mad we can't talk. Lord Jesus, help us to look at each other in love and not anger and give us the answers we need. We're going to discuss this right now, so please be with us. Lord, we need You, and we pray in Your precious Name. Amen.

Part III

Wear
the
Dream

*How to continue to grow in all aspects
of life, communicate on a positive and
enjoyable level, and find meaning and
pleasure in reading God's Word*

Personal and Passionate Devotion

> The men and women He will use in His mighty building enterprises are those who love Him personally, passionately and devotedly. . . . The conditions are stern, but they are glorious.
>
> *Oswald Chambers*, My Utmost for His Highest, *May 7*

Fred

"Those who love Him personally, passionately and devotedly." The Lord demands much from us; He is perhaps a stern Master. He is also generous and gracious, and His blessings are glorious. Until one has experienced the awesome and wondrous might of the Lord, it is difficult to comprehend the magnificence and majesty of His almighty power. One can be told, one can see, and one can hear. But there is nothing that takes the place of experiencing it, of knowing it for yourself.

How can we know this majesty if we have only heard about it? Chambers tells us so clearly that "the only men and women He will use" in His mighty "building enterprises" are those in whom He has done everything . . . "those who love Him personally, passionately and devotedly." His "building enterprises" refers to lives, not to things or places. Chambers is not referring to a magnificent new cathedral, a church that seats five thousand, or a beautiful new center for the Christian elderly. He is talking about lives, human regenerated lives. Are you involved in any way in a mighty building enterprise of His where lives are being transformed by the power of God?

There is no escaping the fact—lukewarm Christians will never experience God's ultimate plan. "One-hour Christians" are those whose weekly Christian experience can be summed up in one hour in a Sunday morning church service. Passionate and devoted Christians are those whose hearts overflow with gratitude and thanksgiving to their Lord and Savior. They are the ones who are involved in the Master's mighty building enterprises.

We have all heard His explicit instructions: "Seek ye first the kingdom of God,"[1] and "Thou shalt love the Lord thy God with all thy heart, and with all thy soul, and with all thy mind,"[2] and "First clean the inside of the cup and of the dish, so that the outside of it may become clean also."[3]

How about You?

Today will you examine together your own commitments to the Lord? Do the words *commitment, personal, passionate,* and *devotion* describe the nature of your heart toward the One who gave His life for you? The One who freed you forever from the bondage of sin and death? Would you be described as a "lukewarm Christian" or a "one-hour Christian"? The Word of God says, "Let not that man think that he shall receive anything of the Lord."[4]

Do you desire revitalized oneness in your marriage, a new fragrance, a renewed relationship flourishing like a fresh new flower bursting forth? Your goal is possible, and it is up to you as individuals to make it happen. It starts with moving from lukewarm to passionate devotion to the Lord God. Are you willing to turn that corner? Are you willing to forsake all to follow Him, as He told the rich young ruler?[5]

This is the starting point. You can read many books, attend many seminars, hear many sermons, but all this will only amount to a pile of good intentions and nothing more unless you are prepared to do all and become all that Jesus is asking of you. There is more to bringing His best into your marriage than just deciding to accept His gift. There are habits to break, confessions to make, and forgiveness to ask. There is repairing and growing and maturing to be done. None of this will happen until you make that commitment. No one can do it for you. You can only do it for yourself. Will you become passionate and devoted to your Lord and Savior? Will you do it today?

Suggested Prayer for Today

Lord, I was hoping for a magic pill, a quick-and-easy solution. I wish there were one. Life would be so much easier. It seems like it is a lot of hard work, but I do remember that You told us that if we would come to You and take Your yoke upon us You would share the load with us as we walk down the road of life. I need someone to share this load with me, Lord, and I am thankful that You are willing. I can't think of anyone else I would rather come to with my hurts and needs.

I know I can trust You, and I am now willing to do it Your way. I guess if I am going to be yoked together with You I don't have much choice! I have to go when You go and stop when You stop. Lord Jesus, I surrender all of me to You. I promise to You today that I will hold nothing back. I want to be on fire for You. I want to be passionately and personally devoted to only You. Though satan will try, I will not permit him to get me to take off Your yoke from my shoulders. I will stand against him with the authority You have given me. Thank You, Lord Jesus. In Your Name I pray. Amen.

82

Personalizing Scripture:
Accepting Each Other

Accept one another, just as Christ also accepted us to the glory of God.

Romans 15:7

Fred

Many, many years ago, shortly after I became a Christian in North Haven, Connecticut, a missionary member of our church, Chuck Tabor, spoke at the Sunday evening service. Most of us can recall certain milestones in our Christian growth—a certain sermon we have never forgotten, a verse or a passage of Scripture that God indelibly inscribed on our hearts, or perhaps an encounter with another Christian who made an especially powerful impact on our lives. That Sunday night was one of these times for me.

Chuck spoke on the "Three Steps of Bible Study." He listed the three steps as questions we should consider as we study God's Word: What does it say? What does it mean? And how does it apply to me? I have never forgotten those steps or Chuck's teaching that night. I have in turn taught the same idea hundreds of times since then myself, passing on Chuck's wonderful ideas.

What his teaching helped me to do was to take Scripture from the impersonal and move it to the personal: where it related to me, where I was, and what I needed. No one in that small church knew it at the time, but Florence and I were at a low point of our life together. Fortunately I was a new Christian and therefore determined to do what I had to do—and to do it right! I studied Scripture diligently, trying to learn all I could. I came across verses that seemed to call me to focus on them. I would ask the Lord, How does this verse apply to me? The idea came to me then to write in Florence's name above certain words to personalize specific scriptures.

Romans 15:7 was one of those verses. I still regularly use the New American Standard New Testament that was given to me in February 1968 as my study Bible. Since that time, that verse in my Bible has read, "Wherefore, accept Florence, just as Christ has also accepted her to the glory of God." With this personal application, the verse meant something special to me! God had sent an instruction just for me, one that both He and I knew I needed.

For many years I had tried to change Florence. My motives were pure, I thought. I was merely trying to polish some of those rough edges so she could become just the wife I wanted, mainly a wife who would please me! I helped her to overcome some of her sparkling Sanguine spontaneity by becoming orderly and meticulous like the Melancholy part of me. I was so successful at remodeling her to conform her to my image that after fifteen years I had a totally different wife whom I didn't care for very much. And who, incidentally, was told by her doctor that her physical problems were psychosomatic and probably due to stress. *What stress?* I wondered.

Then as a new Christian I read Romans 15:7. It told me I was to accept Florence in just the same way that Christ accepted her. He didn't require her to become perfect before He would love and accept her. Why then did I have to try to make her perfect? Why couldn't I love her and accept her the way God created her? If God didn't see a need to change His creation, why couldn't I be satisfied with His workmanship? When I showed Florence what I had written in my Bible and explained to her what I was going to try to do, she wept. This was more than she had ever hoped for. This was the beginning of our rebuilding.

The habits of my "constructive criticism" and "training" did not die easily. After all, they had a fifteen-year head start! At this point I had only good intentions and a desire to do what God wanted me to do. I hadn't learned yet how to come into His presence in prayer and ask for His help. This all happened thirty years ago! I have learned so much since then. Today I am Florence's number one booster. I love her just the way she is, and she knows that I do. There is nothing I want her to change. My main focus in our life together today is to do everything I can to make her life just as enjoyable, comfortable, and stress-free as possible. It's hard for a wife not to feel loved and appreciated when she knows this is her husband's daily goal for her.

I am grateful for all of Scripture, but Romans 15:7 will always hold a special place in my heart. It taught me to accept Florence just as Christ had already accepted her, "to the glory of God"! And thank you, Chuck Tabor, for teaching me how to personalize that verse, to make it apply to me.

How about You?

Is Scripture relevant and meaningful to you? As you study the Word of God, do lights suddenly shine out for you? As you work on the rough edges of your marriage, pay close attention to the kinds of things you hear yourself saying that seem to upset your partner. Does he or she sometimes "clam up" or turn away from you, as if thinking, *what's the use?* These are clear signs of deep, often repeated hurts. Be brave; be strong; determine to get to the roots of these walls between you. Ask God to personalize His Word to you, so you apply His truths specifically to yourself.

Suggested Prayer for Today

Dear God and Heavenly Father, I am thankful today for the mate You have given to me. Help me, Lord, to focus on his/her strengths and good qualities as You do. Help me, Lord, to be blind to those things that have irritated me in the past. I do not ask You to help me to merely overlook them but to be completely blind to them. If I do not see them I will not even know whether or not they are there! Lord, I realize now that my mate is Your creation and therefore it is Your job to do any changing or transforming, not mine. I hereby resign my position as chief character builder and personality improver. I have enough to do to work on myself anyway. O Lord, You are so patient and gentle. I desire to be as tender as You in all my relations with my partner. Help me, Lord Jesus, I pray, to be like You. Amen.

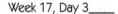

83

Personalizing Scripture:
Giving Preference

Be devoted to one another in brotherly love; give preference to one another in honor.

Romans 12:10

Fred

This is another one of those verses through which the Lord spoke to me loudly and clearly. In looking at the whole passage in Romans, this is a verse that describes how relationships are to be in the body of Christ. And we also see much more here when we look at the verse more closely. Before studying Scripture I always like to pray Psalm 119:18, "Open Thou mine eyes [O Lord], that I may behold wondrous things out of the law" (KJV). When we "pray Scripture" we can always be sure we are praying in the will of God! Scripture is the will of God.

Once again in my study Bible, above the second "one another" in Romans 12:10, I wrote many years ago: "FLORENCE!" That portion of the verse now reads, "Give preference to Florence in honor."

Further study into the meaning of the original Greek word showed me that the phrase "give preference" could even more effectively, I thought, be translated, "outdo one another in giving preference." Naturally I couldn't show this revised translation to my wife, for she might think I was trying to manipulate her to do good things for me! On the contrary, I just wanted to try to outdo myself in putting her in first place in everything I did. When I personalized the verse in this manner, God was able to reach me. He spoke very clearly to me as to how I was to regard and treat Florence!

Here is a simple scenario that may replicate something that has occurred at some time in your home. Let us suppose that a friend visiting you has brought to you both a small box of candy—very rich, very delicious, very expensive chocolates! You open the gold foil box and find eight of the most tantalizing chocolates either of you has ever seen. Since you both love good chocolates, it isn't long before all but one of them is gone.

Later that night as you're both getting ready for bed, you happen to walk alone into the kitchen and see the gold foil box. You lift the cover, and what do you see? Voila! The last of the eight chocolates sitting there alone, just waiting for a friend, all but calling out to you, "Pick me up! Pick me up!" You stop for a moment and count, "Let me see, I think I only had three this afternoon. I should be entitled to this last one."

How about You?

What do you do? Do you eat it secretly? Or . . . do you take it into the bedroom and say, "Honey, I found this one last chocolate in the box. It has your name on it!" Is this ever a test of Romans 12:10! Wouldn't most of us be tempted to add, "I think I only had three this afternoon, but I want you to have this last one"? Now, aren't we being noble to sacrifice our own desires to please our mate? In the natural spirit don't we all want credit for what we do for the other? We are apt to think, *Maybe if I let her know how giving I have been, she'll appreciate it and do something similar for me tomorrow.*

This might be giving preference to one another, but would it be "in honor"? For a no-nonsense answer, it is interesting to read Matthew 6:1–3 in the Good News Bible translation: "Be careful not to perform your . . . duties . . . so that people will see what you do. . . . When you give something to a needy person, do not make a big show of it, as the hypocrites do. . . . They do it so that people will praise them. When you help a needy person, do it in such a way that even your closest friend will not know about it. [What? And not get credit for it?] . . . And your Father, who sees what you do in private, will reward you" (TEV).

Oh, how I love Scripture! Not only is it truth, not only is it the Word of God, but it is so insightful! God knows our every quirk. He knows the carnal nature of our hearts and yet He is so patient to teach us, to train us, and to patiently work to transform us into His own image and likeness. His Word is our guidebook and our measuring stick as well. He makes it so plain and simple when we personalize Scripture: "Give preference to one another in honor."

Suggested Prayer for Today

Dear God and Heavenly Father, my heart is full of thanksgiving to You once again today. I know You love to hear the praises of Your children. I love to praise You and to thank You. You have given so much to me. I have a confidence now that I have never had before. I have the confidence that I already have eternal life, the confidence that You know me and care about what happens to me. I thank You as well, Lord, for the confidence I have that You are always working to perfect in me the work that You began. This gives me hope, Lord. There are days when I very much need that hope! There are days when I feel so forgotten. There are days when I feel no one cares. I am learning that this is only one of the ways the enemy attacks me. I thank You also, Lord, that You have given me Your power and the authority over him. Now all I have to do, Lord, is to remember to exercise that authority. For I am convinced that nothing can separate me from the love of God, but he surely tries. He will not succeed. I will not allow him to have any victory over me. I belong to You and I am Yours. I thank You, too, Lord, for this scripture today. Help me, Lord, to put it into practice in our home. I thank You, my Lord and my God. I praise Your Holy Name. Amen.

84

Personalizing Scripture:
Making Your Mate More Important

Do nothing from selfishness or empty conceit, but with humility of mind . . . regard one another [_____] as more important than himself [_____].

Philippians 2:3

Fred

"I always treat him as more important than myself. Well, I used to."

"I let her make the first choice in everything."

"I'm not selfish; my friends always know they can count on me."

"I let her be in charge at home; she makes all the decisions."

"I'm completely submitted to what he wants; half the time I don't even open my mouth."

"She can go out any time she wants. I don't put any restrictions on her."

Commonly heard phrases, perhaps even in your home. Will you look at those pronouncements again and study them carefully? Don't they sound as though they might have been made to a counselor, maybe on a couple's first appointment? Try to read between the lines. Try saying these sentences out loud with the tone of voice and inflection they might have actually used. Is this a happy couple? Are they well adjusted to each other? Do you think this couple has actually personalized Philippians 2:5?

How would you help them if they came to you? Can you make suggestions to them that they could take home and work on this week to show some improvement before they come back to see the two of you next week? Discuss now together what you would each say to this couple. Figure out what their real problem is versus their "presenting problem."

Couples rarely see themselves as other people see them. As you discussed together their problems and the suggestions you would offer them, have you noticed how much easier it is to straighten out other people than to see why you are having struggles? It always seems to be so much easier to fix others! Aren't we all experts at that? If it weren't true we could cut down the size of the gossip barrel by half!

How about You?

In your home how would you personalize this important "commandment" in the verse at the beginning of this chapter? Notice it's not a suggestion or a recommendation. It's a pretty clear instruction! It starts right out by saying, "Do nothing from . . ." The Scriptures do not pussyfoot around issues! If it's God's directive to us, we had best pay close attention to what He is telling us to do. Begin by putting each other's names in the appropriate place; replace the word *himself* with *myself* and see how it reads. Read it aloud to each other. You might want to add such a line as, "Honey, I have been trying to do this, but now seeing it here in print reminds me that I could do a better job. Will you help me so that I can be a better husband/wife for you?"

Is there a spouse who could say no to such a question? It is so totally selfless. It is asking nothing in return. It is not saying, "I will promise to be better for the next three weeks and then let's see what happens" (meaning, "We'll go on if you show some improvement too!").

The verse also asks us to be humble of mind. The Bible tells us in two different places, "God is opposed to the proud, but gives grace [undeserved favor] to the humble," and in another it warns us that God "mocks proud mockers but gives grace to the humble."[1] What does it mean to be humble? How would you define it?

Humble means to be not proud or assertive, not pretentious and boastful. Would you say these words describe the Lord Jesus? A verse following the one at the top of this day's reading answers the question for us. Philippians 2:5 tells us to "Let this same attitude

and purpose and [humble] mind be in you which was in Christ
Jesus: [Let Him be your example in humility]" (AMP).

Florence knows now without any question or doubt that I always
regard her needs and her interests as more important than mine. As
a result of seeing this selfless attitude in me, which is in stark contrast to the artificial or contrived humility she knew for so many
years, she now treats me exactly the same way. If we ever have a
problem now, it's because we are both trying so selflessly to "regard
the other as more important than myself" at the same time. What a
wonderful problem to have!

Suggested Prayer for Today

Dear Lord Jesus, I want to have that attitude, that mind, that You
exemplified during Your walk here on earth. Master, I want to be
like You. Tell me what I must do so that when my partner looks at
me, self-centeredness or impatience is not seen, and what is seen is
nothing but the love of the risen Lord Jesus Christ. Lord, I desire for
Your unconditional resurrection love to be in me. Help me, dear
Lord Jesus. Help me to be sensitive to my mate's reactions so that
I can be more aware of every word or nonverbal signal that comes
from me that is a negative. Lord, I ask You to give me discernment.
If I can know when I say or do something that is offensive I can
confess it, apologize, and ask forgiveness. I've been doing some of
these things for so many years, Lord, half the time I don't even recognize them at all. Thank You, Lord, for helping me. My partner will
thank You too when the changes are seen in me! In Your gracious
and glorious Name, I pray. Amen.

85

Personalizing Scripture:
Becoming a Servant

Have this attitude in yourselves which was also in Christ Jesus,
who . . . emptied Himself, taking the form of a bondservant, . . .
He humbled Himself by becoming obedient to the point of death.
Philippians 2:5, 7–8

Fred

It probably took much more time than Florence and I wished, but at last we learned something about what makes marriages work. We have been through virtually every struggle any couple could face as we weathered the storms of marital stress. We recognize now that our foundation was weak. Were we different forty-five years ago than any other newly married couple? Probably not. We were young, confident, and frankly naive. What couple on their honeymoon expects that when they get home they will have to begin resolving a cache of buried problems, personality conflicts, and misconceptions? Would you have gone through with your wedding if you had known what was ahead of you?

We have finally weathered all those storms. Our earnest and foremost desire is to enable other couples to sharply cut their own learning curves and profit from the deep waters we waded through.

We all have one basic and very simple problem, and until we understand what it is and learn to overcome it, there is little hope that we can ever reach the zenith that seemed so achievable as we trustingly walked down the aisle and out into the world. What is this ultimate impediment to fulfilling our dreams? Simply that we are all born with a self-centered attitude. From birth through childhood and into adulthood we tend to always think of our own needs and welfare first.

Some never learn. They die miserable, cranky, and hostile. You have no doubt met many such people yourself. Perhaps they never learned, or perhaps they rejected the truth. Let us all be sure we are not eventually one of those. Some of us grow old, and some of us grow up!

If someone had told me what I had to do to be a pleasing and appreciated husband I would have been surprised, but it would have changed my focus drastically. I thought the answer was in *doing*. Nobody told me the answer was in *being!* This is the only answer to our basic problem. It requires a 180-degree turn, from self-centeredness to selflessness! How do we do it?

Jesus is our example. We are to take His attitude and become a "bondservant," humbling ourselves to the point of complete obedience. Obedience to whom? To our spouses? No! To the Lord Jesus Christ only. When I am completely obedient to Him I will have His character, His mind, His attitude. Please notice carefully. This becoming a bondservant is not a doing! Look at Jesus. He was never a doormat. He was never weak. He never lacked self-worth. Yet He was a "bondservant." His servant's nature was an attitude, a frame of mind, a fundamental part of His godliness. He told His disciples that the Son of Man came not to be served but to serve.

Eventually, if we are going to achieve what we desire and fulfill His plans for us, we must learn to exemplify His nature in all that we do, say, or think. Realistically, is this possible? Absolutely! This is what the Christian life is all about, being "transformed by the renewing of [our minds]," and then we will demonstrate by our lives that which is "good and acceptable and perfect."[1] We come to Him every day in prayer, asking without ceasing that He reveal to us whatever in us that is not pleasing to Him.

We "have not, because [we] ask not."[2] If we ask anything in His Name, He will do it! If you ask now, and keep asking, He promises that He will give you the attitude of a bondservant, one whose heart is selfless like His. The Lord Jesus tells us there is no other way to eternal life and to abundant life but through Him.

How about You?

Will you begin today? If you do you will be so glad tomorrow. Your mate will be glad. Your family will be glad, and the Lord Jesus will be glad. The angels of Heaven will rejoice with you and for you. There is no other way. Jesus said, "I am the way."[3]

Suggested Prayer for Today

Dear Lord Jesus, is it really this simple? If it is, why have I made it so complicated? Why have I not been experiencing this perfect peace that Your Word tells me I can have? Why do we still clash over issues that seem so petty later? Why, Lord, do I sometimes overreact and then feel so guilty later? Lord, the first place I want to start my own transformation is right here at home. I ask You now to instill Your mind in me. I ask You to cleanse me of all sense of self: self-centeredness, self-righteousness, and selfishness. I confess to You, Lord, that if others see these in me, even if I haven't, they must be there.

I come to You, Lord, for I know now that You are my only hope of becoming a different person. You are the only way. There is no other way apart from You. I don't want to be apart from You. I want to be always in Your presence. I ask You today to help me to become what You have always intended for me to be. I thank You, Lord Jesus, for hearing my prayer. I worship You, my Lord and my God. Amen.

86

Good Taste

I came to this castle, and I was confronted with tasteless furniture and tasteless pictures. Only then did I realize how closely the bad taste of rulers was connected with their bad way of ruling.
Vaclav Havel, 1st president of Czech Republic after communism fell

Florence

Once Czechoslovakia was set free from the yoke of communism, Vaclav Havel, playwright and imprisoned dissident, became a symbol of the country's future. Born in 1935 into a well-to-do, refined family, Havel became the released country's better self, its moral philosopher promoting values of "courtesy, good taste, intelligence, decency, and responsibility,"[1] traits often missing in American politics. When he took his role as president and entered Hradcany Castle, where the communists had ruled, he was overwhelmed with the lack of taste in furniture and pictures connected with their bad, tasteless way of ruling. Havel defines taste as "a visible manifestation of human sensibility toward the world, environment, and people."[2] He also said a tasteful civility includes speaking kindly to people, paying attention to their opinions, not offending their dignity. "What I really have in mind is something more than just knowing which tie to choose to match a particular shirt," Havel said.

As I read Havel's words, I was challenged to rethink what it means to have good taste in life, to relate with manners and compassion to all people. Without good taste, without speaking kindly to others, we can never become role models for our children, our coworkers, or the people at our churches. When Rehoboam became king after Solomon's death, he asked his father's advisers the secrets to being a respected leader. They answered, "Speak kindly to all, answer all who ask you, and have the attitude of a servant."[3] Rehoboam rejected this message of good taste and chose to rule with an iron fist, bringing the kingdom and himself to ruin.

The advice of Rehoboam's advisers is still useful today. Take a moment and ask yourself: "Do I have good taste? Do I speak kindly to people whether or not they are important to my current activities? Do I answer everyone even those with what appear to be foolish questions? Do I have the attitude of a servant so that I can be an effective leader?

How about You?

As a couple, do you have good taste and courteous manners with each other? If Jesus were the unseen guest at your dinner table, would He be satisfied with your behavior? Would He see that you are the same at home as in public? Would He be touched at the kind politeness you show to one another? If not, what could you do about it?

Give each other permission to say, "I don't consider that comment in good taste."

And when that comment is made about you, instead of getting upset, try to respond, "I'm sorry. I don't want to hurt you. How could I have said that better?"

As you practice this behind the scenes at home, you will soon exhibit for others "a visible manifestation of human sensibility."[4]

Suggested Prayer for Today

Dear Lord Jesus, we haven't thought enough about "good taste" before. We haven't realized that people judge who we are by how politely we treat others and even each other. Give us eyes to see what we do that is offensive to others. So often we just live the day without thinking about things like manners, taste, or dignity. We want to be courteous representatives of You so that others will want to be Christians like us. We ask to be made aware of any crude or rude behavior so that we may be people of good taste. In Your precious Name we pray. Amen.

A Time to Rest

> Then, because so many people were coming and going that they did not even have a chance to eat, He said to them, "Come with me by yourselves to a quiet place and get some rest."
>
> *Mark 6:31 NIV*

Florence

Getting back to nature has never been a real desire of mine; "Camping out" for me is a Holiday Inn with a balcony. Yet every so often Fred gets an urge to go back to Maine to the AimHi Lodge where his parents first took him when he was seven years old. Each time we have gone back there over the forty-five years of our marriage, Fred and I start analyzing how if we bought the place we could do wonders with it. Each little cabin has its own primitive appeal, nestled in pine trees with a porch jutting out over the lake, but once you enter through the screen door and see that you will be sleeping on undersized twin beds redeemed from a Boy Scout camp, you begin to wonder why you came. My attitude about vacationing has always been if you have to pay money to stay somewhere in worse shape than home, you are in questionable mental condition!

The last time we stayed in the cabin named Look Out—which should be a warning in itself—we figured out how to redesign the cabin and add a wing to the side. We'd tear out the tin shower stall in the corner of the tiny bathroom and remove the sign over the toilet that warns of "delicate plumbing." As we got into our plans we had to stop ourselves and realize since we weren't about to buy the place, we had better stop making mental improvements and just enjoy the scenery and go to bed late.

We didn't expect to return, but this year we received a letter telling us we could have Look Out at a substantial discount for the week of July 4. At the last minute, with this book to finish and with Fred longing for nostalgia, we decided to leave California behind and head for Maine. As soon as we entered and unpacked, Fred made his list of needs, and we headed for Wal-Mart to buy civilization items: an electric coffeemaker for those chilly mornings and a cooler chest for chilly drinks, bug spray for the spiders and lighter fluid to coax the fire in the wood stove, a clock radio and a color TV to keep in touch with the world.

We put the reference books and Bibles we had brought with us on the shelves and spread out the magazines we never had time to read on the long, skinny coffee table. We unpacked our bags and hung our clothes in the one closet. Since my pantsuits and sundresses were too long for the closet, I hung some of them on the unbalanced nails that some unbalanced person had many years ago whacked into the knotty-pine walls in no particular order. When Fred asked, "Do I have to look at your clothes hanging in front of me all week?" I tried to convince him to see them as wall hangings, a decorative improvement over plain pine.

How about You?

Have you ever had vacation problems where you wondered why you spent money to be so uncomfortable? Have you had arguments over the poor choice and perhaps blamed each other? As we talk with couples we find some of their worst problems started on vacations. Husbands and wives seem to have unrealistic expectations and then spend months paying off the bills for a best-be-forgotten holiday. We know one man who actually took out a second mortgage on his house to take his family to Disneyland and later went bankrupt because of this decision.

Vacations need to be thought out in advance, agreed upon by both of you, and should not exceed your financial ability at the time. Your children don't love you more because you spent in excess of your means, and you two may end up hostile over the debt you're facing. Sometimes day trips, weekend outings, visits to historical places not too far away, or doing special projects at home can give variety to life as well as—or even better than—a long vacation in an exotic setting.

When I was a child we had one day a year when we took our historical trip to Boston. We all gave Dad suggestions, and then he chose a logical itinerary for our big day. We went on the train and spent almost nothing—and we all remember these trips with pleasure today.

Don't let vacations become a problem. You don't need two costly weeks at the shore in August. Discuss some of your best vacations as children. Why were they memorable? What things at home have you been waiting for each other to do? Why not spend the money on new paint, having the carpets cleaned, or refurbishing the master bedroom? You might be much happier with a new bedspread than with an album full of pictures from Maine.

Suggested Prayer for Today

Dear Lord Jesus, sometimes we think we need to go off to some exotic island in the South Seas to have a well-deserved vacation. Sometimes we think we must spend money we don't have to go somewhere we don't need to go. Lord, make us sensible and show us what we can do that would be fun and not cost beyond our means. Help us not to keep up with the Joneses and then regret the bills later. We know you have a plan for our lives and it includes vacations. We know you pulled away from the crowds to rest without spending much money. Show us what to do that's different, reasonable, and agreeable to both of us.

We will listen for Your leading. In Your Name we pray. Amen.

88

Unfailing Love

What a man desires is unfailing love.

Proverbs 19:22 NIV

Florence

Remember Valentine's Day when we were children? We gave out dozens of little cards saying "I love you"—some to people we didn't even like. We bought those tiny heart candies in pastel colors that said "BE MINE," and if we had a little extra money we'd buy a chocolate heart wrapped in red foil for someone special. Often we evaluated our own worth by how many valentines we received in return: I gave out twenty-five and only received eleven back. Nobody loves me.

As children our feelings of love were often wrapped up in the give-and-take of presents: If I give enough, people will love me. If I receive a lot that shows that people really care. These thoughts, understandable for children, are not appealing in adults, and yet women tell me they are devastated because their husbands forgot their anniversaries: He doesn't love me anymore. I enjoy cards and I get excited over presents, but I want my concept of love to be deeper than the tokens on the table.

Remembering birthdays and special events has always been a major part of our family traditions, and I would put on parties for every occasion I could think of. I made seasonal centerpieces and tablecloths, and we celebrated everything including Ground Hog Day. All of those times are fun memories, positive experiences, but I hope my children would still love me if I hadn't given quite so much.

How important it is that as we mature we see love as more than candy hearts, that we don't evaluate our worth by the price of the present.

How about You?

We women have to understand that men do not have the same sentimental feelings and remembrances we have. And you men, try to find some way to be reminded of family birthdays and at least your anniversary. A well-chosen card, some chocolates, or a pretty little plant are better than a hundred dollars' worth of roses charged to your wife. Women, don't test your husbands to see if they remember and then wail lovelessly when they don't. Help them; don't test them! Say, "Our anniversary is coming up in a few weeks. What do you think would be appropriate to do to celebrate?" Or, "Your mother's birthday is next week, and we're short of money. What could you do to make her happy?"

Men appreciate being helped and resent being put to the test. Don't fail your man who wants an unfailing love.

Suggested Prayer for Today

Dear Lord Jesus, we so want to feel each other's unfailing love—tender, compassionate love that lifts our spirits and warms our hearts. But we're vulnerable to today's materialistic culture, and sometimes we fall into the trap of equating love with things. We come to expect gifts, and we're disappointed when they don't magically appear. Please help us to show each other unfailing love, not by the things we give to each other, but in our attitudes—Christlike attitudes—toward each other. Fill our hearts so that we can express our needs and hear each other's expressions, and open our eyes so that we're better able to see the gifts You have bestowed on us. We ask this in Your Name. Amen.

Night Instruction

> I said to the LORD, "You are my Lord; apart from You I have no good thing." . . . I will praise the LORD, who counsels me; even at night my heart instructs me.
>
> *Psalm 16:2,7 NIV*

Florence

Often I hear Christians say "in me is no good thing"[1] as if this were a badge of humility: If I am a totally worthless worm, I must really be spiritual. But God didn't call the worms to spread the gospel; He called those of us with the strength to carry on even in adverse circumstances. What this oft-misused quote says, in effect, is that without the Lord in our lives, we're not worth much. Now that's true. Left to our own devices, or vices, we are going to have a struggle. We can't handle the problems of life on our own; instead we must bring them to the Lord who, as the verse above promises, counsels us.

How does the Lord counsel us? He doesn't if we don't ask. If I say, "God's too busy for my sad little hurts and pains," He is too busy. He answers those who come to Him in prayer and who desire His response.

Not only will He hear our cries, but when we ask He will instruct us in the night. Before I'd ever read this verse, I taught my leadership classes to "Give your brain an assignment." Before going to sleep at night, I told them, review for the Lord what you are facing tomorrow, what questions you need answered, and what creative ideas you must compose. I always keep pen and paper by my bed so that when ideas pop into my head as I awaken I will be able to jot them down quickly. I've learned that even a short walk to the bathroom may cause fledgling ideas to take flight. I pray for new message outlines, for verses to validate a thought, or for solutions to relationship problems. When I awaken, there is my answer!

How about You?

Are you a no-good-thing-in-me martyr-type Christian? It grieves God to think He created such sad souls when He so much wants confident Christians who joyfully follow His will. Brighten up and thank Him that in His power you are just a little lower than the angels. You are somebody.

To move on in your spiritual growth, start giving your brain an assignment at night and grabbing hold of it quickly in the morning. Jot down what the Lord tells you, and when you feel a little aloof from the Lord, reread the messages He's already given you. Move from "no good thing" to "a new good thing" every day.

As a couple, pray together before going to sleep. Ask the Lord to counsel you in the night. Give your brain an assignment. Pray in faith, knowing that God can work in your minds all night. Remember your bodies are tired, but your minds didn't do that much all day. Scientists have proven we use only 10 percent of our brain potential, so we can rely on the 90 percent that's been resting to perk up in the night and get moving. Once we realize this possibility we can use this untapped mental resource. So together begin a new spiritual program that promises rewarding results. Ask the Lord to activate your dormant abilities, then give your brain an assignment and wake up with a creative plan and answer. Write the message down quickly and praise the Lord that He is never too busy to counsel you in the night.

Suggested Prayer for Today

Lord Jesus, this is a new idea to us, and yet we see that Your Word tells us You are with us in the night. As our hearts pump twenty-four hours a day so our brains are available for round-the-clock instruction. Today, Lord, we each have a question. We will put them before you separately tonight and await Your work in our minds. We don't do this as a test of faith but as additional growth in our spiritual lives. We pray, believing in God the Father and Jesus the Son. Amen.

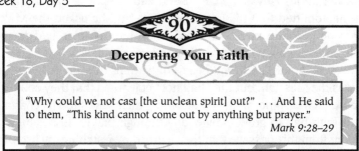

90

Deepening Your Faith

"Why could we not cast [the unclean spirit] out?" . . . And He said to them, "This kind cannot come out by anything but prayer."

Mark 9:28–29

Fred

When Jesus came down from the Mount of Transfiguration with Peter, James, and John, they saw a large crowd gathered around and arguing with the other disciples. When Jesus asked what they were discussing one of the men said to Him, "Teacher, I brought You my son, possessed with a spirit which makes him mute; . . . it dashes him to the ground and he foams at the mouth, and grinds his teeth, and stiffens out. I told your disciples to cast it out, and they could not do it."

Jesus answered, "Bring him to me. . . . How long has this been happening to him?"

The father answered, "From childhood. It has often thrown him both into the fire and into the water to destroy him. But if You can do anything, take pity on us and help us!"

Jesus said to him, "If you can! All things are possible to him who believes."

The boy's father cried out, "I do believe; help my unbelief." Then Jesus rebuked the spirit, and it came out of him.[1]

The disciples who had tried unsuccessfully to remove the "unclean spirit" later asked Jesus privately, "Why could we not cast it out?"

Jesus answered them, "This kind cannot come out by anything but prayer."

What did Jesus mean? Why were the disciples unable to remove this spirit? The answer may be found in the response of the boy's father: "I do believe; help my unbelief." The father had faith. He did believe that Jesus was the Christ and had the power and authority. But he admitted that his faith was weak, and he asked the Master to strengthen him in his unbelief. The nine disciples had not yet realized that walking with Jesus was not enough.

They had faith, and they believed, perhaps in a limited way that he was the Messiah, but they had not yet learned that they could not operate in the spiritual just by attaching themselves to His coattails! Their faith had to grow individually through prayer. It is somewhat evident from this passage that they learned by watching, by listening, and by associating. Now Jesus was telling them that in order to do greater works, to better understand the fullness of God and in order for their faith to grow, there was only one thing needed: PRAYER!

How about You?

You have faith. You believe. But are you by any chance expecting your faith to grow merely by association? Are you expecting to grow spiritually as a result of your partner's prayers and relationship with the Lord? Are you expecting deeper faith from your regular attendance at church, from serving on church boards? Are you perhaps relying on your association with the Lord Jesus for your marriage to be blessed and fulfilled?

Jesus is telling you that those annoying and frustrating specters that interfere with the harmony and oneness that is God's design for the two of you together can only be understood, dealt with, and confessed through prayer. These things "cannot come out by anything but prayer."

There is no shortcut, no substitute, for your regular and committed time of communion with your Savior. Only He has the power to make lasting changes in you. These changes are gradual but will also be a certainty. They do not come by osmosis or by association! They come by an act of your will to spend personal and priority time with the Savior. And only when there are lasting changes in you first will there be lasting changes and strong growth in your love for each other. "Now that you know this truth, how happy you will be if you put it into practice."[2]

Suggested Prayer for Today

Dear Lord Jesus, I desire to do those greater works that You speak of, but even more I desire that those greater works be manifested in my marriage, in the uniting of our two hearts into one. Is this really possible, Lord? Can two separate and distinct personalities who sometimes don't even enjoy living together actually have this kind of harmony? Your Word tells me it is not only possible but that it is Your will for our marriage. I, for one, Lord, want that kind of peace and oneness in our relationship. I am willing to do whatever it takes to iron out every last wrinkle that is undermining our love for each other. Lord Jesus, I pray for the same love for [my mate] as You have for me. Help me, O Lord, to see him/her in the same way that You see each of us: imperfect, growing, and worthy of Your full, unconditional love. I thank You, Lord Jesus, for hearing my prayer that I ask in Your Name. Amen.

His Power over satan

> Behold! I have given you authority and power to trample upon serpents [satan] and scorpions [evil spirits] and . . . over all the power that the enemy [possesses], and nothing shall in any way harm You.
>
> *Luke 10:19* AMP

Fred

One of the best-kept secrets in Christendom is that you and I, because we are Christians, have power and authority exceeding the power of satan. Survey twenty Christians, asking each one individually, "Do you believe in the existence of satan or the devil? Do you believe that he has power?" Chances are that nineteen will give you an unequivocal yes, and the twentieth will at least acknowledge his existence.

Next ask, "Do you think that you as an individual have power and authority that is greater than his? Do you know how to use your authority over him? Have you ever used it?" Many will answer no. But as Christians we do have that awesome power!

The simple truth is that satan—the prince of darkness, lucifer, the devil, or whatever name you wish to use—has already exerted his controlling influence over many unsuspecting Christians. As a result they feel spiritually powerless, ineffective, and defeated. Marriages flounder on foundations of distrust, displeasure, and distemper.

It need not be so! We have nothing to fear in satan! Fear comes only when we become slothful and lazy. The Lord Jesus has already given to us His power and authority over satan. All we have to do is claim and use the power that is ours by inheritance. Why fear someone over whom you can have immediate control and supremacy? When we move forward against him in the name of the Lord Jesus Christ with determination, poise, and conviction, the Bible tells us he will flee! He has no choice. He must obey you.

The most valuable and important weapon God has given us—the weapon of rebuking, binding, and banishing satan—is too seldom used. How often do you personally exercise your God-given authority over satan? If you are like most Christians, the answer is "Seldom, if ever." Try it! You will be thrilled and strengthened at the changes that will take place in your life, your marriage, and your family when you begin to throw your spiritual weight and authority around.

Today's Scripture is an amazing empowerment that is often overlooked. Simply stated, you and I as Christians have already been given Jesus' power over satan, demonic forces, evil spirits, and over "all the power that the enemy possesses." In our own name or power we have absolutely no authority over satan. But the moment we invoke the name of Jesus, satan becomes defenseless, and attacking evil spirits have no choice but to obey. Taking authority over satan should always be done aloud. But you do not need to shout. Your authority is not increased by volume; your authority is in the "Name of the Lord Jesus Christ."

How about You?

Whenever there is strife in your home you can be certain that satan or his spirit servants are attacking. God is not the author of discord! Whenever you burst out in anger, you can know without a doubt your anger is not from the Lord. It is from the enemy. First deal with satan, and then you will be able to calmly trace the roots of your anger. More often than not you will simply find it rooted in selfishness. Other times it may be rooted in unresolved and unhealed longstanding issues.

When you have been in daily prayer communion, you will find that God will give you rapid discernment and recognition of the true source of such disturbances. When satan attacks, strike back immediately! You will be so glad you did. Get in the habit of exercising your authority over satan every single day, whether or not you think he is attacking. You will be building your spiritual "muscles." Use the capitalized portion of today's suggested prayer. I say this out loud each night before Florence and I go to sleep. We both have seen the difference it makes and the peace it brings.

Suggested Prayer for Today

Dear Lord Jesus, I thank You that on the cross You defeated satan, that he is a defeated foe. I thank You, Lord, for giving to me your power and authority over him. In your Name Lord, I now exercise that authority that You have already given to me:

IN THE NAME OF THE LORD JESUS CHRIST, I TAKE AUTHORITY OVER YOU, SATAN! I REBUKE YOU, I BIND YOU, I BANISH YOU! I COMMAND YOU TO LEAVE THIS PLACE. I COMMAND YOU TO LEAVE ME. YOU ARE NOT PERMITTED TO INTERFERE IN MY LIFE. IN THE NAME OF THE LORD JESUS CHRIST, SATAN, I COMMAND YOU AND ALL YOUR EVIL SPIRITS TO BE GONE! BE GONE FROM HERE!

Lord Jesus, I thank You for giving to me Your power over satan. Lord Jesus, I praise You, I thank You, I worship You. Amen.

92

The Taste Test

> How sweet are Your words to my taste, sweeter than honey to my mouth! . . . Your word is a lamp to my feet and a light for my path.
>
> *Psalm 119:103, 105 NIV*

Florence

Is it possible to taste God's Word and to find His personal messages for us to be sweeter than honey? To find that answer we have to take a few bites and find out. As we talk with Christian couples we find many are on a spiritual diet. They are believers in what they know of God's Word, but they don't eat much of it. We know it's not because they can't, but that the pressures of the world keep them too busy, and reading the Bible seems so far down on the priority list.

You are probably not one of them, but let's assume you are. Let's start with the premise that you're busy, you think you couldn't understand the Bible, it wouldn't apply to you personally, and even if you wanted to study, where would you start? Let's pretend at least one of these thoughts has gone through your mind or the mind of a friend of yours who needs God's help and instruction. Let's make it easy to answer these queries.

1. You're too busy. These lessons generally won't take more than five minutes a day to read. Then, if you wish to personalize them and think about the application to your own life, it will add whatever time you want to take. Hopefully, you will look at these lessons together and discuss their meaning.

2. You don't think you'll understand the Bible. We have already pulled the meaning out of the passages presented and we've developed explanations that bring to life these characters of ancient Bible times. This doesn't mean you can't find different or additional truths that apply to the same passages of scripture. No

one has the definitive interpretation of God's Word without the possibility of someone else seeing another message in the same Scripture passage.

3. You don't think Scripture will mean much to you personally. If you don't get into the Word of God, of course you won't be touched by it. Similarly, if you go to the doctor and are handed a prescription for medication that will heal your illness, but you don't take it, you won't feel any different. We have to taste the Word to find it sweet. In the sections of Scripture we have selected for this series of readings, we have applied them to your life as a couple and challenged you to personalize them for your marriage. Even though some of them, like the psalm that appears at the beginning of today's lesson, are not specifically on marriage, but they will open you up to make changes in your attitudes and behavior.

4. I don't know where to start. When I first studied the Bible I started in Matthew. I knew I couldn't understand the Old Testament, plus as a new Christian, I wanted to get right into the teachings of the Master. Soon I was conducting Bible studies in the Women's Club where I was the president. I assigned myself to teach on the characters in the Old Testament to force myself to study them. I got so excited as I "tasted" these stories and found them sweet. I hope you'll feel the same excitement as we look at some of these Old Testament heroes, not just as history or biography, but as human beings like us who knew God but still made mistakes.

As we look at specific passages, we would suggest that you take whatever time you can spare to read the Scripture verses before and after the prescribed section to see what additional truth the Lord will show you individually and as a couple.

Not only did the psalmist tell us that God's Word is sweeter than honey, but that it is a lamp, a light upon our path of life. In those days without paved roads and streetlights, people who had to walk outside at night put tiny lamps on their feet to light their paths. So when this verse talks about "a lamp to my feet and a light for my path," the symbolism was closer to actual practice than it is for us today; however, the idea that God's Word will light up our lives should give us a lift. As we are exposed to the light of God's Word, our days become brighter. As we apply Scripture to our cloudy and confused thinking, the haze should disappear.

How about You?

Are you willing to study these Old Testament stories and search for the truth within the words? Are you willing to eat of God's Word on your spiritual menu and find it sweeter than honey?

Be willing to expose your thoughts to each other and then to the light of the Lord for His examination.

Please don't read these lessons through quickly, although that's better than nothing, but meditate on them and pull out God's application for you both. I hope you will get as excited as I am about tasting God's Word and holding your life up to the lamp of the Lord for His healing touch and hope for the future.

Suggested Prayer for Today

Dear Lord Jesus, we've looked at verses from Your Word before and we've taken tastes here and there, but we are ready now to study some Old Testament sections in hopes we will develop a loving desire to eat of Your Word more and more each day. We ask You to shine a big light on the principles we need to learn and help us to apply these truths to our own lives and not to other people. Lord, we want to wear our dream well and not just settle into the status quo and play pleasant Christian games. Continue to give us the desire to eat whole meals from Your Word as we grow up in our Christian faith. In Your Name we pray. Amen.

93

Request for a King

[The people] said to [Samuel], "You are old and your sons do not walk in your ways; now appoint a king to lead us, such as all the other nations have."

1 Samuel 8:5 NIV

Florence

Many of us spend much of our lives waiting to enter our Promised Land. For us it may be a position, a house, a family; it may be a part of the world we dream of, perhaps Hawaii, Paris, the Riviera. For the Hebrew race the Promised Land was a specific place saved especially for them. God had told Moses where it was and how to get there, yet because of their lack of faith they didn't dare take a chance when they stood facing their dream land. What if the place was full of giants? What if they couldn't trust the Lord? They were a stubborn and rebellious generation. They turned their backs on their Promised Land, and instead of having a homeland to settle in they wandered forty years in the wilderness.

At the time of this verse in 1 Samuel, however, the Hebrew people had crossed the Red Sea and the desert and finally settled in their Promised Land. They were now established in their homeland as stubborn people who refused to do God's will and as rebellious people who wanted to throw off all control.

They came to Samuel, their God-appointed judge, and asked for a king. Samuel pointed out that they didn't need a king, that they had God, their Father who had brought them safely to the land of promise. Samuel gave them God's testimony of salvation, but they seemed to have forgotten all God had done for them, and they were determined to have their own way.

Even God gave up on them and said to Samuel, "Listen to them and give them a king." (1 Samuel 8:22)

This story of the Hebrew people has been a meaningful one to me personally as it tells me how quickly we forget what God has done for us and how stubbornly we insist on taking back control. We cry out to God in time of desperation, He saves us from our sins and our disobedience, He heals our hurts and our situations, and when the crisis is past we go back to our own ways and have little time for the Lord until the next crisis. Sometimes we need to learn the same lesson over and over because we are stubborn. We refuse to learn what God is trying to teach us.

How about You?

Can you think of any time when you were saved by the Lord as you teetered on the brink of disaster? Was it a financial crisis? Illegal activity? Sexual sin? Temptation? Addiction? Did you say, "If You get me out of this, Lord, I'll be Yours forever. I'll never forget what you've done for me"?

The Hebrews were slaves in Egypt, and God brought them out. He pulled them through the waters to the other side. He gave them a country, and yet after all that, they wanted a human king. They forgot the Lord their God.

Spend time today thinking about what Your Father God has done for you. Have you been grateful, or have you forgotten? Have you continued to praise Him, or have you taken back control? Have you ever called on Him in the first place? Are you one of the stubborn and rebellious who, dragged through the lake of fire, would still refuse to give control to the Lord? If you don't know the answers to these questions, ask the Lord. He knows what we don't, and He's waiting for you to ask. Write to Him today a prayer something like this:

Suggested Prayer for Today

Dear Father God, I think I'm similar to these Hebrew people. I remember today how you saved me from _____. At that time I said I'd never forget, but somehow I got busy and I didn't keep You up-front in my mind. In some situations I thought I knew more than You, and I took back control. I have been stubborn, even rebellious at times. Now I want You in control. I don't need a human leader. Forgive me and keep me under Your protective hand. I pray this in the Name of Jesus. Amen.

Reasons for a King

But the people refused to listen to Samuel. "No!" they said. "We want a king over us. Then we will be like all the other nations, with a king to lead us and to go out before us and fight our battles."

1 Samuel 8:19–20 NIV

Florence

When Samuel said no to the pleas for a king, the Hebrew people persisted, "We want a king!" Then they gave Samuel three reasons why they wanted a king to lead them:

1. *We want to be like other people.* Isn't it amazing how the people in Old Testament times had a "keeping up with the Joneses" mind-set? They wanted to be like the others, only better. They knew other countries had kings, majestic rulers with robes and scepters and even palaces. They wanted to be a great nation with a king, too.

2. *We want a human king that we can see.* Samuel told them that a human king was not necessary. "You have God," he reminded them. Then he warned them that a king would conscript their sons and make their daughters become cooks and bakers. The king would take their money, grain, wine, and cattle. He might make them slaves again. But when Samuel had finished his tale of potential woe, they stubbornly cried out again, "We want a king!" The people wanted a king they could see and touch, a king who would listen to them, hear their problems. "We know we have God, and we've heard His testimony a million times," their attitudes said. "Don't give us any trouble. We want a king."

3. *We want a king with a plan who will fight our battles for us.* Not only did they want to be like others and have a king who

293

could fight for them, but they also wanted a leader with a plan who would go ahead of them, who would part all their Red Seas, as God had done before, and who would fight their battles for them. Their minds were so set on what they wanted that they didn't hear the negatives or the warnings.

When Samuel went back to God and told Him of the people's demands, God said—as we might have done at that time—"So give them a king." In effect, He was saying, "You want a human king, you'll get one and you'll rue the day you ever asked for one."

People are the same today. They want what others have, only better. They want a leader they can look up to who will listen and love them. What he does on his off hours doesn't matter. They want someone who has a plan set in motion and who will, if at all possible, do the work for them.

How about You?

1. Are we something like the Hebrew people? Do we want possessions for ourselves like our friends have—only better? Do we want to have the biggest house or newest car? Do we want to make a statement before others? Do we want to go to the most elegant church where the right people go, with the impressive pastor who's on TV? Would we be happy with Samuel if he came along and told us to forget all that and get our eyes on the Lord?

2. Do we know we have a God and yet feel that He's insufficient? That He's a God "afar-off"? We want a human leader who's nearby and who will care for us, who will listen to our problems, who'll give us a hug when we're down. We don't want a Samuel around, saying, "Watch out! If you get too attached to another person and look to that one to be your spiritual alter ego, you will be disappointed."

3. Do we want someone else to make a plan for our lives? To do the hard work for us? To fight our battles so we won't

have to go to the front? Is Samuel saying to us today, "There's no fairy godmother. There's no knight in shining armor. There's no magic kingdom. Stop looking for some human redeemer, get off the dream couch and get moving. Focus your eyes on the real leader and savior who says, 'I will keep you in perfect peace whose eyes are fixed on Me'"?[1]

When Samuel gave this option to the people—it's God or a fallible human—they chose a king and rejected God. How about us? Are we constantly attaching ourselves to different people in hopes of finding the answers to life?

Suggested Prayer for Today

Dear Father God, we confess we have put too much emphasis on people. We've wanted impressive leaders, people who would listen to our problems, people who would come up with a miracle plan for our lives. We've gone to different churches, pastors, counselors, and friends, and we've been disappointed. None of them had the right answers for us, and now we see we are just like those Hebrew people, stiff-necked and rebellious, wanting answers to life from people who don't have all the answers. Lord, help us to put our eyes on You, the only wise counselor we need, knowing that You will keep us in perfect peace.

And Lord, if You would have us seek counsel for a certain reason, open the right door for us that we might not be controlled by people with wrong motives. Thank You for making us think today and for helping us to readjust our focus. We pray in the precious Name of Jesus. Amen.

Called Out by God

> Then Samuel took a flask of oil and poured it on Saul's head and kissed him, saying, "Has not the LORD anointed you leader over his inheritance?"
>
> *1 Samuel 10:1 NIV*

Florence

Once Samuel was convinced the people were adamant about a king and God had said to give them one if that's what they wanted, the question was, Who should that king be?

This story of the people asking God for a king reminds me of how many times my children came to me with requests to go places I knew they should not go. I would give them a brilliant rebuttal about how no one in their right mind would want to do this. At my dramatic conclusion they would look at me unimpressed and say, "We want to go anyway."

Has that ever happened to you? How did you react? Did you say, "You'll rue the day you ever said that. You want a party? I'll give you a party you'll never forget." Does that sound familiar?

I'm sure we can understand God the Father's feelings when the people, against all reason, still wanted a king. So God said, in effect, "You want a king? You'll get one, all right!"

God didn't take applications for the position. He didn't go to the local seminary. He chose someone he knew would please the people, not someone who'd been to king school or who was a judge or a prophet. God chose Saul, "an impressive young man without equal among the Israelites—a head taller than any of the others."[1] Saul was stunned when he was called out by God; he thought it was a mistake. "But am I not a Benjamite, from the smallest tribe of Israel?"[2] he asked, apparently thunderstruck by Samuel's choice. Surely he was wondering, *Could I be a leader? Could God want me?*

Each time I think of this selection of an unlikely person to become a godly leader, I am so grateful God doesn't work through committees. Someone would have surely said, "But he doesn't have any credentials," or "He's not been ordained in the right denomination," or "Isn't he just a Benjamite?"

I'm so glad God didn't use a committee when he called out Fred and me. We were good people, but we had no credentials. We weren't ordained in anything. If God had sent a group out to investigate us for kingship, we might have been turned down when people found we had a token marriage and were each running away in different directions from the grief of our two sons' deaths, when they saw Fred owning a night club, Goodtime Charlie's, and found me traveling around the state of Connecticut with young actors raising money for a theater.

When the committee reported on us, they surely would have turned us down. But God didn't. He saw potential in us, leadership potential, and He called us out.

How about You?

Have you ever felt the call of God on your life? Have you heard Him call your name? When the Lord first called Samuel, he was a young man. "Now Samuel did not yet know the LORD: The word of the Lord had not yet been revealed to him."[3] But when Samuel heard the call he said, "Speak, for your servant is listening."[4]

Are you close enough to the Lord in daily devotion and quiet enough before Him to hear His voice? The great excitement of the Christian life begins when we hear the call and say "Here am I, Lord, send me." Don't ever think God doesn't know who you are or where you are. He doesn't need a committee to locate you, and He isn't interested in your degrees or talents. He's always looking for people who will simply say, "Speak, for your servant is listening." Are you listening?

"The LORD was with Samuel as he grew up, and he let none of his words fall to the ground."[5] How I love that verse! Once Samuel heard God's call, none of his words fell to the ground. That is my desire as God has called Fred and me and we have listened—that none of our words would fall to the ground.

Are you like Samuel in his youth? He didn't know the Lord yet. If so, pause right now and ask the Lord to reveal Himself to you. He is waiting to do His will in your life.

Are you ready to say, "Speak, for your servant is listening"? God is calling out willing servants who will listen to His Word. Are you available for the greatest challenge of your life?

Suggested Prayer for Today

Dear Lord, I am available. I am listening for Your words. [Actually stop, pause, . . . and listen.] Here am I. Use me. I realize I don't have what the world considers credentials, but I have a willing spirit and a contrite heart. Cleanse me and use me. Don't let the words of my mouth fall to the ground. I am ready, Lord. I'm listening for Your call. In Your Name I pray. Amen.

Changed by the Spirit

> The Spirit of the LORD will come upon you in power, and you will prophesy with them; and you will be changed into a different person.
>
> *1 Samuel 10:6 NIV*

Florence

Once Saul had been called out by God and anointed by Samuel as the leader of the inheritance, he was sent to meet a procession of prophets. These were not saintly, sad religious people but ones rejoicing in their faith as tambourines, flutes, and harps were being played before them. Saul was to join in the procession, and when he did, Samuel assured him the Spirit of the Lord would come upon him, and he would be changed into a different person. He would even be able to join in the prophesying, something he had never done before.

Imagine the excitement in Saul's heart as he headed toward the prophets. He had never expected in his wildest dreams that he could be a king! Yet here he was, already called out by God and about to be changed by His spirit. As Saul approached the procession, the prophets welcomed him and "the Spirit of God came upon him in power, and he joined in their prophesying."[1] As Saul became part of the parade of prophets, people who had known him looked on in disbelief and their amazed comments filled the air: "Is this Saul?" "Is this our friend who used to stand on the corner with us?" "This can't be our Saul. He never was religious before." "Is Saul really among the prophets?" Those who knew Saul couldn't believe the change. Whatever had happened?

When Fred and I were called out by God, we didn't know what had happened to us. We had given up on God because of the deaths of our sons. We wondered how a loving God could allow bad things like death to happen to good, church-going people like us. We had no aspirations of becoming Christian leaders when we were asked to house the speakers for a small church conference in New Haven, Connecticut. We listened to the couple's testimony and were amazed that it sounded just like our situation. The couple were attractive and well-dressed professional people who had different personalities and who had drifted apart from each other until they no longer cared.

They had each received the Lord Jesus into their lives and had begun studying God's Word. Fred and I had done that already, and we had started going to church again. If we were going to be Christians, we were going to do it right. This couple told how they'd been called out by God to minister to couples just like them and how they'd been changed by the spirit. Now they really liked each other, they said, and they had fun together.

That evening after their message, they came home with us, and we sat up until two in the morning asking them questions. Their conclusion was, "You two could really amount to something for the Lord if you'd get some training."

We didn't know what "training" was.

"Go out to Arrowhead Springs in California and get some training," they told us.

A few months later Hal Lindsey spoke in New Haven, and he stayed in our home also. After listening to him, the same thing happened. We stayed up late seeking counsel, and he said, "You two could really amount to something if you got some training." He made the same suggestion, and we headed to California. It was at that Lay Institute for Evangelism that Fred and I were called out by God and changed by the spirit. We returned as new people, and just as Saul's acquaintances said, our friends queried, "Are these the same Littauers? The ones who had the nightclub? What has happened? Did they get religion?"

How about You?

Have you heard the call of God in your life? Have you sensed that difference in your attitudes since you were changed by the Spirit?

Can you see your own or your mate's changes? Do people see a difference in you? Do they wonder where this change came from?

If you don't feel confident in your answers, perhaps you should stop and talk together about your commitment to the Lord. Have you been sincere? Have you prayed and asked the Lord for changes, specific changes in your life and in your marriage? Don't go on one more day insecure as to your status with the Lord. As He sees your heart and your sincere desire, He will respond. Be open to the call of God, and be willing to be changed by the Spirit.

Suggested Prayer for Today

Dear Lord Jesus, our Savior, we want to be in Your will and to know Your power in a personal way. We don't want to be average Christians. We want to be leaders in whatever way You desire. We want Your plan for our lives. We want to be listeners through Your Word that we can hear when You call. We want to be called out by God and changed by His Spirit. We want people to see a positive change in us so they will recognize Your power. We pray in Your precious Name. Amen.

Chosen by the People

> When Samuel brought all the tribes of Israel near, the tribe of Benjamin was chosen. Then he brought forward the tribe of Benjamin, clan by clan, and Matri's clan was chosen. Finally Saul son of Kish was chosen.
> *1 Samuel 10:20–21 NIV*

Florence

After the people's demand for a king, Saul was called out by God and changed by the Spirit. It was then time for him to be chosen by the people. Samuel brought all the tribes forth and the name of Saul was chosen, but when they called out for him, he was nowhere to be seen. They asked the Lord where to find him, and the Lord said, "He has hidden himself among the baggage."[1] And so he had.

Saul knew in his heart that he was not qualified to be a king. But in the excitement of the moment, he had agreed. He felt the call of God on his life and knew he'd been changed by the Spirit and had prophesied with the prophets, but it was all so new to him. When he saw the crowds waiting for him to present himself as king he was gripped with fear, and like a child he ran and hid. When they found him and brought him out, he stood a head taller than all the rest.

As Saul stood before the people for their approval and acceptance, Samuel said, "Do you see the man the LORD has chosen? There is no one like him among all the people." Saul reflected the image of what the people desired for their leader, and they shouted, "Long live the king!"[2]

Isn't it amazing that those Old Testament people were so much like us today? We want a leader who looks like a leader, walks like a leader, and acts like a leader. The looks, charm, wit—the outer man is what we look for. If our leaders can smile, give a quick answer, and apologize for minor failures, we as a nation will love them. Little thought or concern goes into their moral values any longer. It's what's up-front that counts.

How about You?

There are several personal lessons for us in this Scripture passage. One is to think about how we choose our leaders and to pray for a return of morality to our government. A second reason is to think about what the people would receive if they chose leaders for their leadership abilities, for their strength of character to stand up for what they believe even when it's not popular.

Third, do we realize that God is still calling people out, and could He be calling us? As God did with Saul, He calls people to be leaders, and they aren't all spiritual giants. He sees the experiences they've been through, and He calls them to give hope to others in similar situations. Fred and I were called out by God from our civic leadership roles, and we were clearly changed by the Spirit—people saw the change even though they didn't understand it. And then we were chosen by the people to teach Bible studies and the personalities. You can't be a leader for long if the people don't want you.

Are you open to being used of the Lord in a leadership role? I can't choose a position for you, but I do know from years of experience that our Father God is ready to call you out at any moment. In my years of training leaders I have seen the Lord put His hand on the unlikeliest of people, change them by His Spirit, equip them for a unique position, and then send them forth to be accepted by the people. I never discount the power of the Lord to select and change those He wishes to use. My job has been to lead people to a point where they can hear God's voice and then to equip those who have heard the call.

Do we all need to become theologians? Do we have to give up all our goods and give them to the poor? Do we all need to become pastors, teachers, and speakers?

Don't worry or fret over what you might become or what God could do with you. "All God's men are ordinary men," Oswald

Chambers said. Ordinary men "made extra-ordinary by the matter He has given them."[3]

God calls those who are listening, and by the power of His Spirit makes them over to conform to what He has in mind, not what we might dream up on our own.

Chambers goes on to say, "When God has put His call on you, woe be to you if you turn to the right hand or to the left. He will do with you what He never did with you before the call came; He will do with you what He is not doing with other people. Let Him have His way."

Are you ready, willing, and listening for His voice?

Suggested Prayer for Today

Dear Lord Jesus, I've not ever thought of myself as a leader. I haven't thought I had the right qualifications, and yet neither did Saul, and You called him out to be the first king of Israel. I know there are no vacancies for kings available, but You are the King and are forever calling out new leaders to bless Your needy people. Lord, I don't know what You want with me, but I'm willing to share my dream with others. I'm listening to You, and I'm waiting for Your direction in my life. Call me, change me, choose me. In the Name of Jesus. Amen.

Committed to Obedience

> Now here is the king you have chosen, the one you asked for; see, the LORD has set a king over you. . . . But if you do not obey the LORD, and if you rebel against His commands, His hand will be against you, as it was against your fathers. *1 Samuel 12:13–15 NIV*

Florence

Once God has called His leaders out and has placed them in positions of some authority, He expects them to be committed to obedience and to remember who it was that placed them there. Once Saul had been appointed and anointed, Samuel brought him before the people and explained to them all their responsibilities. He was duty bound to let them know a kingdom was not just business as usual. They all had to realize what they'd asked for and be willing to support their choices. He told them to "stand still and see this great thing the LORD is about to do before your eyes!"[1]

Samuel then pointed out that they had demanded a king because they didn't want God to be their leader any longer. They wanted someone nearby and not far-off to show them what an evil thing they had done. Samuel called upon the Lord to bring a storm, a feat that Saul, their chosen king, could not do. As they stood there in awe, the rains came, the thunder clapped, and they all cried out, "Don't let us die!"

Isn't it amazing how easily we discount the Lord's power and turn to human leaders for our inspiration? We so easily forget who sent us and who holds control of the rain and the thunder—and of our lives. The people didn't see their desire for a king as a rejection of God, but Samuel made it clear. God is still on the throne.

As they cried out for forgiveness, Samuel assured the people God would not take spite against them "because the Lord was pleased to make you his own."[2] But Samuel did instruct the people to continue to fear the Lord, to serve Him faithfully, and to remember what He had done for them.

The people and their king made new commitments to the Lord to live in obedience to His commands and to remember who has the power to control the winds and the rains.

Saul stood before his people, tall and handsome and only thirty years old, ready to take on the challenges of a kingdom. He'd been called out by God, changed by the Spirit, chosen by his people, and now was committed to obedience. Could anything possibly go wrong?

How about You?

Certainly the tale of the first king of Israel is fairy-tale material. Out of the blue a person is plucked up and seated on a throne to become king of Israel. I always wanted to be a queen. I dreamed of the royal life in a castle and felt my childhood was my Cinderella period. As we daydream of such opportunities, what many of us don't realize in our youthful zeal is that with leadership comes responsibility. CEOs don't sit in big offices because they are tall and handsome but because they've accepted responsibility and have produced what the people wanted.

Samuel didn't just say, "Here's your king . . . Good luck!" He stayed to point out the mutual obedience to God that would bring results and the evil that would fall upon them if they failed to heed God's Word.

We don't have a single Samuel standing before us in the Christian community today, telling us of impending doom if we go astray, and yet it's easy for us to see on our own the rampant immorality and the rejection of God that is leading us all in a humanly hopeless path of destruction. But is all lost? Only if we give up on the God who controls the universe.

Samuel gave words of encouragement for our future: "Be sure to fear the Lord and serve Him faithfully with all your heart; consider what great things He has done for you."[3] What great things has He done for you? Do you keep His gifts to you laid out where you can see them? Do you hold our God in awe and respect and want to serve Him faithfully? Or do you sometimes think you've done it all yourself? So many Christian leaders who started out so grateful for what the Lord had done for them forgot Him when they reached the top and took the credit for their achievements.

Suggested Prayer for Today

Dear Lord Jesus, keep us humble as Saul was in the beginning. Keep us remembering that without You we are nothing. We may look good and stand tall, but we know we can't make it alone. As you bring the thunder and the rain, so You can cause the storms to dampen our lives and ruin our plans when we turn our eyes from You. We confess it's easy to take back control when times get tough and to take the credit when times are at their best. May this lesson of Saul teach us to look daily at what You've done for us and not forget from whence we came. We bless You and praise You, in Jesus' Name. Amen.

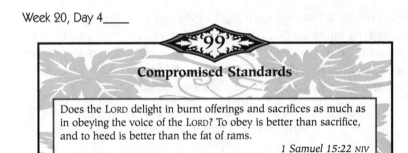

99

Compromised Standards

> Does the LORD delight in burnt offerings and sacrifices as much as in obeying the voice of the LORD? To obey is better than sacrifice, and to heed is better than the fat of rams.
>
> *1 Samuel 15:22 NIV*

Florence

I sometimes feel sorry for Saul. He was put in a position he didn't ask for and was given no on-the-job training. As those of us who are of the Choleric personality would do, he probably determined that if he was the king, he would be the very best king any country had ever had. His only guidelines for the king position were to obey the Lord God and to remember who put him in this new career.

Samuel started the program by telling Saul to stay in Gilgal for seven days, then Samuel would arrive and offer up a sacrifice before the start of a battle. For us it would be like a time of communal prayer with a certain need in mind. But at the end of the seven days Samuel had not arrived, so Saul took things into his own hands. The troops were getting edgy and starting to leave, so Saul made a human judgment: Why don't I do the sacrifice? As the king he felt he had the right to perform this ceremony, and so he did. This was not a bad thing to do; it was a religious offering to the Lord. The wrong part was he had been told to wait until Samuel arrived.

Saul had hardly finished when Samuel appeared and asked, "What have you done?" Saul explained how he needed the Lord's blessing on his battle and the troops were scattering and in his words, "I felt compelled to offer the burnt offering."[1]

When I look back on mistakes I've made I realize that any time I had a compulsion to do something, a compulsion that didn't come from the Lord, the results were a disaster. A compulsion is usually a temptation from the evil one disguised as good works.

Once Saul had explained his reasons for his actions, he expected to be forgiven. However, Samuel said, "You have acted foolishly. You have not kept the command the LORD your God gave you; if you had, he would have established your kingdom over Israel for all time."[2]

Saul had disobeyed.

His second failure came when Saul brought back booty from his battles with the Amalekites. Samuel had warned him to kill all the people and the animals and bring nothing back. But when Saul saw how much there was available to the victor, he spared King Agag and brought back the best of all the sheep and cattle. Again, this was not a bad action since Saul had won the battle, but it was exactly opposite of the command Samuel had given. The Lord spoke directly to Samuel and said, "I am grieved that I have made Saul king, because he has turned away from me and has not carried out my instructions."[3]

Saul was greedy.

The next day a saddened Samuel went to meet with Saul and learned that he had gone to Carmel to build himself a monument. It had not taken Saul long to forget who made him king.

Saul was impressed with himself.

When confronted about his failures, Saul said he was sorry but, "I was afraid of the people and so I gave in to them."[4]

Saul blamed the people.

Samuel explained that offering sacrifices, winning battles, building monuments, and trying to please the people were all worthy aims and activities, but none of them were what the Lord had commanded. "To obey is better than sacrifice," Samuel pointed out. "To heed is better than the fat of the rams."[5]

How about You?

How many times have we done things that weren't bad but weren't what the Lord wanted us to do? How many times have we felt compelled to do something, perhaps something that even sounded religious, and yet knew it wasn't God's will? How many times have we accepted credit for something we didn't do or in some subtle way built a monument to ourselves? And how many times when we were caught in our tricks, our lies, our mistakes, did we find a way to blame other people?

Isn't Saul a perfect example of a well-meaning believer who somehow compromised the standards as set forth by God Himself? From here on when we're not sure, we need to pause and ask the Lord, "Is this what You want me to do?" Religious rites and attendance at services do not take precedence over the Lord's will of the moment. We can't use church as an excuse for not performing the duties the Lord has assigned us. Obedience is better than sacrifice.

Suggested Prayer for Today

Oh Lord Jesus, how easy it is for me to do good works when You are calling us to obey a different plan. How easy to make excuses as to why it's not my fault. How easy to rationalize why anyone would have done what I did. Lord, forgive us our narrow focus; forgive us our self-centered nature. Lord, we know You have given us all we have and if we needed more You'd gladly give us a bonus, and yet so often we think we've done it all alone. In spite of all our mistakes You don't reject us, for You love us more than we have ever loved You. Dear Lord, we come before You in repentance and ask Your forgiveness and Your grace even though we haven't earned it. We thank You and praise You in the Name of Jesus. Amen.

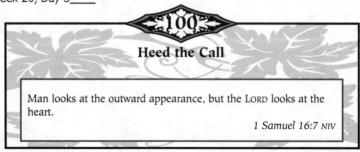

100

Heed the Call

Man looks at the outward appearance, but the LORD looks at the heart.

1 Samuel 16:7 NIV

Florence

Once the Lord God had decided to remove his blessing from Saul, He told Samuel to go and find a new candidate for a future king. "Fill your horn with oil and be on your way. I am sending you to Jesse of Bethlehem. I have chosen one of his sons to be king."[1]

Carrying the horn of anointing oil with him, Samuel went to Jesse's home and asked to see his sons. When he looked at Eliab, he knew this must be the one. He reminded Samuel of Saul's handsome face and impressive physique. *Surely, he is the Lord's anointed,* Samuel thought. But just as Samuel was thinking this, the Lord spoke to him: "Do not consider his appearance or his height, for I have rejected him. The LORD does not look at the things man looks at. Man looks at the outward appearance, but the LORD looks at the heart."[2]

From that point on Samuel made no judgments without first looking to the Lord for His selection. As seven sons passed before Samuel, the Lord gave no indication that He had a choice. Samuel wondered if he had misread the Lord's comments, and he asked Jesse, "Are these all the sons you have?'

"Well, there is still the youngest," Jesse answered, "but he is tending the sheep."

Samuel said, "Send for him; we will not sit down until he arrives."[3]

Can you imagine how Samuel felt as he sat there waiting for the youngest son to come in from the fields? Here he'd come all this way at his old age and had looked over seven sons with no word of affirmation from the Lord. _What if this young one isn't right either? Then where do I turn?_ he must have worried.

Once Samuel saw David he knew this was the Lord's choice. David was handsome and tanned from his days in the field. Although he was young he had an air of confidence about him, and Samuel liked him instantly.

The Lord spoke clearly to Samuel, "Rise and anoint him; he is the one."[4]

David did not know what he was chosen for, but he stood as Samuel poured on his head the oil from the horn. The Scripture tells us that the Spirit of the Lord came upon David with power and at the same time the Spirit of the Lord was removed from Saul. The power he'd been given to be king was taken from him, although the Lord allowed Saul to continue to reign for forty-two years.

As I have studied this Scripture passage I have realized that even though we always want to look our best on the outside, the Lord is searching straight into our hearts. He looks where man can't see, and He knows what we are really like inside.

I've also found that God gives a special power from His Spirit to the leaders he has selected. When we fail Him and stray from the course He has prepared, when we take things into our own hands, when we build monuments to ourselves and blame others, He gives us time to repent. But if we don't, if we continue down an ego path, He ultimately pulls this extra power away from us, and we fall right off the pedestal.

Many of the most recent fallen Christian leaders are ones I have known personally. They were each called out by God to fill a very special purpose. They were changed by the Spirit, and each one had a genuine testimony. They were chosen by the people. Television viewers and church congregations worshiped them and gave them large donations. They were initially committed to obedience. They started out with pure motives.

What happened? Along the line they compromised their standards. They decided the rules weren't for them. Some got greedy, some built monuments, buildings, colleges, ministries in their own names, some were involved in financial mismanagement, and some fell into sexual sin. In each case the Lord gave them time to repent. Some did repent and were restored. Some blamed others when the truth was exposed.

God still controls the power. He gives it and He takes it, and there's nothing more pitiful to observe than a preacher who's lost his power and is still trying to preach.

How about You?

What lesson does this have for each one of us who might be called to leadership? What can we all learn from Saul's story? Saul was tall, handsome, and impressive; he could have run for president, and we would have elected him. Saul was young, inexperienced, and needing the Lord, but somehow he forgot the source of his power and lived a troubled life to the very end. May we be spared the fate of Saul.

Suggested Prayer for Today

Oh Lord, teach us to look on the inside and not be fooled by slick packaging. Lord, teach us to be discerning and to know Your true servants from those masquerading as angels of light. Lord, help me to keep my eyes focused on You and not on other people. Help me to always remember where the power comes from and not to think it originates with me. Keep me from building monuments to myself and compromising my standards. Lord Jesus, I want to be an earthly representative for You. I want people to look at me and see You. I want people to be drawn to the saving power of Jesus Christ to change lives. I'm ready to be called out by God, changed by His Spirit, chosen by the people, and committed to obedience. In Jesus' Name, I pray. Amen.

Heed the call; don't fall like Saul!

◄❖101❖►

How Good People Get into Trouble

We all, like sheep, have gone astray, each of us has turned to his own way.

Isaiah 53:6 KJV

Florence

When I present the story of David before a group, I start by asking, "How many of you here are good people?" Almost every hand goes up. Then, "Keep your hand up if you are a good person who has at some time gotten yourself into trouble." More hands go up amid groans and laughs. "I see some of you have gotten into trouble who aren't even good," I tease.

It's an amazing part of human nature that we're more apt to admit that we've been a little bit bad than to raise our hands for being good. Yet we as Christian people do feel we're basically good, but we also know we should be humble, so we shouldn't, at least publicly, be thinking well of ourselves.

Let's assume right now that we are good people. We don't even have to be great; good is good enough. Wherever we stand on the goodness scale, let's think about any trouble we've gotten ourselves into. Not the "natural disaster" type of trouble where the roof fell in or the crops failed or floods washed our homes away but the kind of troubles where we really knew better but got involved anyway. For those few of you who are so very, very good that you've never stepped over God's line in the sand, have fun with these following lessons anyway and keep thanking God that you "are not like other men."[1]

I've learned that God never wastes our time or His Word. If He gives us a particular directive that isn't applicable to our own lives at that moment, within twenty-four hours He will send us a person who does needs this help. We have had individuals take this material and teach it to teenagers with startling results, and some have used the story of David in marriage classes. Start first by applying these challenges to yourselves individually, then as a couple, and when you have talked it through, use the principles with your teenagers—not in a preachy way but as amazing truth from God's Word. Let them know that it is human nature to be like sheep and go astray, to want to do your own thing, but that all bad decisions bear responsibility and consequences. David never set out to get in trouble, but by putting himself in a position of temptation, he fell. Forbidden fruit may be the sweetest, but we have to live with the aftertaste a long time.

We've already ingested the lessons of Saul, a good man who wasn't looking for trouble but who was open to the temptations that go with leadership and power. He disobeyed God's clearly stated Word, he got greedy when presented with available booty, he built monuments to himself when he forgot it was God who made him king, and when he was confronted with his sin he blamed the people, insisting, "I was just trying to keep the people happy."

These mistakes may not seem high on the sin scale, but God isn't checking to see how bad we are but whether or not we are obeying what we know God wants from each one of us. How do we know? When we are in tune with the Lord, He deals with our consciences, and He nudges us before we get into trouble. He customizes our restrictions. What's not right for me might be permissible for you.

When Fred and I were new believing Christians and didn't even know God could speak to us, we were sitting at the country club one Saturday evening. It was the monthly formal dance, and we were really dressed up! This country club and the people in it were very important to us as we were founding members and had been instrumental in the planning and decorating.

That night as I sat next to a wealthy man with whom I was highly impressed, I realized for the first time that he was a drunk. Now I knew he drank, but I'd never seen him as he really was, a slobbering, repulsive drunk. It was as if a veil had been removed, and I saw an unpleasant truth before me. As he pawed at my arm and tried to kiss me, the thought went through my head, *What are you doing here?*

I looked around and realized I had no real attachment to any of these people although I knew them well. On the way home I said to Fred, "Do you know what thought went through my head tonight?"

Before I could tell him, he said, "Let me tell you first. As I looked around at our friends tonight, it came to my mind, *Fred, what are you doing here?*"

We look back in amazement at how the Lord said the same thing to each of us at the same time. We never went back to the country club again, and to this day no one seems to have missed us. This lesson to us does not mean that *you* shouldn't belong to a country club, but it was very clear that *we* shouldn't.

We are God's good people, and when we listen and respond to Him, He will keep us out of trouble.

Suggested Prayer for Today

Lord Jesus, we so easily go on our own way without thinking of Your will for our lives. We are those well-meaning sheep who somehow go astray. Lord, give us the mental alertness to sense potential trouble and not enter in where we shouldn't be. Help us to be examples to our children of what real Christians are like. Let them see us practice what we preach. Thank You, Lord, that You are always with us no matter where we go. Thank You for constantly watching over our thoughts and deeds. We praise You for Your loving care of us and pray for our willingness to listen. In the powerful Name of Jesus, we pray. Amen and Amen.

Making Poor Choices

> And it came to pass, after the year was expired, at the time when kings go forth to battle, that David sent Joab, and his servants with him, and all Israel. . . . But David tarried still at Jerusalem.
>
> *1 Samuel 11:1 KJV*

Florence

David was a good person. Even people who have never opened a Bible know about David. They know that when he was but a lad he volunteered to kill a giant when adult soldiers were too afraid to try, and soon Goliath lay dead on the ground.

We know, beyond that, he had faith in God and was sure that the God who protected him from the wild beasts out in the fields with the sheep could also guide him into killing Goliath with only one stone. We know David had overcome any feelings of rejection caused by his family's forgetting him as he tended the sheep. He looked upon his isolation as God's provision for his life at that time.

We know David had rugged good looks, because when he walked down Main Street next to Saul, the tall and handsome king, the women only had eyes for David. They would call out to him and throw rose petals in his path.

We know David had musical talent. He played the harp so beautifully that when Saul was depressed he called on David to play the harp and comfort him. Saul didn't need happiness pills when he had David. We also know David as a poet, a psalmist, and a songwriter. He worshiped the Lord in music and in words, and David could hear God's voice. As he matured David became an able administrator, a military leader, a spiritual giant, and at God's choosing, the king. David wasn't just a good person. Scripture tells us that David was a man after God's own heart!

When we examine the positive attributes of David we can see an exceptional man. Who among us could amass all of David's strengths? How then could God's favorite son, a good person, possibly get into trouble? Let's look at 1 Samuel 11.

It was spring, the time of year when all kings had to check their boundaries and make sure there had been no unseen invasions. It was the time of year when good kings went to battle. Since we know David was a good king who understood the rules, we have assurance that David would go to battle and once more lead his men to victory. However, the verse describing the army's departure from the city has a "but." A "but" in a sentence is like a wall constructed between the first and second part. It says, "No matter what you just read there is a contradiction here." "David sent Joab, and his servants . . . , and all Israel; . . . But David tarried still at Jerusalem." What is wrong here? David knew what God and the people expected of him. But he chose not to do it. The first step in getting into trouble is not going where God wants you to go or conversely going where you know you shouldn't be.

How about You?

Very few of us get trapped into trouble. Our woes are usually the results of our making a conscious decision to take a chance and go where we know we shouldn't go.

Have you ever done this? Have you ever been in the wrong place at the wrong time? Have you ever taken a careless risk and been caught?

As our children were growing up, we taught them a simple statement, "If in doubt, don't!" We tried to show them how to make value judgments on their own, how to consider, *Would God be happy with my choice? Would my parents be thrilled to find me here?* One night when our teenage son first had his driver's license, he went out to do what was the relatively harmless Friday night activity for the local teens: go "cruisin' E Street." Shortly after midnight he came into our bedroom and woke me up. "I thought you would like to know that something you said made sense," he said.

Some mothers die without ever hearing those words. I sat right up and said, "Tell me about it."

He then explained that while cruisin' E Street a friend had called over to him. "There's a party at Mike's house. I'll meet you there." He drove over to Mike's, parked the car, and walked up the steps and across the front porch. "As I went to open the door," he said, "it was as if I heard your voice say, 'If in doubt, don't.' I was in doubt. I didn't know what was going on in there. I stood for a moment and kept hearing your voice. I turned and went back down the steps and to my car. As I was driving down the street, police cars drove up. They raided the place and found drugs. I just thought you'd like to know while you are comfortably in your bed my friends' mothers are all down at the police station bailing them out."

Sometimes God speaks in a mother's voice: "If in doubt, don't."

Think today about the times as a youth that you got in trouble. Share these experiences with each other. Were there times when you were in doubt and didn't go somewhere that could have led to trouble? Were you a believing Christian as a teen? Did that make a difference? Are you teaching your children to make value judgments? Do they understand, "If in doubt, don't"?

Suggested Prayer for Today

Dear Lord Jesus, we have made mistakes; we have been in the wrong place at the wrong time. We have talked over these mistakes together and agreed to be more careful in the future. We want our children to see us as examples of people who make right choices. Help us to teach them "If in doubt, don't" without being preachy. We see that the first step to getting into trouble is being somewhere you don't want us to be. We love You and pray in Your Name. Amen.

Get Tempted

> And it came to pass in an eventide, that David arose from off his bed, and walked upon the roof of the king's house: and from the roof he saw a woman washing herself, and the woman was very beautiful to look upon.
> *1 Samuel 11:2 KJV*

Florence

David had already made a poor choice. He did not go where he knew God and man expected him to be. Perhaps David was like some of us who have taught Sunday school for years. It's time for a new term, and we say, "I've done this long enough. Let the younger ones teach. Send Joab instead."

Because David made this first step into trouble, he was open for temptation. The moment we step out from under God's umbrella of protection and head off into our own direction, satan is right there to display appealing activities before us. David should have been at the front with his men, but instead he was at home. Because he didn't go to work, he wasn't tired and couldn't sleep.

So in the late evening he arose off his bed and went wandering around on his roof. Now if you couldn't sleep, you probably wouldn't go wandering on your roof, but you probably don't have a roof like David's, a flat roof with plants and trees and flowers, a veritable garden. As David was strolling on his roof, he looked over the edge and saw a naked woman taking a bath. Scripture doesn't tell us how this woman dragged the bathtub out on the patio under the floodlights or even why, but it does tell she was there for David to see.

Now, if you men were wandering on your roof because you couldn't sleep, because you weren't tired because you hadn't gone to work, and you looked over and saw a naked lady, you would immediately turn your head the other way and go inside, right? But David didn't do that. Instead he took a good look and saw she was "beautiful to look upon." You can't tell that in a fleeting glance.

It is obvious that David had not been neighborly because he didn't know who this woman was who lived so close to the palace that he could look right down upon her. He had not had any potluck suppers with those stick-on nametags that say, "Hello, I'm David."

How do good people get into trouble? They don't go where they know the Lord wants them to be; therefore, since they are out of God's will, they are open to temptation. We tend to think that satan comes in a red suit with horns and a pitchfork but conversely he comes disguised and beautiful, with temptations custom made for each one of us, for he knows our weaknesses.

How about You?

We looked yesterday at times when we have not been in the right place at the right time or even with the right people. Not one of us is planning to become a bank robber, but if we hang around with bank robbers and go where they go, there's a bigger chance that some day we might rob a bank. If your Christian teens hang around with druggies, there's a likelihood they might someday take drugs themselves. If you men have a female coworker who's home sick in bed and you go to visit her alone, there's more of a chance you'll be tempted than if you hadn't gone or if you'd brought your wife along with you.

When we are in the wrong place under the wrong set of circumstances, we are quickly tempted, and unless we have developed a strong "If in doubt, don't" pattern of response, we may find ourselves in trouble.

No matter who we are or how spiritual we may be, the devil can get us if we put ourselves in a vulnerable position. One pastor told me he thought he was the purest, most moral person he knew. He had eaten of God's Word to the full and had led revivals where hundreds had been saved. Then a young woman in his church came to see him for counsel. She had a pitiful background of abuse and was in a marriage to a brutal man. He felt so sorry for her. He prayed with her and encouraged her and tried to lift her spirits. She needed such comforting that he scheduled her appointments in the evenings in his office after everyone had gone. His reasons were all from sympathy for this poor, downtrodden soul. This was a good man who meant well, but he made a poor choice and was in the wrong place with the wrong person at the wrong time, and he got in trouble.

The best way to stay out of trouble is to make sure you don't put yourself in places of possible temptation. No matter how altruistic your motives might be, never allow yourself to be alone with a person of the opposite sex. No matter how spiritual you may be or how many verses you may know, don't go wandering on your roof!

Suggested Prayer for Today

Dear Lord Jesus, we have such compassion for people in need that we sometimes allow ourselves to be out there on the roof, peering over. Lord, give us new discernment where we can help others but not put ourselves in foolish positions where we could be open to temptation. We don't want to ruin our marriage or devastate our children. Help us to learn from David's poor choice. We know, Lord, that You have the power to observe our goings out and our comings in, and we ask when You see our hand on the doorknob to whisper, "When in doubt, don't." We pray in Your Name and power. Amen.

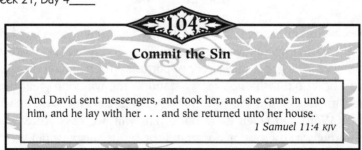

Commit the Sin

And David sent messengers, and took her, and she came in unto him, and he lay with her . . . and she returned unto her house.

1 Samuel 11:4 KJV

Florence

We have already seen that David's troubles started when he made a conscious choice not to go where he knew he should be. Because he was out of God's will, he was tempted by a beautiful woman next door who didn't even know the king was looking at her. Since every able-bodied man but David was out at the front, he felt safe to play around. There was no one in town but David and a few eunuchs, so he sent one of them to see who she was.

The answer was: Bathsheba, wife of Uriah the Hittite. David, who taught the Ten Commandments to others, knew he should not covet his neighbor's wife. This was not a situation where David had no available women; he had several hundred wives in the back room, but somehow the forbidden fruit was most appealing. Besides, who would ever know? (It's amazing how many poor choices we make when we don't think anyone will ever know.)

So David sent for Bathsheba, and as his loyal subject she had no choice but to come. While Scripture doesn't tell us what he said to her or how he seduced her, it does say, "and he lay with her." David has now committed both covetousness and adultery. This is not an admirable record for a spiritual leader who stands as a moral example to the nation of Israel. Then the Word tells us that he sent her back to her own house. He didn't even take her out to Denny's for breakfast. This was not to be a meaningful relationship. If it were a movie, it might be called, *Sin for a Season,* or *A Fling with the King.*

How about You?

In our current amoral society a leader who did what David did would be neither unusual or out of line. Today we're told to do whatever feels good, take every opportunity for personal pleasure, and not let old-fashioned mores stand in the way of a great time. But Christians know this line of reasoning doesn't measure up with God's Word and when we're out of His will, we have to reap the consequences of our actions and bear the responsibility. Just because no one knows doesn't make it right.

This is not a time for you to dump any past infidelities on each other or try to hurt each other but only to discuss what this story of David has taught you both so far. What lessons can you pass on to your teens that might make a difference in their lives? If both of you have been as pure as the driven snow, you may think this saga of David doesn't need to be told to Christians, but Fred and I work almost exclusively within Christian churches, and we find adultery to be one of the major hidden sins in the body of Christ.

One attractive lady named Karen told me this story: She and her husband were pillars of the church, and he was chairman of the board of elders. He was a good man who never got into trouble but who never complimented her either. They had a calm but unexciting marriage, and she had not kept herself up as well as she should have.

Karen joined the church choir, and one night at rehearsal she sat next to Bill, a salesman who often gave his testimony at business luncheons. He greeted her and leaned over. He took a deep breath and sighed, "My, you smell great." Karen told me her whole insides turned over at that comment. She could hardly wait for choir rehearsal the next week. She had her hair frosted and spent more time on her makeup. (If you think she smelled good last week, you should stand near her this week!) She and Bill sat next to each other again, and once more he took a deep sniff. "Wow, that's great perfume," he said.

Surely, we should be safe in church . . . But Karen's husband hadn't been enchanted about any part of her in years and these affirmations were what she longed for.

As you can imagine, these two were the most faithful choir members; they began to sing duets together and practice in their mutual spare time. Can you get into trouble singing in the church choir? Not if singing is all you do. But by the time Karen was telling me this tale, she was taking day trips with Bill and making up stories to cover the truth.

Let's hope that neither of you is involved with anyone else, but one way to prevent the possibility is to converse positively with each other and lift each other up so you won't be seeking compliments from someone else. Everyone needs to feel loved and appreciated, but in so many of the cases we deal with, neither spouse feels the other cares. They put each other down instead of building each other up. This type of behavior is apt to prepare your mate to be open to the advances of an admiring pursuer. It's time for you to renew your efforts to make your mate the "apple of your eye." And remember: All your children will learn of marriage is what they learn from observing you.

Suggested Prayer for Today

Dear Lord Jesus, we've been too casual in our behavior with each other. We've stopped doing some of the nice things we used to do. We see that now. We're sorry. We know the Christian churches have the same problems as the world has, and we don't want to be one of those bad statistics. Help us to keep our focus on building each other up, not tearing down. We thank You that You have the power to change us when we ask sincerely. We love You, Lord, and we love each other. In Your Name we pray. Amen.

Cover It Up

> And the woman conceived, and sent and told David, and said, "I am with child."
>
> *2 Samuel 11:5 KJV*

Florence

We all know that David never set out to get himself in trouble, but by the time he got the phone call from Bathsheba and she gave him the news all philandering males dread to hear, he was truly ashamed of what he had done. Can't you just see him think, *How did this ever happen to me? I didn't mean anything by it. I just wanted to have a good time. She's a nice girl but . . .*

What happens when good people get into trouble? Young girls are told today that it's easy to have an abortion, but the truth is, once there is a pregnancy there is no good option. I talk with women who had abortions twenty years ago and still carry the guilt and shame and pain even though no one knows about it. I talk with others who gave the baby up for adoption and spend the rest of their lives looking for the lost child, crying on his or her birthday, wondering what he or she looks like. We know about this, because our adopted son found his birth mother. I talk with some women who kept the child and have held him or her accountable for their lonely life as a single mother and continually spill anger toward the absent father on the child.

Once there is a pregnancy, there is no good answer. Even a forced marriage doesn't bring the unity needed to provide a happy home for the child. With no ideal options, what does David do? He's the king; surely he can think of some way to cover up what he now sees as a sin unto the Lord.

David came up with Plan A: Bring Bathsheba's husband home from the battle, send him into his wife, and David's troubles would be over.[1] How simple! David was proud that he had thought of this because it would be a little embarrassing to have Uriah come home next year and find an unexpected baby.

Notice how friendly David was with this common soldier, a man so insignificant that even though he and Bathsheba had lived next door for years, David didn't even know their names. When Uriah came in, no doubt amazed that he had been brought before the king, David asked, "How's the war going?"[2]

They passed the time of day as old buddies, then David sent him on his way, saying, in effect, "Go home to your wife, and as a reward for your devotion to duty I'm sending along a prime-rib dinner for two."[3]

Oh, noble David!

At last he would get a good night's sleep. David's troubles were over. How easy it is to overcome problems when you're the king! But when the morning was dawning and David was yawning, his servants came in with the morning paper and the news that Uriah had not gone into his house.

At this news, David had to think, There must be some mistake! He knew any full-blooded soldier brought in from weeks in the trenches would be thrilled to spend the night with Bathsheba. But not Uriah.

David couldn't believe his ears, so he sent for Uriah. Picture David in his bathrobe, trying to ask calmly: "Why didn't you go home last night?"

Uriah answered, "With all my friends still encamped on open fields, I'd be a traitor to go in and enjoy the pleasures of my home and wife. I will not do this thing!"[4]

Who's noble now? David had not counted on a man of principles. The king would like to shake Uriah and send him home, but he had to stay calm. He asked Uriah to stick around another day, and David began to plot out Plan B.

As with Watergate, the act itself was bad enough, but the cover-up was worse. Have you ever told one little lie only to be forced into many larger ones to protect the first? When we knowingly disobey God's plan for our lives, we are headed for trouble. Likewise, David's trouble got deeper and deeper, and he had to institute Plan B: If

Uriah's too nice to go home to Bathsheba sober, let's get him drunk.[5] Why, David is that you? Is that our spiritual leader planning to get Uriah drunk?

Why, yes it is. David had an intimate palace party with his pal, Uriah, and when the decent man was drunk David sent him home to his wife. Now good King David's woes would surely be over, but look: Uriah "went not down to his house."[6] Uriah drunk is more noble than David sober! Plan B had failed.

Now David was truly desperate, so he came up with Plan C: Have Uriah killed in battle. David would never murder—we all know that—but he did need to get Uriah out of the way. If only Uriah had gone along with Plan A or B he would not have been put in position C! It was really his own fault for being so above it all.

So David wrote a letter to Joab: "Set ye Uriah in the forefront of the hottest battle, and retire ye from him, that he may be smitten, and die."[7] In his own hand David wrote the kiss of death for poor Uriah. I'm sure it wasn't easy. David didn't have a thing against Uriah, yet he issued the death warrant on an innocent man to cover up his own sin.

To save postage and get it there faster, David sent the letter in Uriah's own hand. How could you, David? Then the news came back, "Uriah the Hittite is dead."[8]

David's troubles were over! He was home free!

Bathsheba mourned the loss of her husband,[9] and David, wanting to do things properly, waited till the period of mourning was past before he married her to live happily ever after.

David got away with it. Because he was in a position of authority he was able to manipulate circumstances to his advantage so that no one would be the wiser.

But the Bible says, "The thing that David had done displeased the Lord."[10]

How about You?

Before I studied the Old Testament with an eye to applying it in my own life, I just looked at it as a series of stories, a history of the

Hebrew people, but as I delved below the surface, I saw a panorama of people behaving true to the basest standards of human nature as we live it and observe it today.

What troubles have you gotten yourself into that are still giving you pain today? Share with each other things that don't have to do with your marriage relationship, difficulties of the past that have altered your behavior of today. What cover-ups did you devise in your desperation? Did anyone ever find out? We'll look later to see what David did to receive forgiveness.

In the story of Karen and Bill, she came to me before the situation had become known, and we took some quick steps. First, she found a church nearer to their home and prevailed upon her husband to change. When he saw it would be nearer and easier for her, he agreed. She stopped even communicating with Bill, and he began to realize how wrong this whole alliance was. They each repented to the Lord, told no one, and got to work on bringing excitement into their own marriages. Karen and her husband have made it, but Bill went on to other affairs, and eventually his wife divorced him. Karen saw how she could have ruined her marriage and deeply hurt her children if she had put her trust in Bill.

Are there any areas of division in your marriage? Repair them before one of you is tempted by another person in what seems like a more exciting situation. David was a good person who, because he wanted a little illegal pleasure, committed covetousness, adultery, and murder of an innocent man—the theme of the Ten Commandments that he taught to others.

Suggested Prayer for Today

Dear Lord Jesus, we ask You to forgive us of our sins, those we each know about and those we have kept hidden. Your eye sees inside of us, and You know full well what we've done. Lift the guilt from us and give us new joy and love for one another. In Your powerful Name we pray. Amen.

⟨106⟩

Faced with the Truth

Thou art the man.

2 Samuel 12:7 KJV

Florence

David never intended to get into trouble, and he did all he could do to repair the sins of covetousness, adultery, and murder. He married Bathsheba, brought her to his house, and intended to raise their son along with his other children. He could have abandoned her, but he chose to do the right thing. That's all we can do once we've gotten ourselves into trouble: Stop, look at the situation, ask for the Lord's forgiveness, and do all we are able to make amends.

David had recovered from the crisis. No one knew what he had done, but the thing that David had done displeased the Lord. Someone did know! The Lord sent Nathan the prophet to speak to David about the situation. Nathan didn't blurt out that he knew; instead he told a story about two men. One was rich, and one was poor. The rich man had "exceeding many flocks and herds."[1] His hills were dotted with little white sheep.

The abundance of sheep in Nathan's story didn't relate to me personally until I visited New Zealand. A lady there drove me through a park where newborn sheep and their mothers were cavorting down into the street. "Why don't you fence them in," I asked, "so people can't steal them?"

"Steal them? We can't get rid of them!" she answered. Exceeding many flocks!

In Nathan's story, the poor man next door to the rich man had only one little sheep, which had been his children's pet. He had raised this sheep, and it drank out of his cup, ate from his plate, slept in his bed, and "was unto him as a daughter."[2] That's a very close relationship with a sheep! This reminded me of the time I stayed overnight at a friend's house and at breakfast she gave me a bowl of cereal. As I was about to eat it, a cat jumped up on the table and began to lap out of my bowl. As I looked surprised, my friend said, "That shows she loves you."

I wasn't sure I needed that much love!

The rich man had company, and he went out to get one of his "exceeding many flock" to kill for dinner; however, when he walked out the front door, there before him was the pitiful little lamb from next door. He thought to himself, *Why take my own? Why not take this one from my poor neighbor?* So he did take the other man's lamb.

David, upon hearing what this man had done, was furious. His "anger was greatly kindled against the man." Instantly, David meted out the judgment. He didn't think about it or pray about it. He lashed out, "The man that hath done this thing shall surely die."[3] An immediate death sentence! Plus David said, "And he shall restore the lamb fourfold because he did this thing and because he had no pity."[4]

No pity? Look who's talking! Nathan looked David straight in the eye and stated, "Thou art the man."

How about You?

Reread this story in 2 Samuel 12 and consider our human nature that is so quick to pass out judgment on other people in areas where we have failed ourselves. Here David, the spiritual leader, the one chosen by God to set an example for his flock, has reached next door and taken the one wife of Uriah for his own amusement when he had "exceeding many" wives of his own. Worse than that, he had her husband killed. He then wanted to have the rich man executed over the theft of one sheep "because," he added, "the man had no pity."

Do you know someone, perhaps in your own family, who is quick to condemn and yet is far from blameless himself or herself? Somehow we have the feeling if we quickly jump on someone else, we will be perceived as discerning and without fault ourselves. Mature Christians don't leap to judgment and make pronouncements on others. Before placing any blame we need to hear both sides, pray for the Lord's leading, discuss the issue with other informed and stable believers, and then handle the situation privately. I'm always wary of Christians whose main ministry is cutting down any leadership people who don't agree with them.

What part of this message applies to you two? Do you tend to jump to judgment? Do you blame each other? Do you have a need to place blame?

Many years ago before the changes the Lord made in Fred had come about, he had to know instantly who had done the bad deed. "Who left the front door open and let this fly in?" We learned that all of life came to a halt until we had a culprit. Since Fred wasn't going to punish us except to say "Don't do that again," we developed a method to handle these types of situations. Whoever was near would say, "I did it," whether or not or she did. We called this method, "Admit blame so we can move on."

We now see what a foolish waste of time the blame game was. In eternal values a fly is only an inconsequential dot, and God doesn't really care who left the door open.

Suggested Prayer for Today

Heavenly Father, we come to You today as people who find it so easy to judge others and so hard to accept our own blame and sincerely repent. We know we have jumped on others, on each other, on our children, on coworkers, on hypocrites in the church. Lord, show us where our own faults are that we might apologize. We don't want You to grab us one day and say, "Thou art the man." Thanks again, Lord, for this story of David so that we can see how easy it is for good people to get in trouble. We love You, Lord, and we praise the Holy Name of Jesus. Amen.

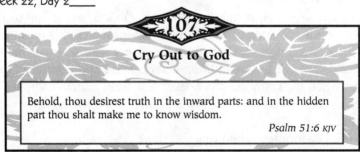

107

Cry Out to God

Behold, thou desirest truth in the inward parts: and in the hidden part thou shalt make me to know wisdom.

Psalm 51:6 KJV

Florence

After the story Nathan told David to convict him of his sin, God Himself cried out to David, saying, in essence, "How could you have done this? I made you king, I gave you riches, a palace, and wives, and if that hadn't been enough I would have given you more. But you didn't ask. Instead you stole the little lamb next door."[1]

Does that line sound familiar? How many of us had parents who cried out, "How could you do this to me after all I've done for you?" Have any of us put this guilt upon our children?

God did not strike David down, but He didn't let him go unpunished either. Be sure you read 2 Samuel 12 to see what punishments David endured, the death of his son among others. David never had real peace again. In his psalms David was constantly calling out to God, who had loved him as a favorite son, and begging for forgiveness and for protection from his enemies.

How about You?

In Psalm 51 David comes before the Lord in a time of repentance. Read this psalm over line by line, asking the Lord to show you what He wants you to learn.

What did David do in his hour of grief and pain? Open to Psalm 51 and follow his lead. Perhaps you both might benefit from these steps today.

1. Ask God for mercy

David says, "Have mercy upon me, O God, according to thy lovingkindness" (verse 1). When we ask for mercy this means we know we don't deserve God's forgiveness, but we also know that He loves us enough to give it. We are never more appreciative of love than when we know we don't deserve it. This principle applies as well to your relationship with your partner when you have hurt him or her.

You beg for mercy, knowing you don't deserve it.

Your partner, through the love of God, forgives you.

You are so grateful for undeserved forgiveness that you love more deeply than ever before.

Your partner responds, and the healing begins. Don't expect instant miracles, for the hurts may be deep.

2. Admit your mistake.

"For I acknowledge my transgressions: and my sin is ever before me" (verse 3). David has a guilty conscience, and he can't get his bad behavior out of his mind. He knows that to be rid of this black cloud hovering over him he must openly acknowledge his mistakes, and he does. Notice that he does not add a "however," as we are apt to do.

"I know I was wrong; however, anyone married to you would have done the same thing." God wants us to admit that we have sinned and not try to water down the act with "howevers."

Your mate needs to hear the same words from your lips as David spoke if you hope to reconcile your marriage. It takes a mature person to admit the complete blame for the problem without casting a few "howevers" of correlating responsibility on his or her partner.

3. Tell the truth

"Behold, thou desirest truth in the inward parts" (verse 6). God wants to hear the truth, out in the open. David knew he had been deceptive. In coming clean with your partner you do not need to add details that will ruin the possibilities of recovery and make the whole scene so vivid that your mate will never get it out of his or her mind. The aim is to heal, not to hurt. We should tell the truth in love.

4. Be willing to change

"Wash me . . . cleanse me . . . purge me . . . hide thy face from my sins, and blot out mine iniquities. Create in me a clean heart" (verses 2, 7, 9–10). David felt dirty from his sin. He asked God to wash him clean. Once we have asked for mercy, admitted our mistakes, and told the truth, we have taken care of the past. Now it's time to clean up ourselves, get our heads straight, and live right.

To start, ask your partner to share with you all the things you should do differently, and write them down without argument or defense.

At this point do not make deals such as, "I'll do this if you'll do that." Be mature. This is your sin that has to be dealt with, even if you feel your partner contributed to it. You make plans to restructure your life and please your partner. To insist that your mate change at this moment of your sin is only a childish way to ease your guilt and keep you from shouldering the blame. Be willing to make all the improvements, and let God work in your partner's heart in due time. Chances are that if your mate sees genuine shifts in a positive direction, he or she will more easily forgive and forget and will also want to improve.

5. Restore fellowship with God and your partner.

"Renew a right spirit within me" (verse 10). When we openly disobey God's clear rules for our lives, we fall out of fellowship with God. When we realize our errors and confess our sins, we are restored. How uncomfortable we are when we have a wrong spirit within us. How deeply we desire to be renewed and have spiritual fellowship with God and our partner!

"Cast me not away from thy presence, and take not thy Holy Spirit from me" (verse 11). David asked God to renew him, to give him a right attitude. He begged God not to cast him out and not to remove the power of the Holy Spirit from him. (David had seen what happened to Saul when God took His power away. He had seen the deep depression, the irrational moods.) David knew that God had used his life greatly and had lifted him up to the top position in the land, not on David's merits but on God's mercy.

Suggested Prayer for Today

Oh Lord, we do need Your help. Until we read this psalm we didn't realize how much we needed Your mercy and each other's forgiveness. We're facing the truth and admitting our mistakes. We are now, finally, each willing to change instead of blaming each other. Renew a right spirit within us. Don't cast us out of Your fellowship. We love You, Lord Jesus. Amen.

(Go back through these steps together.
Discuss them openly and then go through the prayer again.)

Ask for Joy

Restore unto me the joy of Thy salvation; and uphold me with Thy free Spirit. Then will I teach transgressors Thy ways and sinners shall be converted unto Thee.

Psalm 51:12–13 KJV

Florence

Once we have gotten ourselves in any kind of trouble caused by our stepping outside of God's will for our life and disobeying what we know He wants us to do, even if we've gotten away with it, the joy is gone. We can have happy moments when we've repressed the memory for a period of time, but the joy we used to know is no longer a part of our daily life. There's a burden on our shoulders, a little black cloud hovering over our head.

When we think of this lack of joy, we can imagine how David felt as he faced the Lord and cried out to Him for mercy. Mercy is asking for forgiveness when you know you don't deserve it. If any one of us needs forgiveness from the Lord, we need to follow David's steps as he wrote them in Psalm 51.

Ask God for mercy—He gives it in abundance.

Admit your mistake—don't place blame on others.

Tell the truth—no more hiding the facts.

Be willing to change—yourself, not your mate.

Restore fellowship—with God and your partner.

Once David was willing to face the truth and not rationalize around his cover-ups, he was ready to ask God to restore his joy. Do you often pray for joy—not happy days but inner joy and peace? Once we have confessed and told the truth to the Lord, He is willing to give us joy. David wanted the kind of joy he had experienced as a young boy alone with God out in the fields. He wanted the joy and excitement he remembered when God spared his life as Saul pursued him. He wanted the thrill he felt as God the Father put him on the throne of Israel. Even though David was still king the thrill was gone, and guilt was in its place.

Ask for the joy of the Lord. I remember the joy of my salvation, the lift of the guilt and shame I felt from producing two brain-damaged sons and going through their agonizing deaths. I asked the Lord Jesus to come into my life and change me, to lift my guilt, and to heal my marriage. I started going back to church again, I realized our marriage problems weren't all Fred's fault, I began to study God's Word in a personal way, and I found out through the personality studies that it was all right for me to be real. I remember how Fred turned our nightclub into a church and how the piano and the singing were fresh and bright. The "Old Rugged Cross" became new for me, and in my heart there rang a melody. For the first time in my life I knew the joy of my salvation.

Thank God for a broken spirit. We don't often thank the Lord for what seems to us to be a negative. We don't want our lights to burn out or our spirits to be broken. As we learned in our lessons on Saul, God is not so impressed with physical sacrifices and donated money as he is with a truly humble heart and a contrite spirit. When we feel broken we must be thankful in knowing we are right where God wants us, and it's a big step up from there.

Give testimony of a changed life. A person who has never been wrong and is self-righteous is unattractive to others, but one who is willing to admit his sin and the depth of God's forgiving power has much to share with others. When I was young and self-assured, thinking I could control my destiny, I had no compassion for people with problems. I felt that mistakes were a sign of weakness, and I respected only strength.

Once I suffered the loss of my two sons after doing everything humanly possible to heal them, I knew what heartbreak was, and I could feel for others.

Once I was brought to my knees with a broken spirit, I was open to the claims of Christ, and I was restored. The Lord Jesus gave me a new life to use for His glory.

David tells God, "When this is over, I'll teach others about You, and many will be converted."

How about You?

May I urge you to go back and read 1 and 2 Samuel and ask the Lord to personalize these stories of Saul and David for you. In each verse you study be open to hear what God wants you to learn. As you apply Scripture to your life, you'll see how inspiring and fulfilling it is to hear from God personally, and you, as David did, will desire to share your faith with others.

The reason so many people are fearful of standing up and speaking before others is that they truly have nothing exciting to say. Not until we have seen our broken spirits laid out before us and asked the Lord to restore our joy do we have anything of value to share. But once we have a changed life, the guilt is gone, we're no longer ashamed, the joy is bubbling over, and then we can't keep quiet! We have to share with others. As we do, many sinners will repent because of our testimony.

I've given my testimony publicly so many hundreds of times that I sometimes think, *I can't do this one more time.* Yet, once I get on the platform and realize I'm sharing what the Lord has done for me, His power floods over me, and I give my story of the joy of my salvation with gratitude and enthusiasm.

I pray sincerely that you both have found the study of Saul and David as exciting as I have and that you have applied it in such a way that your lives have already changed. Remember:

Be available to be . . .
Called out by God,
Changed by His Spirit,
Chosen by the people,
Committed to obedience, and don't
Compromise your standards.

Remember David, and if in doubt
Don't be in the wrong place,
Don't compromise your standards,
Don't give in to temptation,

Don't enter into immoral relationships,
Don't ignore the Ten Commandments.

If you get yourself in any trouble
Ask God for mercy,
Admit your mistakes,
Tell the truth,
Be willing to change,
Restore your fellowship.

Ask for the joy of the Lord,
Thank God for your broken spirit, and
Share your testimony with others.

Suggested Prayer for Today

(By now you can easily pray on your own. Go back over the steps listed above and pray through them one at a time. If you wish to stop and make a comment as you're praying, that's all right. There are no prayer rules except to have a thankful heart and a spirit full of praise. Remember to close your prayer in the Name of Jesus, for it's in His Name that every knee will bow and every tongue confess that Jesus Christ is Lord.[1] Amen and Amen.)

See His Face

> Keep me as the apple of your eye; hide me in the shadow of your wings from the wicked who assail me, from my mortal enemies who surround me.
>
> *Psalm 17:8–9* NIV

Fred and Florence

As David called out to the Lord in his time of rejection and pursuit, he remembered, perhaps with nostalgia, back before his fall when he had known for certain that he was God's favorite child, that he had received blessings beyond all others, that he was the apple of God's eye. Here in his time of punishment and rebellion of family and friends, David called out to God again: "Hide me in the shadow of your wings."

Can you picture a huge, eagle-like bird swooping down as the enemy approaches and lifting David up to the heavens? That's his desire, and many times it's our wish too. He asked his God to keep him and hide him from the wicked, the mortal enemies who were assailing him.

David had sinned against God. He disobeyed the very One who had so richly blessed him. Now the consequences of the choices he made were catching up to him. he felt oppressed on every side, and indeed he was.

When we too make choices that are contrary to what we know God wants for us, there are usually consequences we must face. We might prefer to hide in the shadow of His mighty wing, but that is rarely possible.

If we are stopped for speeding on the highway we'll probably have to pay the fine that is sure to be imposed.

If we avoid declaring some income on our tax returns, thinking naively, *They'll never know,* we may be very shocked, dejected, and probably fearful when we receive the inevitable IRS notice of an impending audit.

If we find ourselves getting emotionally involved with someone who is not our spouse, we may find it not only difficult to break off the relationship when we come to our senses, but the third person may be unwilling to do the same and cause much grief and heartache to fall on us.

It is at this point we cry, "Oh, that I had never strayed. Oh, that I had never bent the rules in the first place!"

How about You?

There is probably not one of us who can look back on the years that have passed without seeing a decision we made, a word we said, or an action we took that we now regret. Fortunately, most of us do not have mortal enemies attacking us as David did. But many of us may still be struggling with the guilt or shame, or even the consequences of those choices we now wish we had never made.

We cannot undo the past. We cannot change the facts of our personal history. We can, however, come with a contrite and remorseful spirit to the Lord and ask His forgiveness. This He always freely gives. And the Scripture says that when the Lord forgives, He forgets. He washes the slate clean.[1]

Unfortunately, the traffic court, the IRS, and those who assess our fragile personal reputations are seldom so gracious and forgiving. Are there still unresolved issues, unrepented mistakes, or unforgiven sins that must be made right in your life? If they are with your mate, go and confess, be open, and ask forgiveness while giving assurance of complete repentance, a permanent turning away from the act that caused the problem in the first place. Confess, as well, to your Father in Heaven, also assuring Him you will walk your pathway of life close to Him and never again stray from His expectations of you.

Clean up yesterday's mistakes and avoid tomorrow's miscues by living your life in perfect harmony with the standard Jesus exemplified for each of us. Then you will not need to cry out, as David did, "Lord, hide me in the shadow of your wings."

Suggested Prayer for Today

Blessed Lord Jesus, I am thankful that You raised a standard for me to follow in my life. I do not ever again want to bend any rule or law to accommodate my needs or desires of the moment. I want to live as You lived. I want my own name to be respected as much as I respect Your Name. I want my family, my friends, and my brothers and sisters in Christ to think of me as one who is always truthful, whose word can be accepted without question, and as one who can be trusted to do as he/she promises to do.

I confess I have fallen short of this in the past. But now I realize that I must change. I must put all the undesirable habits and patterns behind me and move forward in Your will, guided by Your light. You, O Lord, are light. You are truth. Help me, O Lord, to be like You. In Your Name I pray. Amen.

And We Know Who Wins

> In all these things we overwhelmingly conquer through Him
> who loved us. . . . Thanks be to God, who always leads us in
> His triumph in Christ.   *Romans 8:37, 2 Corinthians 2:14*
>
> That you may be able to stand firm.   *Ephesians 6:11*

Fred

"We overwhelmingly conquer! . . . Always leads us in His triumph!"

There is no doubt. The battle has already been won. Our Lord clearly overcame all the forces stacked against Him at the Cross. We are partakers of His victory. Therefore there is no more "warfare," even though that is a popular term. There remains only "spiritual skirmishes" with an enemy who knows himself that he is already defeated.

What then do we have to fear? We have nothing to fear, for we already have all the spiritual weapons we will ever need. We only need to learn to use them so that when the enemy attacks we will quickly gain the victory that has already been ordained for us. "We overwhelmingly conquer through Him!" "He always leads us in His triumph!" The outcome has been determined in advance, and we know who wins! We do!

The powers of darkness are real and are attacking wherever they can today. You may be under attack at this very moment and not even be aware of it. Ephesians 6 tells us we must always be prepared with our spiritual armor and our weapons of victory, the shield of faith and the sword of the Spirit.

What are some of the ways that we can recognize satan's attacks upon us as individuals and on our marriage? Here is a partial list to help you have discernment. We are not referring to evil spirits or demons but the "fiery darts" or "flaming missiles" of the evil one that Ephesians 6:16 speaks of, the "zingers" that satan delights in firing at us:

1. Any form of anger, suppressed or expressed, that is not specifically directed at sin

2. Any evidence of lack of faith, feeling, or believing that this issue is beyond God's ability

3. Any unwillingness by either partner to communicate feelings

4. Any sexually based activity or attraction with someone other than your spouse

5. Any form of bonding, especially emotionally with another person outside of the marriage

6. Any disinterest in Scripture, prayer, or in God Himself

7. Any form of fear, anxiety, or worry

8. Depression in any of its nefarious forms

Some of these manifestations may surprise you. Upon researching the Word, you will find that each one is contrary to God's promise and plan for us. Knowing this, the vast effect of satan's attack becomes obvious when we realize how widespread the malady of depression is today. *USA Today* reported, "Since FDA approval in 1987, the number of Americans taking . . . anti-depressant [Prozac] has grown to 18 million" in 1996![1]

What Can You Do about These Attacks?

First of all, remember the comment, "I've read the end of the Book, and we win!" We have absolute and complete authority over satan and any and all fiery darts that he may fire at us. Second, be alert to the fact that he will target you. He will do all he can to separate you from commitment to your Lord and to each other. Third, know your authority (read Luke 10:19 again right now if you don't remember it) and do not hesitate ever to exercise it. Fourth, use that powerful spiritual weapon regularly, even daily, to bind him and to command him to leave you, always IN THE NAME OF THE LORD

JESUS CHRIST, and always aloud. For reminders on how to do this, see chapter 91, "His Power over satan."

You will be amazed at how quickly he flees when you command him to go. Once again, we don't merely suggest, we urge every Christian husband to take authority over him every night, in the presence of your wife. Not only will be you be exercising the power that the Lord has already given to You, but also your wife will especially appreciate you for protecting her against his attacks.

Suggested Prayer for Today

(Today, let every husband go back to page 286 and pray out loud, in the presence of your wife, the suggested prayer given there, taking hold of your God-given authority over satan and commanding him to leave you!)

When I Awake

They have tracked me down, they now surround me, with eyes alert, to throw me to the ground. They are like a lion hungry for prey. . . . Rise up, O Lord, confront them, bring them down; rescue me from the wicked by your sword.   *Psalm 17:11–13 NIV*

Florence

Have you ever felt that the whole world was against you? They've tracked you down, their eyes are following your every move, they've got you surrounded? Do you wake up in the night and see a lion crouching in the corner? How brilliantly the psalmist David, so many years ago, described the fears we have today. As he was literally surrounded by enemies pursuing him he called out to God to save him. Probably none of us have been hiding in caves hoping our foes won't find us, but how many of us are emotionally running away, hoping no one will find out who we really are, how we really feel, believing, If you really knew me you wouldn't like me?

When these times of fear and insecurity overwhelm us, what do we do? Do we call friends for assurance of our worth? Do we push our feelings down or deny them? Do we blame our mates or the fates for our fears? Or do we call upon our Lord to confront what haunts us, bring down our emotional giants and cut away those mean people who have offended us? O Lord, save us from such men!

How we react to hard times shows us how close we are to the Lord and how much faith we have in His protective care. In David's psalms, he calls out from his point of problem. He tells God what's wrong, then he asks for salvation plus a good night's rest.

Each night before we go to sleep, Fred prays out loud; he brings our needs before God, and he binds satan and his evil spirits from tormenting us in the night. He prays in the name of Jesus Christ our Lord and Savior. Since he has begun these bold, clear prayers we both sleep better, and when we awaken we are rested, ready, and satisfied.

How about You?

Many of us as Christians suffer from fears, insecurity, and depression. Often we cover these up, deny we have problems, and then feel guilty. Are any of these lions pursuing you? If so, David tells us to bring these fears to the Lord, ask Him to confront our lions and bring them down. As we call to the Lord before going to sleep, as we bind satan aloud in the name of Jesus, we will awaken in the morning with a feeling of peace and spiritual satisfaction. Discuss your lions with each other. So many couples we talk with have never told their mate about their fears assuming the other one will ridicule them and tell them they are stupid. Be open and honest with each other and then pray for your own needs and those fears of your mate. Don't preach, pray!

Husband's list of "lions":

_____

_____

Wife's list of "lions":

_____

_____

Suggested Prayer for Today

Father God, we feel like David today. We each have our own set of fears. We each feel pursued at times by lions that we are too weak to fight off. We pray, as David did, for You to confront our lions and bring them down. We know we must confront them too and bring them specifically before You.

Give us wisdom to know what to do ourselves as we await Your rescue. We bring these fears before You, knowing You are not the Creator of fear but of power, love, and of sound minds. Show us Your face in the morning, Lord, and we will be satisfied. We thank You and praise You. In Jesus' Name. Amen.

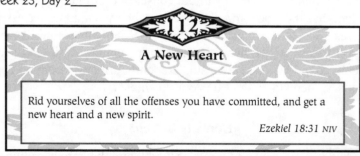

A New Heart

> Rid yourselves of all the offenses you have committed, and get a new heart and a new spirit.
>
> *Ezekiel 18:31 NIV*

Florence

Before I started studying the Bible seriously and realizing it applied to real people, I assumed that everyone in the great Book was godly and well behaved. But as I read, I realized Adam and Eve disobeyed the only rule they had. Abraham lied, Rebecca deceived her husband, Jacob stole from his father-in-law, and Joseph's brothers sold him into slavery. These were not perfect people!

Throughout the Old Testament the Hebrew people had a running battle with their morals and their God. When they were in trouble they called out to God, and each time He saved them. When their barns were full in times of plenty, they forgot their God and did what was right in their own eyes. They worshiped idols and disregarded the promises they had made to God when times were tough. Like recalcitrant children, they would repent of their wickedness, the Father would forgive them, they'd be grateful and praise God, and then they would forget what He did for them and head into trouble again and again.

At the time of this verse, Ezekiel was a priest among the exiles in Babylonia. God chose him to go and warn the Israelites of their sins. The Spirit of the Lord lifted him to his feet and told him of the difficult mission ahead of him. God told Ezekiel that the people were rebellious, stubborn, hardened, and obstinate. They refused to listen to advice; they thought they knew more than the Lord Himself. Does this perhaps sound like some of our friends? Some of our teenagers? Some of our in-laws? Perhaps even some of us?

In Ezekiel 18, the Lord gave a list of some of the sins this rebellious nation committed: murder without conscience, adultery, oppressing or ignoring the poor and the needy, robbery, charging excessive interest, and other detestable behaviors. Does this sound like our nation today? As we head toward the millennium, will God send Ezekiel to us? Will he say again, "Repent! Turn away from all your offenses; then sin will not be your downfall"?[1]

How about You?

We live in a crooked and perverse world, and the Lord is calling us to repent. You don't have to be in a cathedral or at a revival meeting; you can make a personal commitment today. Start by asking the Lord to show each of you what you have done that grieves Him. Write down everything that comes to your mind. Then pray through each item. To repent means to be conscience-stricken about past actions and to be so overwhelmed by recalling those transgressions that you vow never to behave that way again. To repent is not to toss a casual "I'm sorry" toward the Lord but to grieve over each action, feeling remorse, and then knowing you are forgiven.

Even though our circumstances have been so jaded that we can watch news reports of murder, rape, robbery, and disasters while eating dinner, God our Father is still calling us to a life of purity and holiness. Even though our teens think drinking and drugs are cool and have hardened their hearts to the point a girl can give birth to a baby during the prom, throw it in the trash, and then go back to dancing the night away,[2] God our Father calls us to accountability. Rid yourselves of all the offenses you have committed and get a new heart and a new spirit.

Suggested Prayer for Today

Dear Lord Jesus, You want us to repent, and yet we keep making excuses for why we did the wrong thing. We rationalize why it's not our fault, believing, If those other people were better, I could be too. Lord, today I do repent. I am conscience-stricken over this whole list of failures. I will pray through each one. [Make a list of all offenses that come to mind.] You promise us, Lord, that You will forgive us of these offenses, and even more, You will give us a new attitude of the heart and a new spirit. We thank You and praise You. Amen.

Your Reading Program:
The Scriptures

Study to show thyself approved unto God, a workman that
needeth not to be ashamed, rightly dividing the word of truth.

2 Timothy 2:15

Fred

How much time have you each spent in Bible study—not in church
or in a group but in personal Bible study in the past seven days?
Count up the number of actual minutes or hours you have spent in
undistracted prayer with your Father in Heaven during those same
seven days. The minutes or hours that you come up with will indicate how devoted you really are to your marriage, to your Lord, to
building that personal and passionate devotion to Him.

Why do we men so often allow our wives to surpass us in Bible
study, in seminars, in personal growth—and then expect them to
recognize and accept us as their spiritual "head"? There is something that doesn't add up when we think of it that way.

How do you feel about the total number of minutes or hours that
you arrived at? Does it indicate that you are putting the Lord in
"first place" in your life? I too struggled for many years with these
same conflicts. Bible study itself never was a problem for me. I
enjoyed studying, learning, and growing in my knowledge of God's
Word. The problem was finding the time to do it. Too frequently the
pressures of my daily schedule, the "tyranny of the urgent," would
crowd out my best intentions. Weeks, maybe months, would go by
before I realized I had been skipping my daily Bible study. It is not
surprising that satan would keep us so busy, so occupied even with
good works, that we never seem to manage to find the time to get
into our Bibles for in-depth study. Nevertheless, that is how we
grow. God speaks to us in numerous ways; one of the most certain
ways is through His Word.

When we see something in Scripture, when we learn something, when "the lights suddenly go on," we can know it is from God and is truth. There is no need to wonder. God's Word is truth! How then can you learn? How will you grow if you do not make a good and strict habit of consistently setting aside time each day for study?

We seem to find time for everything else in this world. Have you ever had a problem finding time for your favorite television program, for the newspaper or a magazine? We can always manage to find time for those things that are important to us, the things we want to do.

I wish I had a simple solution for you. I don't! I think every Christian struggles with finding regular daily time for Bible study and prayer. It is a battle that most of us will always have to wage. The only way I have had success is through determination and recognizing this must be a priority. We simply have to obey God's order to put Him in first place. We always have time for what is important. We can always manage to postpone those things that are less urgent, uninteresting, or unexciting. We must decide that He is important. We must become personally passionate and devoted to Him.

There is one thing I have done to help me maintain self-discipline over prayer and study time. I am basically a recordkeeper, especially in my "personal electronic organizer." It helps me to keep a record of the number of days in a row that I have been in daily written prayer and study. Each day I add to my total number. I have been doing this for the past six or seven years and find it most effective for keeping my self-decreed discipline. Once that number builds up, I hate to have to go back to "zero" and start all over again because I forgot.

How about You?

Have you developed a system to enable you to find time for the Word and to have a prayer time each day? Have you even moved these two essentials of the Christian life to the top of your own priority list? Is it possible that each of you could help the other? Do your daily schedules make it possible for you each to have your own time with the Lord at the same time? You can study and pray together, but most couples find it more effective to study on their own what is most meaningful to them at the moment, and at their own pace.

Let us remember once again, since opposites attract, we tend to like to do our study time in our own way, which often doesn't happen to be the way of our mate. It is not essential that we study together or that we study the same thing. If you like to do that and your joint study time is enriching to you both, by all means continue. There are only two criteria: Are you making sure to do it, and are you being blessed by the way that you are doing it?

Suggested Prayer for Today

Heavenly Father, I confess to You once again that I have not been putting You in the priority-one position in my life because I do not manage to have time to spend with You. I am consumed by the tyranny of the urgent. There is so much to do and so little time to do it. There are so many demands on my time, Lord. I don't have to tell You this; You already know it. Nor do I have to give You any excuses. I need to confess my failures to You and to ask Your forgiveness. Then I have to be concerned enough about those failures to do something about them. I am concerned, Lord. In the final analysis of life, "Only one life, 'twill soon be past. Only what's done for Christ will last." Help me, O Lord, to get and keep my priorities in order and then to stay consistent. I thank You, my Lord and my God. In Your Name I pray. Amen.

Your Reading Program: What Are You Reading?

> Life being very short, and the quiet hours of it few, we ought to waste none of them in reading valueless books.
>
> *John Ruskin*

Fred

The problem for so many of us is not that we are reading valueless books but that we aren't reading any books. Secondly, many of us who are reading are in fact reading what might be called valueless. Another word often used is *trash*.

Charlie "Tremendous" Jones, a highly respected motivationalist, has often said, "The difference between what you are now and what you could be in two years is the people you meet and the books that you read." Let's focus then for today on the books that you have read and the books that you could read in the next two years. Will there be any difference in who you are or where you are in life or in your marriage in the next two years? Another oft-quoted proverb is, "Today is the first day of the rest of your life!" The decision to change the course of our life must be made today.

Robin Williams starred in *Dead Poets Society,* a movie with an unforgettable message: *Carpe diem,* two Latin words that translate "Seize the day!" Let us begin today to make a difference, to "Seize the day!" Let us begin by agreeing to improve or add to our reading programs.

The first step is to review the books you have read in the past twelve months. In the spaces provided list the titles of the last four books that each of you has read. In the parentheses following the title evaluate the relative significance to you of each of the books you have listed. Write in a word such as: Enjoyable, Valuable, Minor, Don't Know, a Waste! or Can't Remember, etc.

WIFE:

1. _____ (_____)

2. _____ (_____)

3. _____ (_____)

4. _____ (_____)

HUSBAND:

1. _____ (_____)

2. _____ (_____)

3. _____ (_____)

4. _____ (_____)

As you review the books you have read, have you tended to read "how-to" books or business, Christian, or inspirational books, or have you focused on "recreational" reading, pulp novels, or the other category, "none"? In her excellent book, *Dare to Dream,* Florence emphasizes the importance of reading and recommends a balanced diet.

So what should you read? She suggests:

1. Select a subject, something you are interested in, perhaps related to your work or home life.
2. Get acquainted with a person as either an author or a subject. Florence has read widely on and by Winston Churchill.
3. Pick a period of history. Can you see the endless possibilities of reading both fiction and nonfiction of a chosen point in time?
4. Become an armchair traveler. Bookstores and libraries are filled with fascinating volumes of places you may never be able to visit. Reading is in some ways even better than being there.
5. Get motivated. In this era of how-to books, there is no excuse for any of us to say, "I'd like to, if only I knew how."

6. Enjoy romance and mystery. Do some things just for the sheer pleasure of it!

7. Reread the classics. They're called classics because they are! In high school, most of us were striving so hard for a grade we never even thought to capture the beauty of the author's style or content.

How about You?

Are you seeing confusion, disillusion, or despair in your days? Learn to love life! And what more marvelous way to begin than to start your reading program. *Carpe diem!* Start with a time of study in God's Word. Cut down on the TV time. Add in to your day periods of educational, recreational, inspirational, or just plain enjoyable reading. You will amazed at how much more you have to talk to each other about when you read good books.

Suggested Prayer for Today

Heavenly Father, every good gift and every perfect gift "cometh down from heaven," from You. We thank You today for the gift of good books that You have given to us through authors who have used the skills and talents You have given to them so that they can give us the gift of good reading. Father, help us to not waste our time on pointless and meaningless activities that have no redeeming or lasting value. We thank You for each new tomorrow that gives us a new start for the rest of our lives. We bless You and praise You, our Lord and our God. In Jesus' Name we pray. Amen.

115

I Love You

Husbands, love your wives, just as Christ also loved the church.
Ephesians 5:25

Fred

It has been said the two most wanted phrases in human relation-ships are "I'm sorry" and "I love you." And it's not only husbands and wives who desire these words. Children, especially teenagers, also long to hear these same two expressions from their parents. Many tell us they seldom do; instead, they tend to hear more often what they're to do, how they should do it, and why they shouldn't have done it!

Is it any wonder that so many of us leave the teen years and head into marriage with an unfulfilled longing to hear those magic words, "I love you"? During the courtship period, when we are trying to win or be won, "I love you" comes easily and natu-rally. It's part of the arsenal we use to help us put our best foot forward.

Isn't one of the major problems the fact that too often courtship doesn't last much beyond "I do"? Wouldn't it be wonderful if "I love you" flowed from the lips of husbands and wives as easily after twenty or thirty years of marriage as it did in the beginning?

One thing all married couples eventually come to realize is this: One day there will be just the two of us. The children will be gone. They'll be involved in their own lives and may seldom call or come and visit. Then the time will come when both of you are retired from your work and family responsibilities, and you have the good for-tune—or the problem—of vast amounts of time to spend together. Which will it be for you?

How about You?

What will you do then if you have not built your marriage on a strong foundation of love, mutual respect, and trust? What will you do then if you have not become "best friends" who enjoy living together and working together?

We can assure you from our own experiences and from ministering to and helping other couples, becoming best friends does not just happen. It takes effort, caring, and the love of the Lord Jesus flowing through you and into each other to reach the satisfying and selfless bonding of two people with different minds and personalities who "become one" in every sense of the word.

Ensuring that kind of future means you liberally and sincerely use now the words "I love you." It means a tender and caring embrace of each other. It means hugs and kisses. It means looks to each other that say, "You're special," and "You're important to me." It means you do some menial household chores for your partner as a means of saying, "I'm doing this for you because I love you."

The Scriptures clearly tell us, "Husbands, love your wives." I would like to suggest to you men, especially, if saying (and meaning!) "I love you" has not been a frequent part of your expressions to your wife that you begin now by saying those coveted words to her. Transport your mind back to your courting days and remember how you looked into her eyes and won her heart with these beautiful and always appreciated words.

I enjoy speaking English in foreign dialects. Every once in a while I will take Florence's hand and begin to plant kisses up her arm, saying to her in my best French-flavored accent, "Mon, cherie, I love you so much." Can you believe after forty-five years of marriage she still loves it and giggles like a little girl? It's fun for both of us! Isn't that what marriage should be—fun for both of you? Start working on it now. Make your marriage even more fun than it already is. Start with "I love you." You might even try it with a French accent!

Suggested Prayer for Today

Dear God and Heavenly Father, I thank You for giving us permission as Christians to have fun with each other. I am thankful that our Christian marriage does not have to be straight-laced, sober, and sad. Lord, we are thankful You have given us Your joy. Together we want to exhibit to each other more of the joy that is available to us. It makes sense, Lord, that if I allow Your joy to fill me then we both can have more fun together.

Show each of us, Lord, the areas of our life that are resistant to being filled with Your Spirit and bringing Your joy into our lives. Help us, O blessed Lord and Savior, to be like You. Help us to see each other as You see us—imperfect but growing, maturing, and created in Your image and likeness. Help me, Lord, to see as You see. I thank You, my Lord and my God. In Jesus' Name I pray. Amen.

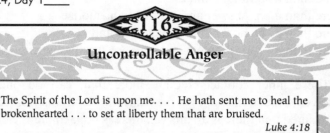

Uncontrollable Anger

The Spirit of the Lord is upon me. . . . He hath sent me to heal the brokenhearted . . . to set at liberty them that are bruised.

Luke 4:18

Fred

No matter how hard they try,
no matter how much they pray,
no matter how often they exercise their authority over satan,
no matter how often they seek godly counsel, and for some,
no matter how vehemently they deny or justify its existence,
. . . there are some Christians who never seem to gain victory over anger that erupts on occasion into an uncontrollable rage. This kind of volatile emotion will inevitably become a destroyer of relationships, of families, of lives, and frequently of marriage. Unless the scriptural steps are taken to bring identification, understanding, cleansing, and healing to the deep hurts that are evidenced by these outbursts, there is little hope of achieving the abundant life our Lord Jesus has promised us.

This type of deep emotion is almost always an indication of some type of early childhood trauma. If you feel trapped in this tormenting situation, commanding satan to depart from you three times a day will be helpful, but it is merely "first aid" for deep wounds. Those repressed and even forgotten incidents become an open door into our souls that the prince of darkness will attack again and again. He knows where to find them, because he likely has been responsible for originally causing them.

Identifying and rectifying these issues is not something that can be ignored, for they can be disastrous forces in any marriage. They require:

more than a spiritual band-aid,
more than a pat answer and a verse to memorize,
more than a "go home and pray more," and
more than a "Your problem is you're not submissive enough."

These inner conflicts require more than can be offered or resolved through the pages of the *Daily Marriage Builders*. However, be assured that there is an answer, there is hope, there is cleansing, and there is healing. The Lord Jesus said He has been sent to heal the brokenhearted, to set free those who are in captivity. He is our hope. He is our answer. He Himself has said, "Every plant, which my Heavenly Father hath not planted, shall be rooted up."[1]

How can we be so confident? How can we offer you such assurance? If it weren't for the truth of the Word, we could not. If it were not that we ourselves were forced to walk through deep waters ourselves, we could not. But we did, and we are now standing on the solid ground. We are standing on the Rock . . . and His Name is Jesus! There is room for you here. If you are facing seemingly insurmountable struggles, we want you to be here on the Rock with us. There may be some walking through uncharted deep waters ahead for you. Fear not! Go forth! "I am with you always, even to the end of the age."[2]

How about You?

Are there seemingly unresolvable conflicts that are keeping you apart from each other? Is one of you suffering from anger, fears, depression, inner struggles for which there seems to be no answer, no hope? In the Addenda at the conclusion of this book we list several resources that we highly recommend to you. They are in the section entitled, "For Inner Struggles." Start working through them in the order in which they are listed. "Working through them" means carefully and prayerfully considering each one, underlining and highlighting those that impact you most significantly.

If you have already studied the four different personality types and have found that the issues you are facing go even deeper, determine today to get to the bottom of those issues. Find any roots that were not planted there by your Father in Heaven. Find them and root them up as the Lord Jesus has directed! Those who have done so have been overjoyed by the new life of peace and contentment they are able to experience today.

Suggested Prayer for Today

(Pray this prayer if you suspect today's chapter
applies to one of you.)

Dear God and Heavenly Father: Why do we struggle so? What is preventing us from overcoming these walls that seem to be around us? Almighty God, we pray for answers and knowledge. How can we break this bondage that seems to have a grip on us? We ask you, Lord, to open our minds and our hearts that we may know truth. We ask You, Lord, to show us how to cut these ropes of bondage that seem to be about us. Father, we surrender our will to Yours now as we ask You to speak to us. We ask for discernment and guidance. We thank You, O gracious Lord, for hearing our prayer that we ask in the Name of the Lord Jesus Christ. Amen.

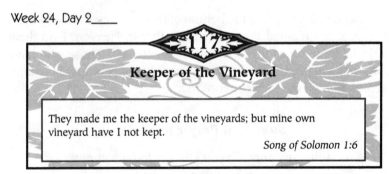

117

Keeper of the Vineyard

They made me the keeper of the vineyards; but mine own vineyard have I not kept.

Song of Solomon 1:6

Fred

One of the joys of Bible study is the mining of hitherto undiscovered nuggets of treasure—scriptural gems that prompt us to say, "It was there all the time, but I just never *saw* that truth before." Countless times as we have delved deeper into the Word, each of us has found some thrilling new understanding that convinced us all the more of the awesome content that God has stored for our use in His Scriptures.

Most of us can still recall when we had first become Christians that verse or two God used to illuminate our minds to something He wanted us to see. We remember our enthusiasm when we made what we thought was our personal and secret strike in God's gold mines.

God clearly had something He wanted me to see about myself that day when He first opened to me today's verse from the Song of Solomon. After hearing the gospel message every Sunday for a year, I surrendered my will to His will in August 1966. As a new Christian I wanted to do it well. Being part Melancholy, I always believed that anything worth doing is worth doing right! So I plunged into studying my Bible with newfound interest and comprehension.

I was a young husband, a young father, hustling to build my business empire, and at the same time very involved in church and community activities and civic organizations. I was at that age when I thought that I could conquer anything I tackled. I wholeheartedly believed the adage "If you want something done, give it to a busy man." I was the busy man! (I was also young and foolish, but I didn't know it yet!)

Then one day, this verse from the Song of Solomon literally leaped off the page at me. God showed me that I was taking care of all the other vineyards, but "mine own" I had failed to keep! I saw that my time was overly invested in things outside the home, and therefore I had little or no time for my own vineyard.

I rushed into the kitchen to show the verse to Florence, confessing that I had just seen that I was overinvolved in things outside the home and didn't have time for my wife and family. Florence was in emotional shock, but it was a positive shock! She told me she was overwhelmed that I had seen this. She had seen that my heart was focused on the community and our business. She felt I put everything else ahead of her needs and those of the children.

Later that week I showed my exciting discovery to my pastor. "This Christianity is really working!" I told him. My well-meaning but young pastor promptly punctured my bubble by explaining to me that this was not what the passage meant at all. He proceeded to give me some theological seminary explanation that had no relevance to where I was or what God was trying to teach me. For the first time I learned that there is not necessarily only one explanation to the message of a Scripture verse. If God chooses to reveal something to you through it, no one else can tell you, "That is wrong."

How about You?

How often do you experience the joy of personally mining a nugget from God's gold mine? If you have not seen any lately, is it because you haven't been out digging? God speaks to us through many means. Two of the three most important means are through prayer and through His Word. When we are too busy, too occupied with the vineyards of life, and have no time for prayer and meditative study, we lose out on these two avenues to hear from our Lord. The third means the Lord uses to get out attention is the direct impression of the Holy Spirit into our mind. But if we are too busy to pray and read, it is highly unlikely that we will ever be able to discern these nonaudible messages.

Would it not be a good idea for the two of you now to set aside some time to evaluate individually and together how you are spending your time and energy? Are the things that are occupying your life God's will for you or your will for you? Put your conclusions down on a piece of paper. Commit together to make the necessary changes. Then, on your calendar sixty days from now, schedule one hour to review together how well you have progressed in effecting the desired improvements.

Suggested Prayer for Today

Almighty God, we ask You to help the two of us as we evaluate our life and commitments now to see what areas You might desire for us to deemphasize or even eliminate. I pray for your Spirit to fill us both that we might speak in a gentle, patient, and not in an accusatory tone. Remind us, Lord, of the principles of good communications and help us to see when we slip and break one of those rules.

Lord, it is important to us both that we get our life heading more in the direction of the plans and purposes that You already have for us. We do not intend to be disobedient or disrespectful to You, Lord, but we do see ourselves so easily getting off the track. We therefore once again surrender ourselves to You, saying, "Here am I, Lord. Take me as I am and mold me and shape me however You will." In the life-changing Name of Jesus, I pray. Amen.

Is Life Wasted?

> Guard what has been entrusted to your care. Turn away from godless chatter and the opposing ideas of what is falsely called knowledge.
>
> *1 Timothy 6:20 NIV*

Fred

It was a beautiful autumn Saturday in 1976 as I headed my rental car from the Bradley Field Airport west through the rolling hillside of northern Connecticut. It was one of my monthly business trips from California, but this was to include one of my periodic visits to see my son, Larry, sixteen.

I only saw Larry about once a year. That was all I could emotionally handle. Larry was a living vegetable, having been born with a defective and rapidly deteriorating brain. By the time he was one year old he had no normal human faculties. He was blind, deaf, and unable to speak. He only cried when the seizures gripped his little body in pain.

Larry was the second son I had visited at this children's nursery. His older brother, Freddie, had suffered the same disease and had succumbed there at age two. It was one week later that we had learned that Larry's condition was the same and equally hopeless. We knew we had no choice but to take Larry to that nursery where he would receive the same loving care that Freddie had received.

Upon arriving at the nursery, I found an attendant who led me upstairs through a room full of cribs and then onto a small enclosed porch. She pointed to the little baby boy dressed in a tiny, well-worn suit, lying on a cushion on the floor. She then left me alone to visit with my son. Even though it had been almost a year since I had last seen him, Larry had changed very little; he was still no bigger than he had been when he was a year old.

(Twenty-one years later as I write these words, I still have to pause to swallow the lumps that are in my throat and wipe the tears that want to run down my face. I also take time to thank my Lord for Larry and for his brief life here on earth.)

How does one visit with a tiny little child who is lying on the floor six feet below you, who doesn't even know you are there and wouldn't even know who you are if he did? All I knew to do was to stand over him and pray. Among other words, I prayed, "Lord Jesus, I ask You to take him home because his life is so wasted."

Instantly, I heard God's answer to me. It came in words so clear that it was almost audible. "His life is no more wasted than is your life when you're not serving me, or is the life of any Christian who simply sits in church on Sunday morning!"

I continued to pray and to stand over my son for the next fifteen or twenty minutes. I had driven an hour and a half for this brief visit. The time was not wasted, for God had brought me there that day for the message He wanted to give to me. Later that afternoon as I drove south to Westport, Connecticut, to my brother's home, God's message reverberated in my mind: His life is no more wasted than is your life when you're not serving me, or than the life of any Christian who simply sits in church on Sunday morning.

I continued to thank the Lord for this word that He gave to me. I have never forgotten it. I have endeavored to always heed what He said to me that day. I have thanked the Lord regularly for my two sons' lives. Now I know they weren't wasted!

How about You?

Our lives, each one of us, was purchased at great price. We understand that. Nevertheless, with the passage of time some of us begin to take lightly the costly and amazing work that was done for us. Perhaps our seeds fell into rocky soil and never took deep root to flourish and bear much fruit. It is not too late. We can still take steps to rectify that condition. The Lord, through Paul, directed Timothy to guard what had been entrusted to him, to avoid foolish and worldly chatter. Think of how much of our "chatter" is worldly and foolish. Isn't it easy to get caught up in what everyone else is doing? Don't we all want to be accepted? We do. We have already been accepted. When we are accepted into the kingdom of our God, we also accept an enormous responsibility: to fulfill the purposes our Lord has for us.

What are those purposes? In short, to grow into complete and perfect trust in Him, to depend on Him alone and on His power, to allow Him to bring us to the end of our self-sufficiency, to glorify Him and enjoy being in His presence, and to allow Him to fulfill whatsoever purpose in our lives He desires. In other words, His purpose for us is complete abandonment to Him. Start today to rectify any conditions in your life that are not a satisfaction to Jesus.

Suggested Prayer for Today

Gracious God and Heavenly Father, I ask You to forgive me if I have taken lightly the price You paid so that I might have eternal life, the promise that I might be with You forever. I am reminded that the Lord Jesus hung in agony to free me from the bondage to sin and to satan. I am thankful for so great a gift. I ask You now to help me get serious about strengthening my relationship with You. Draw me to Yourself, Lord, I pray. I will come. I will come unto You daily. I will endeavor to the best of my ability to keep my mind and spiritual eyesight centered on You. I thank You, my Lord and my God, that You are always patient with me and ready to welcome me with open arms whenever I turn back toward You. Thank You, O blessed Lord and Savior. Amen.

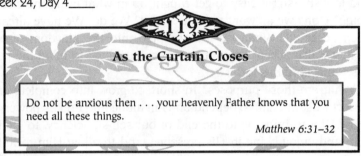

As the Curtain Closes

Do not be anxious then . . . your heavenly Father knows that you need all these things.

Matthew 6:31–32

Fred

In June 1976, I flew from California to Miami, Florida, for one of those unique appointments with life we are all privileged on rare occasion to experience. I thought I was making the trip for my grandfather's ninety-seventh birthday. That was the basic reason, but it was not the special purpose that my Heavenly Father had in His mind for me.

As he began his ninety-eighth year, my grandfather had most of his mental, physical, and spiritual faculties intact. The only readily noticeable differences were that he wore a hearing aid and walked slowly and carefully. He was somewhat physically weak, for he spent much time resting in bed.

I know little of his early spiritual background. I suspect that there wasn't much of a foundation, although he would always be described respectfully as moral, upstanding, and well-regarded by his peers. Somewhere in the late 1930s he became involved in the same cult that the rest of our family was caught up in. Much, much later, probably in the early 1970s, through what means only the Lord Himself knows, Grandfather must have committed his life to Him.

He never talked much about his faith but the fact that something had happened to him spiritually was clear to those of us who had ourselves taken that life-changing step forward. That June of 1976, he was a "young" Christian but not necessarily a "baby" Christian, for he spent many hours in Bible study, learning and growing.

It was early Friday evening when I arrived at his apartment from the airport. My mother was preparing dinner. She suggested that I go into his bedroom to visit with him before she called us all to eat. I will never forget the next forty-five minutes as I sat at my grandfather's bedside. This was the special time God had planned for me. He had a message to give to me through my grandfather!

His voice was clear; his words were coherent. He recognized me and knew that I had come to visit him. What was so significant to me was that he kept saying the same few sentences over and over. "Thank You, God, for all the blessings You have given to me. Thank You for sending my grandson from California to visit me. Thank You, Lord, for all Your goodness."

This was about all he said for that forty-five minutes as I sat with him. He kept repeating it over and over. Any attempt that I made to commence conversation seemed to go nowhere. I would never have said that my grandfather had lived a happy life. He did achieve some material success, despite his lack of education, but I also never heard of a day in his seventy-six-year marriage that was not marked by stress. Two strong-willed people lived those many years together but never seemed to learn the secret of harmony. All they knew to do was to tightly bite their lips and avoid the inevitable argument.

What I did not know that evening was that just three days later, after I had left Miami to fly to New Haven, Connecticut, I would receive a call to come back. Grandfather had died. He had gone to be with his Father in Heaven. Perhaps he had some premonition that the curtains were about to close on his life here on earth. One thing, however, is clear. He had only one thing on his mind, his relationship and thanksgiving to his Father in Heaven. Nothing else mattered. He was in fact simply offering prayers of gratitude the entire time I sat by his bed! Nothing else was important to him in what would prove to be his last days, only praise and thankfulness to His Lord and Savior.

I was also thankful to the Lord for giving that message to me. When the curtains are about to close on the final act, there is only one thing that is important, our Lord and our gratitude to Him! I will never forget June 1976.

How about You?

Are you still trying to make monuments of material things that will have no value to you when the curtain closes on your final act? Are you placing your focus and priority on those things that have no heavenly worth? Do you need to heed and apply the lesson the Father had for me as I spent that quiet evening in my grandfather's bedroom? I trust and pray that I will never lose my perspective on eternal values versus temporal things. What about you?

Suggested Prayer for Today

Dear Lord Jesus, in Your earthly walk among us, You never lost sight of Your relationship to Your Father in Heaven. You already knew that Your stay here would be brief and that You would go back to Your Father. You never amassed treasures for Yourself. You never ignored the needs of those around You. You never turned anyone away. You always had time, and yet You too had only twenty-four hours in each day just as we have. You finished Your work in only three years, Lord. We have already been given so much more time than You had, and yet we often feel we have so little to show for it. Help me now, Lord, to remember the lesson You taught Fred through his grandfather. Help me remember that when my final curtain closes there will be only one thing that is important. Lord Jesus, I want to make You the priority in my life right now! I thank You, and I praise You. In Your Name I pray. Amen.

Give Out the Music

Many of us die with the music still in us.

Oliver Wendell Holmes

Florence

Have you been giving out Silver Boxes—gifts of encouraging words—since we first talked about them in chapter 20? Have you been considering ways you can live your life, as Ralph Lagergren told me he was doing (see Chapter 33)? Ralph said, "I'm banging my cymbals and playing every other instrument I can. The music is not going to die in me." Today let's conclude our marriage-building time together by assessing where we've come from and where we're going. To do so, we will look at two areas of questions, one area dealing with others and the other area dealing with ourselves. First, ask yourself, *Am I encouraging others to be the best they can be? Am I giving out Silver Boxes? Am I making sure that my children and my mate will not die with the music still in them?*

Then ask, *What am I doing with myself? Is there some hidden talent I haven't yet used? Have I held back because someone once said, "You really don't have much talent"?*

Fred's mother once told me she had always wanted to be an opera singer. She majored in music in college and wanted to go for further study. When I asked her why she didn't do it, she gave a reply I've heard from many others also, "My mother said, 'You don't have that good a voice—singers are a dime a dozen. No one can understand opera anyway.'" Her father had added, "Singers never make much money. Forget that foolishness and come into the family business where you'll make some money."

Fred's mother, interrupting her story, got up from her chair, went down the hall to a closet, and brought back a box full of pictures.

She pulled one out and showed it to me. It was a stage setting for an opera; the cast was in costume, and she was sitting in the center of the set on a wing chair. "See," she pointed, "I'm right there in the middle. I had the lead in the opera."

"When was this?" I asked.

"My senior year in college. It was the last time I ever sang."

She handed me the picture and said, "Here, you can have this. No one else knows this story. Give it to your daughter, Marita. She's named after me. Let her know that her grandmother could have been somebody if only she'd heard some encouraging words."

If only my mother-in-law's parents had lifted her up instead of cutting her down. If only they had given her Silver Boxes.

In her latter years she had something akin to Alzheimer's disease and eventually couldn't recognize us or talk to us at all. One day I asked the nurse, "Does Mother ever talk?"

"No, she never says a word," the nurse answered. "But every once in a while, she stands up and sings opera."

Isn't it amazing that no matter how we repress our desires and suppress our talent, they still sit there in our minds inside of little boxes of broken dreams, the evidence of what could have been if only someone had given us some encouraging words.

Fred's mother died with the music still in her. I don't want that to happen to you!

How about You?

Do you have some talent that you've left in the box and never taken out?

Do you want to play the piano? The violin? The trumpet?

Did you want to be a dancer? An actor? A speaker?

Did you want to write poetry? Drama? The great American novel?

Did you want to be a teacher? A doctor? A politician?

Discuss these hidden dreams with each other. Dare to dream once more that you could fulfill your desires.

Prepare the dream by studying at home, by reading the right

books, and by listening to tapes on your subject. Go back to school, take lessons, get a job with a future. Don't worry about what others think. Encourage each other. Give Silver Boxes!

Wear the dream. Stay the course and don't give up. Follow your dream. Study God's Word for His leading. Keep yourself clean. Good people do get into trouble when they step out of God's will. Don't be in the wrong place at the wrong time. Continue to give Silver Boxes to everyone you meet—and especially to each other.

After I spoke on Silver Boxes at a network marketing "Family Reunion," I received a letter from Jim Brehm. He wrote: "Raised in a family of quick-witted, stingingly sarcastic, put-down artists, I really took to heart your Silver Box approach to communication. Now my challenge is to melt, then re-cast my silver bullets into Silver Boxes."

Have you been shooting out silver bullets instead of giving Silver Boxes?

Suggested Prayer for Today

Dear Lord Jesus, we don't want this time of dreaming to end, and we ask You to keep us moving ahead, practicing the gift of giving Silver Boxes. Lord, we confess it's easier to shoot those silver bullets than it is to wrap up our words in silver, but we want to do this. We want to be remembered for our positive words, for our Silver Boxes with bows on top. Forgive us for any unkind words we've said to each other and help us encourage one another every day. Lord Jesus, keep us daring to dream forever, direct us in preparing that dream and never giving up, and most of all, keep us standing close to You, protected, under Your wing. We want to wear the dream for others to see so they will want to follow You. We promise not to be lazy or indifferent. We don't want to die with the music still in us. In Your gracious and glorious Name we pray. Amen.

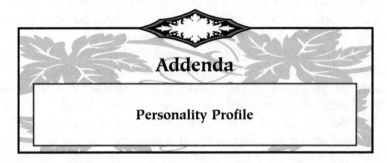

Addenda

Personality Profile

Directions: In <u>each</u> of the following rows of <u>four words across</u> place an X in front of the <u>one</u> word that most often applies to you. Continue through all forty lines. Be sure each numbered line is marked. If you are not sure which word most applies, ask a spouse or a friend, or think of what your answer would have been *when you were a child.*

Strengths

1.	___ Adventurous	___ Adaptable	___ Animated	___ Analytical
2.	___ Persistent	___ Playful	___ Persuasive	___ Peaceful
3.	___ Submissive	___ Self-Sacrificing	___ Sociable	___ Strong-willed
4.	___ Considerate	___ Controlled	___ Competitive	___ Convincing
5.	___ Refreshing	___ Respectful	___ Reserved	___ Resourceful
6.	___ Satisfied	___ Sensitive	___ Self-reliant	___ Spirited
7.	___ Planner	___ Patient	___ Positive	___ Promoter
8.	___ Sure	___ Spontaneous	___ Scheduled	___ Shy
9.	___ Orderly	___ Obliging	___ Outspoken	___ Optimistic
10.	___ Friendly	___ Faithful	___ Funny	___ Forceful
11.	___ Daring	___ Delightful	___ Diplomatic	___ Detailed
12.	___ Cheerful	___ Consistent	___ Cultured	___ Confident
13.	___ Idealistic	___ Independent	___ Inoffensive	___ Inspiring
14.	___ Demonstrative	___ Decisive	___ Dry humor	___ Deep
15.	___ Mediator	___ Musical	___ Mover	___ Mixes easily

16. ___ Thoughtful	___ Tenacious	___ Talker	___ Tolerant
17. ___ Listener	___ Loyal	___ Leader	___ Lively
18. ___ Contented	___ Chief	___ Chartmaker	___ Cute
19. ___ Perfectionist	___ Pleasant	___ Productive	___ Popular
20. ___ Bouncy	___ Bold	___ Behaved	___ Balanced

Weaknesses

21. ___ Blank	___ Bashful	___ Brassy	___ Bossy
22. ___ Undisciplined	___ Unsympathetic	___ Unenthusiastic	___ Unforgiving
23. ___ Reticent	___ Resentful	___ Resistant	___ Repetitious
24. ___ Fussy	___ Fearful	___ Forgetful	___ Frank
25. ___ Impatient	___ Insecure	___ Indecisive	___ Interrupts
26. ___ Unpopular	___ Uninvolved	___ Unpredictable	___ Unaffectionate
27. ___ Headstrong	___ Haphazard	___ Hard to please	___ Hesitant
28. ___ Plain	___ Pessimistic	___ Proud	___ Permissive
29. ___ Angers easily	___ Aimless	___ Argumentative	___ Alienated
30. ___ Naive	___ Negative attitude	___ Nervy	___ Nonchalant
31. ___ Worrier	___ Withdrawn	___ Workaholic	___ Wants credit
32. ___ Too sensitive	___ Tactless	___ Timid	___ Talkative
33. ___ Doubtful	___ Disorganized	___ Domineering	___ Depressed
34. ___ Inconsistent	___ Introvert	___ Intolerant	___ Indifferent
35. ___ Messy	___ Moody	___ Mumbles	___ Manipulative
36. ___ Slow	___ Stubborn	___ Show-off	___ Skeptical
37. ___ Loner	___ Lord over	___ Lazy	___ Loud
38. ___ Sluggish	___ Suspicious	___ Short-tempered	___ Scatterbrained
39. ___ Revengeful	___ Restless	___ Reluctant	___ Rash
40. ___ Compromising	___ Critical	___ Crafty	___ Changeable

Now transfer all your Xs to the corresponding words on the Personality Profile Scoring Form.

Created by Fred Littauer. All rights reserved. Not to be reproduced. Copies may be ordered from: CLASS Book Service, 4065 Oceanside Blvd., Suite 4, Oceanside, California 92056. Telephone: 888-678-1235.

Personality Scoring Form

Place an X beside the corresponding words you marked on the Personality Profile Test. Then, giving one point for each x, add up your subtotals.

Strengths

	Sanquine-Popular	Choleric-Powerful	Melancholy-Perfect	Phlegmatic-Peaceful
1.	___ Animated	___ Adventurous	___ Analytical	___ Adaptable
2.	___ Playful	___ Persuasive	___ Persistent	___ Peaceful
3.	___ Sociable	___ Strong-willed	___ Self-Sacrificing	___ Submissive
4.	___ Convincing	___ Competitive	___ Considerate	___ Controlled
5.	___ Refreshing	___ Resourceful	___ Respectful	___ Reserved
6.	___ Spirited	___ Self-Reliant	___ Sensitive	___ Satisfied
7.	___ Promoter	___ Positive	___ Planner	___ Patient
8.	___ Spontaneous	___ Sure	___ Scheduled	___ Shy
9.	___ Optimistic	___ Outspoken	___ Orderly	___ Obliging
10.	___ Funny	___ Forceful	___ Faithful	___ Friendly
11.	___ Delightful	___ Daring	___ Detailed	___ Diplomatic
12.	___ Cheerful	___ Confident	___ Cultured	___ Consistent
13.	___ Inspiring	___ Independent	___ Idealistic	___ Inoffensive
14.	___ Demonstrative	___ Decisive	___ Deep	___ Dry humor
15.	___ Mixes easily	___ Mover	___ Musical	___ Mediator
16.	___ Talker	___ Tenacious	___ Thoughtful	___ Tolerant
17.	___ Lively	___ Leader	___ Loyal	___ Listener
18.	___ Cute	___ Chief	___ Chartmaker	___ Contented
19.	___ Popular	___ Productive	___ Perfectionist	___ Pleasant
20.	___ Bouncy	___ Bold	___ Behaved	___ Balanced

Strengths Subtotals

___   ___   ___   ___

Weaknesses

21. ___ Brassy	___ Bossy	___ Bashful	___ Blank
22. ___ Undisciplined	___ Unsympathetic	___ Unforgiving	___ Unenthusiastic
23. ___ Repetitious	___ Resistant	___ Resentful	___ Reticent
24. ___ Forgetful	___ Frank	___ Fussy	___ Fearful
25. ___ Interrupts	___ Impatient	___ Insecure	___ Indecisive
26. ___ Unpredictable	___ Unaffectionate	___ Unpopular	___ Uninvolved
27. ___ Haphazard	___ Headstrong	___ Hard to please	___ Hesitant
28. ___ Permissive	___ Proud	___ Pessimistic	___ Plain
29. ___ Angers easily	___ Argumentative	___ Alienated	___ Aimless
30. ___ Naive	___ Nervy	___ Negative	___ Nonchalant
31. ___ Wants credit	___ Workaholic	___ Withdrawn	___ Worrier
32. ___ Talkative	___ Tactless	___ Too sensitive	___ Timid
33. ___ Disorganized	___ Domineering	___ Depressed	___ Doubtful
34. ___ Inconsistent	___ Intolerant	___ Introvert	___ Indifferent
35. ___ Messy	___ Manipulative	___ Moody	___ Mumbles
36. ___ Show-off	___ Stubborn	___ Skeptical	___ Slow
37. ___ Loud	___ Lord over	___ Loner	___ Lazy
38. ___ Scatterbrained	___ Short-tempered	___ Suspicious	___ Sluggish
39. ___ Restless	___ Rash	___ Revengeful	___ Reluctant
40. ___ Changeable	___ Crafty	___ Critical	___ Compromising

Weaknesses Subtotals

___   ___   ___   ___

GRAND TOTALS

___   ___   ___   ___

The following table shows how the typical strengths and weaknesses of the personality types are revealed emotionally, with friends and at work.

Table 1
Comparison of Strengths and Weaknesses by Personality Type

STRENGTHS

Sanguine-Popular	Choleric-Powerful	Melancholy-Perfect	Phlegmatic-Peaceful
EMOTIONS	**EMOTIONS**	**EMOTIONS**	**EMOTIONS**
Appealing personality	Born leader	Deep and thoughtful	Low-key personality
Talkative, storyteller	Dynamic and active	Analytical	Easygoing and relaxed
Life of the party	Compulsive need for	Serious and purposeful	Calm, cool, and
Good sense of humor	change	Genius prone	collected
Memory for color	Must correct wrongs	Talented and creative	Patient, well balanced
Physically holds on to	Strong-willed and	Artistic or musical	Consistent life
listener	decisive	Philosophical and poetic	Quiet, but witty
Emotional	Unemotional	Appreciative of beauty	Sympathetic and kind
Enthusiastic	Not easily discouraged	Sensitive to others	Keeps emotions hidden
Cheerful	Independent and self-	Self-sacrificing	Happily reconciled
Curious	sufficient	Conscientious	to life
Good on stage	Exudes confidence	Idealistic	All-purpose person
Wide-eyed and innocent			
Lives in the present			
Changeable disposition			
Sincere at heart			
Always a child			
WORK	**WORK**	**WORK**	**WORK**
Volunteers for jobs	Goal oriented	Schedule oriented	Competent and steady
Thinks up new activities	Sees the whole picture	Perfectionist	Peaceful and agreeable
Looks great on the	Organizes well	Detail conscious	Has administrative ability
surface	Seeks practical	Persistent and thorough	Mediates problems
Creative and colorful	solutions	Orderly and organized	Avoids conflicts
Has energy and	Moves quickly to action	Neat and tidy	Good under pressure
enthusiasm	Delegates work	Economical	Finds the easy way
Starts in a flashy way	Insists on production	Sees the problems	
Inspires others to join	Makes the goal	Need to finish	
Charms others to work	Stimulates activity	Likes charts, graphs,	
	Thrives on opposition	figures, lists	
	Can run anything		
FRIENDS	**FRIENDS**	**FRIENDS**	**FRIENDS**
Makes friends easily	Has little need for	Makes friends cautiously	Easy to get along with
Loves people	friends	Content to stay in back-	Pleasant and enjoyable
Thrives on compliments	Will work for group	ground	Inoffensive
Seems exciting	activity	Avoids causing attention	Good listener
Envied by others	Will lead and organize	Faithful and devoted	Dry sense of humor
Doesn't hold grudges	Is usually right	Will listen to complaints	Enjoys watching people
Apologizes quickly	Excels in emergencies	Can solve others'	Has many friends
Prevents dull moments		problems	Has compassion and
Likes spontaneous		Concern for others	concern
activities		Compassionate	
		Seeks ideal mate	

WEAKNESSES

Sanguine-Popular

EMOTIONS
Compulsive talker
Exaggerates
Dwells on trivia
Can't remember names
Scares others off
Too happy for some
Has restless energy
Egotistical
Blusters and complains
Naive, gets taken in
Loud voice and laugh
Controlled by
 circumstances
Gets angry easily
Seems phony to some
Never grows up

WORK
Would rather talk
Forgets obligations
Doesn't follow through
Confidence fades fast
Undisciplined
Priorities out of order
Decides by feelings
Easily distracted
Wastes time talking

FRIENDS
Hates to be alone
Needs to be center
 stage
Wants to be popular
Looks for credit
Dominates
 conversations
Interrupts and doesn't
 listen
Answers for others
Fickle and forgetful
Makes excuses
Repeats stories

Choleric-Powerful

EMOTIONS
Bossy
Impatient
Quick-tempered
Can't relax
Too impetuous
Enjoys controversy
 and arguments
Won't give up when
 losing
Comes on too strong
Inflexible
Is not complimentary
Dislikes tears and
 emotions
Is unsympathetic

WORK
Intolerant of mistakes
Doesn't analyze details
Bored by trivia
Rash decisions
May be rude or tactless
Manipulates people
Demanding of others
End justifies the means
Work may become god
Demands loyalty in the
 ranks

FRIENDS
Tends to use people
Dominates others
Decides for others
Knows everything
Can do everything
 better
Is too independent
Possessive of friends
 and mate
Can't say, "I'm sorry"
May be right, but
 unpopular

Melancholy-Perfect

EMOTIONS
Remembers the
 negatives
Moody and depressed
Enjoys being hurt
Has false humility
Off in another world
Low self-image
Has selective hearing
Self-centered
Too introspective
Guilt feelings
Persecutive complex
Tends to hypochondria

WORK
Not people oriented
Depressed over
 imperfections
Chooses difficult work
Hesitant to start projects
Spends too much time
 planning
Prefers analysis to work
Self-deprecating
Hard to please
Standards often too high
Deep need for approval

FRIENDS
Lives through others
Insecure socially
Withdrawn and remote
Critical of others
Holds back affection
Dislikes those in
 opposition
Suspicious of people
Antagonistic and
 vengeful
Unforgiving
Full of contradictions
Skeptical of
 compliments

Phlegmatic-Peaceful

EMOTIONS
Unenthusiastic
Fearful and worried
Indecisive
Avoids responsibility
Quiet will of iron
Selfish
Too shy and reticent
Too compromising
Self-righteous

WORK
Not goal oriented
Lacks self-motivation
Hard to get moving
Resents being pushed
Lazy and careless
Discourages others
Would rather watch

FRIENDS
Dampens enthusiasm
Stays uninvolved
Is not exciting
Indifferent to plans
Judges others
Sarcastic and teasing
Resists change

You'll see from Table 1 that we've added some descriptive adjectives to the personality types: Popular Sanguine, Perfect Melancholy, Powerful Choleric, and Peaceful Phlegmatic. We find that these terms help people remember which characteristics are typically associated with those personality types. And while we call some of those characteristics strengths, it's important to note that, when carried to extremes, these traits can become weaknesses—or even compulsions, as shown in Table 2.

Table 2

Strengths Carried to Extremes

Popular-Sanguine

NATURAL STRENGTHS	STRENGTHS CARRIED TO EXTREMES	COMPULSIONS
Magnetic personality	Depends on charm and wit	Can become a con artist, bigamist
Entertaining storyteller	Constantly talking	Must be talking to feel secure
Loves to go shopping	Buys and charges irrationally	Becomes a debt-laden shopaholic
Life of the party	Too loud, too wild	Makes fool of self, becomes party animal

Perfect-Melancholy

NATURAL STRENGTHS	STRENGTHS CARRIED TO EXTREMES	COMPULSIONS
Schedule oriented	Can't function without schedule	Obsessed with punctuality
Knowledge on health and nutrition	Constant physical attention	May become hypochondriac
Neat, immaculate dresser	Can't go out until perfect	Constant washing; has fetish about looks
Wants things done perfectly	Wants others to be perfect	Nitpicks and criticizes constantly

Powerful-Choleric

NATURAL STRENGTHS	STRENGTHS CARRIED TO EXTREMES	COMPULSIONS
Born leader	Angry if people buck authority	Obsessed with power
Decisive	Decides for everyone	Manipulates own way
Quick and active	Makes impulsive choices	Becomes irrational
Loves to work	Works beyond the norm	Becomes a workaholic

Peaceful-Phlegmatic

NATURAL STRENGTHS	STRENGTHS CARRIED TO EXTREMES	COMPULSIONS
Low-key emotions	Hides emotions	Blocks out all feeling
Easygoing	Lets others decide	Can't make any decisions
Cooperative	Compromises standards	Easily becomes a pawn
Low motivation	Becomes lazy and laid back	Refuses to budge

After you have transferred your checked words from the Personality Profile Test to the Personality Scoring Form, calculate your score and see which personality you score highest in. If you do not feel right about your results, consider these possibilities that may have distorted the profile:

1. You may have taken the test incorrectly. You should have made one check on each of forty lines (twenty strengths and twenty weaknesses). Sometimes people check no response or more than one response on each line, or they check only one response in each vertical column rather than on each horizontal line.

2. You transferred your responses incorrectly. For instance, instead of putting an X by the word *adaptable* on the scoring form you may have put the check in the same position on the scoring sheet as it was on the test, instead of on the same word.

3. You scored yourself as you would like to be, as other always wanted you to be, or as good Christian people should be instead of how you really are.

4. You are somewhat confused about who you really are and you need help interpreting the score.

Recommended Reading

For Marriage
After Every Wedding Comes a Marriage, Florence Littauer (Harvest House).
Get a Life without the Strife, Florence and Fred Littauer (Thomas Nelson).
Personality Plus, Florence Littauer (Fleming Revell-Baker)
Wake Up, Men! Fred Littauer (Word).
Wake Up, Women! Florence Littauer (Word).

For Inner Struggles
Blow Away the Black Clouds, Florence Littauer (Word).
Hope for Hurting Women, Florence Littauer (Word)
Freeing Your Mind from memories That bind (Fred and Florence Littauer (Thomas Nelson).

The Promise of Healing, Fred Littauer (Thomas Nelson).
Touched by the Master, Fred Littauer (Creation House).
The Promise of Healing, audiocassette album with manual presenting a live, three-day prayer workshop for recovery from childhood trauma (CLASS Book Services).

For Understanding Personalities

Getting Along with Almost Anybody, Florence and Marita Littauer (Fleming Revell-Baker).
*Personality Plus, Florence Littauer (Fleming Revell-Baker).
Personality Puzzle, Florence and Marita Littauer (Fleming Revell-Baker).
Put Power in Your Personality, Florence Littauer (Fleming Revell-Baker).
Your Personality Tree, Florence Littauer (Word).
Personality Profile, complete testing instrument, Fred Littauer (CLASS Book Service).
* All-time bestseller—over 750,000 copies!

Inspiration and Motivation, and Other Helps

Dare to Dream, Florence Littauer (Word).
The Gift of Encouraging Words, Florence Littauer (Word).
I Found My Keys, Now Where's My Car, Florence Littauer (Word).
It Takes So Little to Be Ave Average, Florence Littauer (Harvest House).
Raising Christians, Not Just Children, Florence Littauer (Word).
Silver Boxes, the Gift of Encouragement, Florence Littauer (Word).
How to Get Along with Difficult People, Florence Littauer (Word).

Many of these books are available in foreign language editions. For information and to order any of these resources:

> CLASS Book Service
> 4065 Oceanside Blvd., Suite R
> Oceanside, California 92056
> Call 888-678-1235
> e-mail:classbooks@aol.com

Notes

How to Get the Most Out of This Book
1. Johnny Carson, quoted in *Time* magazine, 26 June 1989.

Chapter 4. When the Going Gets Tough
1. *USA Today,* 3 July 1997.
2. Oswald Chamber, *My Utmost for His Highest,* July 7.

Chapter 5. Reaping Bountifully
1. Matthew 19:6 KJV.

Chapter 15. Poor Dreams
1. *U.S. News & World Report,* 2 June 1997.

Chapter 17. Creative Conversation
1. *Newsweek,* 23 June 1997.

Chapter 34. Moral Leadership
1. Matthew 26:11 NIV.
2. See Matthew 22:14.
3. See Isaiah 6:8.

Chapter 36. Who Is the Head? Who Is the Authority?
1. For a more detailed explanation of the relevant Scripture, please see chapter 13, "How Can the Husband Be the Head of the Wife?" in Fred Littauer's, *Wake Up Men!* (Dallas: Word Publishing, 1994).
2. Matthew 28:18.

Chapter 40. The Husband, the Partner
1. Spiros Zodhiates, Th.D., *The Complete Word Study New Testament* (Chattanooga, Tenn.: AMG Publishers, 1991), 944.

Daily Marriage Builders for Couples

Chapter 74. Sometimes Dogs Make Better Mates!
1. With thanks to Bob and Yvonne Turnbull Ministries, who no doubt picked up some of these in their e-mail before the list was forwarded on to us.

Chapter 81. Personal and Passionate Devotion
1. Matthew 6:33 KJV.
2. Matthew 22:37 KJV.
3. Matthew 23:26.
4. James 1:7 KJV.
5. See Mark 10:17–31.

Chapter 84. Personalizing Scripture:
    Making Your Mate More Important
1. See James 4:6, 1 Peter 5:5, and Proverbs 3:34 NIV.

Chapter 85. Personalizing Scripture:
    Becoming a Servant
1. See Romans 12:2 NIV.
2. See James 4:2 KJV.
3. John 14:6.

Chapter 86. Good Taste
1. Interview with Vaclav Havel, *Time* magazine, 3 August 1992.
2. Ibid.
3. Paraphrase of 1 Kings 12:7.
4. Havel, *Time*.

Chapter 89. Night Instruction
1. See Psalm 16:2.

Chapter 90. Deepening Your Faith
1. See Mark 9:14–29.
2. John 13:17 TEV.

Chapter 94. Reasons for a King
1. See Isaiah 26:3.

Chapter 95. Called Out by God
1. 1 Samuel 9:2 NIV.
2. 1 Samuel 9:21 NIV.
3. 1 Samuel 3:7 NIV.

4. 1 Samuel 3:10 NIV.
5. 1 Samuel 3:19 NIV.

Chapter 96. Changed by the Spirit
1. 1 Samuel 10:10 NIV.

Chapter 97. Chosen by the People
1. 1 Samuel 10:22 NIV.
2. 1 Samuel 10:24 NIV.
3. Chambers, *My Utmost For His Highest,* October 25.

Chapter 98. Committed to Obedience
1. 1 Samuel 12:16 NIV.
2. 1 Samuel 12:22 NIV.
3. 1 Samuel 12:24 NIV.

Chapter 99. Compromised Standards
1. See 1 Samuel 13:11–13 NIV.
2. 1 Samuel 13:14 NIV.
3. 1 Samuel 15:11 NIV.
4. 1 Samuel 15:24 NIV.
5. 1 Samuel 15:22 NIV.

Chapter 100. Heed the Call
1. 1 Samuel 16:1 NIV.
2. 1 Samuel 16:7 NIV.
3. 1 Samuel 16:11 NIV.
4. 1 Samuel 16:12 NIV.

Chapter 101. How Good People Get into Trouble
1. See Luke 18:11.

Chapter 105. Cover It Up
1. See 2 Samuel 11:6.
2. See 2 Samuel 11:7.
3. See 2 Samuel 11:8.
4. See 2 Samuel 11:10–11.
5. See 2 Samuel 11:13.
6. 2 Samuel 11:13 KJV.
7. 2 Samuel 11:15 KJV.
8. See 2 Samuel 11:14, 24 KJV.
9. See 2 Samuel 11:26 KJV.
10. 2 Samuel 11:27 KJV.

Chapter 106. Faced with the Truth
 1. 2 Samuel 12:2 KJV.
 2. 2 Samuel 12:3 KJV.
 3. 2 Samuel 12:5 KJV.
 4. 2 Samuel 12:6 KJV.

Chapter 107. Cry Out to God
 1. See 2 Samuel 12:7–9.
Chapter 108. Ask for Joy
 1. See Philippians 2:10 KJV.

Chapter 109. See His Face
 1. See Jeremiah 31:34.

Chapter 110. And We Know Who Wins
 1. *USA Today,* 9 July 1997.

Chapter 112. A New Heart
 1. Ezekiel 18:30 NIV.
 2. A true occurrence recently reported in the news.

Chapter 116. Uncontrollable Anger
 1. Matthew 15:13 KJV.
 2. Matthew 28:20.